The Failure to Protect

The Failure to Protect

The Path to and Consequences of Humanitarian Interventionism

Timo Kivimäki

Professor of International Relations, University of Bath, UK

Edward Elgar
PUBLISHING

Cheltenham, UK • Northampton, MA, USA

Published by
Edward Elgar Publishing Limited
The Lypiatts
15 Lansdown Road
Cheltenham
Glos GL50 2JA
UK

Edward Elgar Publishing, Inc.
William Pratt House
9 Dewey Court
Northampton
Massachusetts 01060
USA

A catalogue record for this book
is available from the British Library

Library of Congress Control Number: 2018959279

This book is available electronically in the Elgaronline
Social and Political Science subject collection
DOI 10.4337/9781788111010

FSC
www.fsc.org
MIX
Paper from
responsible sources
FSC® C013056

ISBN 978 1 78811 100 3 (cased)
ISBN 978 1 78811 101 0 (eBook)

Typeset by Servis Filmsetting Ltd, Stockport, Cheshire
Printed and bound in Great Britain by TJ International Ltd, Padstow

Contents

Preface

Peace research is committed to helping the reduction of violence in the world. It is based on a pragmatist approach: knowledge serves agency for peace. The mainstream of peace research is increasingly committed to a philosophy of social science that is borrowed from natural sciences and rejected by philosophers of social sciences already in the 1960s. Pragmatism of such peace research aims at finding exogenous conditions that mechanistically cause conflict behaviour either deterministically or probabilistically. With this knowledge it will then help peace actors to solve conflicts by changing these conditions.

This book tries to build on slightly more developed philosophical foundations – ontological premises that do not analyse social structures and agency away from the developments in the reality of conflict. The objective of this book is still pragmatic. It studies approaches of actors of peace and conflict and investigates how they lead to peaceful or belligerent outcomes as they interact with social and material structures. Therefore, the focus of this book is not on objective, exogenous material conditions that cause peace or war, but on approaches to the protection of civilians from violence. Knowledge in this book is not only intended simply as an instrument for the identification of what should be done, but also as an articulation that constitutes more peaceful realities, or that challenges knowledge that is part of the conflict problem. I called this approach to scholarship 'constructivist pragmatism' in my book on *Paradigms of Peace* (Imperial College Press, 2016). The knowledge that this book challenges as part of conflict reality is the understanding of Western masculine agency as an exclusive, natural agency of global protection of civilians, and the understanding of protection as a politically uncontroversial and impartial, positive activity. The articulations this book offers aim at creating horizons to a more democratic and what I call more 'matriotic' approach to global peace.

The idea of this book was born out of my investigation on the surprising pacification of East Asia at the end of the 1970s (*The Long Peace of East Asia*, Routledge, 2014). It turned out that average annual conflict fatalities in Southeast and Northeast Asia had declined by 95 per cent if the period after 1978 was compared with the post-World War II period and that the main reason for this staggering decline in conflict fatalities was the refusal, sometime in the 1970s, of the region to accept external military help in their internal struggles. It seemed clear to me that allies with the intention to help their Cold War partners had done more damage than good in their eagerness to defend their partners. This to me seemed to go against the conventional wisdom from political rhetoric and the media, and I became curious whether this discovery could be generalized beyond East Asia and beyond the Cold War era. Thus, I wanted to explore whether in the post-Cold War era too, protection had harmful consequences, and if so, why. This was the first intellectual path towards the investigation for this book.

While working on *The Long Peace of East Asia*, I worked closely with conflict data, especially data on conflict fatalities. In that process I also became acquainted with theories with a much longer perspective on conflict developments than the one I was studying myself. Steven Pinker's book, *The Better Angels of Our Nature: Why Violence Has Declined* (Allen Lane, 2011), Francis Fukuyama's book on *The Origins of Political Order from Prehuman Times to the French Revolution* (Farrar, Straus and Giroux, 2011) and Anthony Giddens's book on *The Nation-State and Violence* (Polity, 1985) alerted me to the megatrends of violence and to the idea that peace expanded with the expansion of zones of order. The seminal book on *New and Old Wars* (Stanford University Press, 1999) by Mary Kaldor linked these megatrends to the more recent trend in which people of the world were about to abandon their nationalist selfishness for the benefit of global human security. Could the new trend of getting involved in the prevention of violence in faraway places – the saving of strangers – be part of the final megatrend, after which the whole world could be part of one single security community?

Putting the experience of the long peace of East Asia together with the experience of expanding security communities created a puzzle that needed a solution. If cosmopolitan protection could be part of the next pacific megatrend then how does that fit with my own discovery in East Asia, according to which the ending of military protection had contributed to the long peace? Could it be that while cosmopolitan protection of global civilians is part of a positive megatrend, in the shorter run its distortions are part of the problem of violence? This was the puzzle I wanted to solve with the project that this book is part of.

In the process of research, I have had an endless number of discussions with my closest colleagues in the project and in my department at the University of Bath. I am greatly indebted to these conversations, and owe a great gratitude to Wali Aslam, Mattia Cacciatori, Brett Edwards, Salla Huikuri, Emanuela Koskimies, Mauricio Rivera and Scott Thomas. For the insights on feminist theory, especially for Chapter 8, I am indebted to discussions with Alexandra Kivimäki. I am also grateful for ideas and comments related to this study to Gordon Burt, Judith Large and Hugh Miall of the Conflict Research Society, another intellectual home of my thinking. Finally, I am grateful to the Edward Elgar Publishing team for the work in polishing the manuscript and finishing this book project. My readers do not have access to the previous versions of this book, but if they had, they would also be grateful to Edward Elgar.

Timo Kivimäki
Bath, June 30, 2018

1. Introduction

THE PARADOX OF PROTECTION

There are three paradoxes in current warfare. The most immediate of the paradoxes is related to the rise of fatalities in many of the conflicts that explicit effort at protecting civilians has escalated. The declaratory objective of 12 of the latest Western war participations in Kosovo, Sierra Leone, Afghanistan, Yemen, Iraq, Pakistan, Central African Republic, Somalia, Mali, Mauritania, Libya and Syria, has been to protect civilians from terror, conflict criminals, dictators or weapons that are exceptionally dangerous for global civilians – weapons of mass destruction (WMDs). Yet, many of these wars have only been escalated after and by these Western protective interventions (see Chapter 4). Many of the civilians that the United States, United Kingdom, France and others tried to protect were against these Western interventions to start with (Brown, 2014; Hussain, 2016; Rayment, 2005). Eventually, many of these civilians were killed due to the escalation of the conflict by the Western intervention. Fatal protection is, indeed, a paradox and it is the failure to protect that this book focuses on. The record of military action that has claimed its legitimacy from cosmopolitan thinking on protection (but which was not necessarily an accurate reflection of the theory) will be reviewed in Chapter 4 of this book.

The second paradox is in the incompatibility of the perceived reality of cosmopolitan protection and the expectations of it as a less power-centric, more feminized approach to world politics. While it could be assumed that protection of civilians is focused on caring and nurturing ordinary people – global civilians – and to be the opposite of the Cold War logic of geopolitics (Hooper, 1998), it seems that operations with a protective declaratory motive have never been far from state-centric power politics (Chapter 8). The rationale of protection has offered ways to play down global institutions in favour of states. It has offered justifications for nationalist direct military action that tend to ignore the voice of the civilians, just as the logic of Cold War does. The preference for measures that require the use of power to change someone else's behaviour by means of deterrence, pressure, or destruction instead of engaging in direct protective and nurturing action (by accepting refugees or offering development aid, for example), and the effect of this power-centricity on conflict fatalities, will be investigated in Chapter 8.

The third paradox is related to the fact that the consequences of cosmopolitan protection in the protective operations of the past two decades have gone against a global historical pattern. Usually, when zones of order expand at the expense of zones of anarchy, a lot of violence disappears (Elias, 1982; Fukuyama, 2011; Giddens, 1985; Pinker, 2011; Tilly, 1990). According to Pinker, for example, the move of humanity from hunting and gathering groups to larger agricultural, sedentary communities 5000 years ago reduced violent death by 80 per cent. The transition from feudal city states to kingdoms was associated with the decline of homicidal violence by 90–98 per cent (Pinker, 2011, Chapters 2–7).[1]

The association between expansion of security communities and decline in violence is understandable as more interaction takes place within, rather than between, communities, and thus more dyads of interaction take place in order than in anarchy. In the realist and neorealist theories of international politics and international relations, the lack of community and order, the existence of anarchy, is often a permissive cause of conflict (Waltz, 1979). In interaction within an existing order, say a nation-state, we cannot even imagine warfare. A war between Birmingham and London in the UK would be unimaginable, and today a war between Germany and France would be almost as unimaginable, given the developing European security community. In addition to the realist theories of anarchy and order, all this has been explained in the theories of communities, common identities and common norms in the constructivist and English schools (Adler and Barnett, 1998; Burke, 2013; Buzan and Wæver, 2003; Deutsch, 1955; Kratochwil, 1989; Linklater, 2011; Taylor, 1982; Wæver, 1996).

Cosmopolitan protection has therefore been seen as a sign of gradual transformation of national security thinking and the national security communities into global security thinking and a global security community (Burke, 2013; Gholiagha, 2015; Kaldor, 2003, 2012, 2013; Linklater, 2002; Mello, 2010; Münkler, 2002; Seybolt, 2007; Shaw, 2003). Yet, this expansion of security communities has not brought about peace. This is the third paradox of current warfare.

This book will explain and make sense of these three apparent paradoxes. It will explain why protection leads to escalation, why it leads to power-centric national selfishness, and why it does not lead to a global security community. This is the focus of this book.

CHAPTERS OF THE BOOK

To answer the question of why protection fails, we need to follow the path to failure backwards – from the end to the beginning. The first instrumental question we need to answer, for example, is why efforts to protect global civilians are resisted. The answer to this question may make sense of the reasons for the escalation of conflict. Second, we need to answer how the practice of military protection fuels resistance and offers perceived justification for the enemy's violence. Before we can answer these questions, however, we must answer the question of how much, and in what ways, the practice of military protection of civilians has been a failure. This book assumes that the number of fatalities is the main criterion of success and failure of a military operation to protect. An operation has been a failure if it has failed to reduce the number of fatalities. Of course, civilians also need protection against brutal treatment, not just against killings, but if we make sense of the scale of fatalities, it is likely that brutality is in proportion to the number of fatalities too.

Since the situation in fragile states before protective interventions was one of a lack of norms, structures, institutions and enforcement of order, then, to discover whether military protection has failed or succeeded, the question we must also pose is whether and in what ways have international protective interventions affected these structures and state fragility. In other words, before trying to explain why cosmopolitan protection fails or succeeds, we must investigate how the consequences of these protective operations are associated with conflict fatalities and state fragility.

These two questions – has protection failed, and why – will be approached in this book, first in Chapters 2 and 3, by identifying the conditions under which current warfare takes place. Here, this book first drills down to the concept of state fragility, the condition that allows opportunistic violence against civilians in the first place. I will first examine the analysis of the so-called new wars and then I will link the analytical definitions with operations on existing data on state fragility and identify stable and fragile states. Next, I will create a definition and operationalization of and a distinction between new wars and protection wars. I will start with the empirical discovery that almost all contemporary conflict fatalities are produced in intrastate conflicts of fragile states. Then I will show how these wars can be distinguished between those that are intervened in by well-intentioned great powers, and those that are not. The first category of wars will be termed 'protection wars', and the latter 'new wars'.

In Chapter 4, I will then use the identification of fragile states and protection wars and new wars to analyse the consequences of protective interventionism on conflict fatalities and state fragility. This analysis will consider all intrastate conflicts since 1995 until 2016[2] and study the effect of interventionism on:

- overall global numbers of fatalities and overall global development of state fragility;
- state fragility and number of fatalities in countries where interventions took place and in countries where they did not take place;
- the number of fatalities in specific conflicts.

The main conclusion of Chapter 4 is that most conflicts that were intervened in by great powers with good intentions, escalated and contributed to the increase of global as well as conflict-specific numbers of fatalities, at the same time as increasing state fragility and fatalities in the countries concerned. The chapter will then conclude that, compared to similar conflicts where great powers did not intervene, so far, protective interventions have, indeed, been failures. However, the chapter will also show that failure has been uneven, with some cases, most clearly the UK's intervention in Sierra Leone in 2000, more successful than others. In general, it seems that the first humanitarian interventions, Kosovo, 1999, Sierra Leone, 2000, and the first years of the intervention in Afghanistan, were particularly more successful than the interventions that took place after the beginning of the war in Iraq, and after the transformation of interventions into a pattern of air operations rather than boots on the ground.

After Chapter 4, the book then aims to make sense of the developments that have led to the failure of protection. In Chapter 5, it will review the sources of escalation of protection wars by looking at how enemies of protection justify their violence once there is international intervention. This chapter will look at the interaction between the hostile discourses of the Slobodan Milošević, Saddam Hussein, Muammar Gaddafi and Bashar al-Assad administrations and the terrorist discourse of ISIS and Al Qaeda on the one hand, and the US presidential discourse on the other, and trace the mutual constitution of legitimate violence in world politics. The chapter demonstrates which elements of US practices and rhetoric were successfully used by dictators and terrorists in the construction of the legitimacy (within their own communities) of violence against intervening forces and the original civilian targets. This analysis reveals that the main sources of perceived legitimacy of violence against civilians were related to the perceived selfishness, unilateralism and militarism of Western approaches to protection. Here the exceptions, and the case of Sierra Leone in particular, will be studied too. The chapter will investigate why the UK intervention did not give rise to motivations and justifications for increased rebel (and rebel soldier) violence in this exceptional case.

In Chapters 6, 7 and 8, the analysis moves an additional step backwards on the path to the failure of protection. These chapters will look at why Western protection has taken forms that can be viewed as selfish, unilateralist and militaristic, by tracing the roots of selfishness, unilateralism and militarism in the process of interaction between material and social structures and presidential agency in US foreign policy. US presidential papers from 1989 have been analysed for their method, agency and referent object of protection to reveal the trends and to identify the main texts that have then been subjected to further qualitative analysis. The sources of legitimacy of selfishness, unilateralism and militarism in US protection are then revealed and analysed, and at the end of each of these chapters, trends in methods, agents and referent objects of protection are related to the practices of protection (new and ongoing protective military operations), to prove that these discursive changes had an impact on the types of practices of protection the US had adopted. Also, these chapters will pay attention to the exceptions and try to explain the variation in the degree of success or failure of protective operations.

Chapter 9 concludes with the recipes for failure in Western protection of global civilians and suggests that global democratization and inclusiveness on the one hand, and feminization of protection on the other, could be recipes for better practices of protection. This chapter returns to the theories, one that rejects the whole idea of failure in protection and the other that tries to make sense of it. Before that, though, below we introduce the existing theories and their claims for and approaches to the protection of civilians.

EXISTING LITERATURE ON ANARCHICAL INTRASTATE CONFLICTS AND THE IMPACT OF EXTERNAL INTERVENTION

Anarchy is the fundamental underlying concept in the theory of international relations. It is the condition that distinguishes this field from the rest of political science. For Kenneth Waltz, the underlying cause permitting war to arise is anarchy – the lack of a regulatory system on the international level. While this general, enabling cause alone does not explain wars, it does pave the way for other particular causes, which for Waltz are often accidental and trivial, but are the more immediate causes of war (Waltz, 1968, p. 231; see also Suganami's analysis of Waltz's permissive or logical causality in Suganami, 1996, pp. 35–48).

Empirical work on conflicts has already shown that the dominant type of conflict after World War II has been intrastate warfare (Holsti, 2006; Lacina and Gleditsch, 2005; Sarkees and Wayman, 2010). Already in the 1980s, 1990s and 2000s, scholars of post-colonial security (Ayoob, 1991; Azar and Moon, 1988c) and theorists on new wars (Duffield, 2001; Kaldor, 1999; Mello, 2010; Shaw, 2003) as well as some rationalist scholars (Fearon, 1995; Fearon and Laitin, 2014; Posen, 1993; Van Evera, 1994) pointed to the fact that, while in the West (and the Global North), states had grown out of intrastate anarchy, the Global South states still lived under conditions of disorder. There, the regulatory system of states did not exercise a monopoly on legitimate violence. Therefore, according to theorists on post-colonial security and the theorists on new wars, conflict studies ought to focus on intrastate anarchy rather than interstate anarchy. Despite the fact that the study of international relations is often seen as the 'political science of the context of anarchy' we should be alert to the fact that much of international relations is, in fact, orderly. Meanwhile, a significant amount of intrastate politics is not. Between states, order does exist – for example, within the EU; and intrastate anarchy is also prevalent – for example, in Somalia.

The claim that post-Cold War conflicts have generally been fought in fragile developing countries gets support from empirical studies of civil wars. These studies posit that the nature of current conflicts is largely ethno-nationalist. As Snyder argues, ethnic nationalism 'predominates when institutions collapse, when existing institutions are not fulfilling people's basic needs and when satisfactory alternative structures are not readily available' (Snyder, 1993, p. 86; see also Brown, 1996, p. 17). Rationalist theorists of intrastate conflict, such as Posen, Fearon, Laitin and Van Evera (Fearon and Laitin, 2014, p. 3; Posen, 1993; see also Tilly, 1975; Van Evera, 1994), have explicitly applied models from international relations theory to the analysis of security dilemmas between ethnic groups within developing states with a weak regulating authority. According to this analysis, the lack of a monopoly on legitimate violence because of state security fragility means that even without any interest in violence, intrastate groups need to resort to their own capacity to defend themselves. Because of internal anarchy, ethnic and religious groups may see each other as potential threats, and this common sentiment fuels mutual antagonism (Fearon, 1995; Posen, 1993).

Those who study the specific problems of Third World security (Ayoob, 2004; Azar and Moon, 1988c) have specified the internal sources of this insecurity typical of conflicts of today. Post-colonial scholars argue that the main conflict threat in fragile developing countries is related to the intrastate political software problems (rather than military hardware problems) of the state (Azar and Moon, 1988a). Such problems are first the lack of government performance and the lack of capacity to produce intended policy outcomes (security, welfare, etc.); second, the lack of national unity or common interests and mutual identity inside the nation; and finally, the lack of legitimacy of the state and its leaders (Azar and Moon, 1988c, p. 8).

Nevertheless, while the existing analysis of the conditions of current warfare tends to emphasize the failing states as the main condition of warfare in the post-Cold War era, scholarship has major disagreements on the following questions that are crucial for the justification of protective intervention. The existing literature on ethical and empirical dimensions of protection will be used as clarification of the alternative ethical and factual knowledge behind the practice of protection, while the empirical generalizations of existing literature related to the rationales of protection will also be used for the creation of hypotheses for this investigation on the path to the failure of protection. The following questions are essential for our investigation:

- Ethics:
  - Is it permissible to intervene in another country to protect its citizens?
  - Who has permission to protect?
- Diagnosis:
  - Does state fragility cause opportunistic and greed-motivated violence by perpetrators and innocent civilians, or does it (also) cause grievance-based violence without a clear-cut distinction between the justified and the unjustified parties?
  - Are states failing and thus is there an emergency that requires urgent international action?
  - Is military protection a feasible and useful strategy?

On Ethics of Cosmopolitan Protection

Cosmopolitanism is an ethical theory and thus should not be confused with theories that make empirical generalizations on the consequences of acting on cosmopolitan prescriptions. Yet, there are commonalities in the thinking of cosmopolitan scholars with regard to the diagnosis of the world, some of which are almost necessary for cosmopolitan ethics to be relevant in the realm of global military governance. Therefore, this book has a loose definition of cosmopolitanism and includes the empirical generalizations of those scholars who define themselves as cosmopolitan theorists of international relations (Kaldor, Duffield, Ralph, Hayden) in the term cosmopolitanism.

From the point of view of a study on interventions, there are at least two relevant ethical principles. The first is related to the claim that:

> [. . .]all persons stand in certain moral relations with one another by virtue of the fact that they are all members of a universal community. All persons possess equal moral worth deserving of our respect, and certain obligations of justice with regards to other persons place constraints on our conduct. (Hayden, 2005, p. 2)

The principle that state borders have no moral relevance to the obligations and rights of people, and that thus, human rights and obligations are universal and general, and the same regardless of borders, is common to all cosmopolitan theories of interventions and theorists of new wars. This cosmopolitan ethical position is also clearly stated in the UN documents related to the doctrine on the Responsibility to Protect as codified in the Resolution adopted by the General Assembly on 16 September 2005 (United Nations General Assembly, 2005). While some view cosmopolitan morality from the point of view of common utility (Singer, 1972), rights (Vincent, 1986) or obligations (O'Neill, 2000) this is not important for our study of interventions, but since the analysis in this book will continue along a consequentialist path, it will itself commit to some kind of utilitarianism, in which the virtue of protection is based on its utility in the prevention of fatalities of war and fragility of structures that should prevent such fatalities from occurring.

An important normative distinction between cosmopolitan theories is in the question of who can intervene when conflict entrepreneurs, terrorists or dictators threaten the lives of citizens in a country that is too fragile to be able or too distorted to even want to protect these people from such violence. The main difference in the theories that focus on the global protection of civilians is not so much whether a theory allows unilateral actors to act to protect civilians in another country, but rather whether the theory pays serious attention to the very question of agency of protection. While the Kantian tradition is clearly contractarian and assumes that norms of protection should somehow be owned by all those in the global community (Kant, 1999), Hayden (2005) represents a most elaborate ethical analysis that largely ignores the question in the exploration of the real world, while international relations specialists in the cosmopolitan school often simply skip the question of agency (Duffield, 2001; Kaldor, 2012).[3] Yet, as will be further analysed in Chapters 5 and 7, this question has tremendous consequences for the success of protection of civilians from conflict violence.

Both in scholarly and in political literature, the moral question of who has the right and responsibility to protect depends partly on the nature of conflicts and thus on the diagnosis. As will be shown in Chapter 7, a diagnosis that sees conflicts as criminal violence makes a moral judgement of protection by anybody easier than a diagnosis that claims that conflicts are more complicated, and that it is not possible to simply identify the bad guy from the good guy.

The political discourses that will be focused on in this book mostly subscribe to the moral position that either ignores the question of agency in protection, or use rhetorical strategies (criminalization of the opponent, hegemonic logic of global agency, the end of history discourse, etc.) to make the question of who protects irrelevant or confusing, as also will be shown in Chapter 7. However, the UN doctrine on the Responsibility to Protect is rather explicit about the question of agency. Already in 1999, the UN Secretary-General Kofi Annan raised the question and warned that humanitarian interventions that were not authorized by the UN Security Council could be 'setting dangerous precedents for future interventions without a clear criterion' (Annan 1999). Annan and the UN resolutions on the Responsibility to Protect emphasize the agency of the UN Security Council in cosmopolitan protection, even if soliciting cooperation and help from regional organizations in their own areas (United Nations General Assembly, 2005). Neither the Secretary-General's Annual Report of 1999 to the UNGA, that initially introduced some cosmopolitan principles involving resisting violence within member states, nor the UNGA resolution of 2005 on the Responsibility to Protect mention NATO as an agent or even as a collaborator in protection.

Diagnosis: Greed and Opportunities or Grievances – Protective Intervention as a Cure or a Curse?

Does state fragility simply offer opportunities for conflict entrepreneurs? Does it create asymmetrical wars in which opportunistic perpetrators threaten innocent civilians (Bellamy, 2016; Buchanan and Keohane, 2015; Duffield, 2001; Kaldor, 2012; Mello, 2010; Münkler, 2002; Thakur, 2016), or does it also create grievances that cause conflicts between equally justified or unjustified conflicting parties (Ayoob, 1991; Azar and Moon, 1988c; Gurr, 2000; Nafziger, Steward and Väyrynen, 2000)? While the latter type of diagnosis would prescribe conflict resolution, the former can lend support to an interventionist prescription, assuming that interventionist protection is morally right and strategically feasible. This study will show that the former diagnosis of conflicts underlies the cosmopolitan interventionism that this book focuses on.

There is a wealth of empirical analyses of conflicts that agree that the prevalent type of violence in conflicts is opportunistic rather than ideological or political. Heupel and Zangl have shown convincingly that war economies based on criminal activities are important contexts of warfare of today. The fragmentation of warring parties and the economization of their war motives facilitate the application of brutal violence against civilians (Heupel and Zangl, 2010). According to most theories that support the interventionist approach to new wars, conflicts are motivated by greed rather than grievances: potential wealth is a much more important context of wars than desperation and grievances and poverty (see, for example, Duffield, 2001; Kaldor, 2012, p. 2; Münkler, 2002, p. 7).

Yet, the transformation of war from grievance motivations to opportunistic greed motivations is not necessarily anything new. It may have been highlighted by the decline in the ideological interstate competition between the communist and anti-communist great powers, yet this decline did not necessarily change the situation in conflicts of fragile states. In fragile states, the motives for war may have been diverse and also related to opportunities and greed. Despite the fact that Kaldor and Münkler seem to suggest that some of the changes after the end of the Cold War contributed to the emergence of opportunistic violence that targets innocent civilians, Kalyvas has suggested that the criminal, rather than the political, nature of warfare is not something new (Kalyvas, 2001, p. 99).

Yet, despite the existence of criminal, opportunistic motives of violence, wars can still be mainly motivated by grievances. Gurr, Lichbach and Nafziger et al. have argued that grievances still dominate as predictors of conflicts (Gurr, 1970, 1993; Lichbach and Gurr, 1981; Nafziger et al., 2000), and that only this can explain why compromises, rather than enforcement of norms, have been associated with the decline of conflict fatalities, especially in the 1990s (Gurr, 2000). Regardless of whether conflicts in fragile states are driven by opportunities and greed, or by grievances, it seems clear that the diagnosis based on greedy, opportunistic and criminal conflict motives drives the reality of political interventions. When conflicts were not considered as political and as being motivated by political disputes on the terms of order, who was controlling the 'local thugs' or 'mad mortar-men' did not make such a difference (Clinton, 2000d, p. 2146). According to Bush Jr:

> [t]hese are people that you just cannot reason with. You can't negotiate with them. Therapy is not going to work with them. [Laughter] They're coldblooded people. That's the way they are. And we have a solemn responsibility to the American people to bring them to justice. We must deal with them in foreign lands so we do not have to face them here at home. That's our job. (G.W. Bush, 2005c, p. 1317)

While it seems clear that the scholarly ideas of criminal conflicts interact with the dominant interventionist political discourse and help identify the logic of justification of interventionism, the claim that conflicts are opportunistic and therefore can be ended simply by taking away the opportunities for violence can, and will be, tested in this study.

The urgency of new war theories to protect civilians has been partly based on the diagnosis that state fragility is increasing and that this is why the international community has to develop robust mechanisms of intervention urgently. According to new war theory, after the end of the Cold War, the lack of interest by the international community in the suffering of people in the anarchic zones of the Third World created a new situation that was providing opportunities for violence and new wars. This allowed brutal, senseless violence to continue unchecked:

> [T]he end of the Cold War has been accompanied by an apparently reduced willingness and ability to control internal violence. . . Governments and potential insurgents no longer have ideological patrons who provide them with the wherewithal to commit violence and then expect some influence over how that violence is carried out. (Snow, 1996, p. 46; see also Daalder, 1996, p. 462; Kaldor, 1999, p. 3)

Thus, the policies of relative non-intervention that the US and its allies implemented during the genocides in Bosnia and Rwanda represented exceptions in which great powers did not interfere in opportunistic chaos in these anarchic states, even though violence and human suffering was evident.

Even though rationalist theory focuses mostly on where state institutions have failed, Fearon and Laitin suggest that anarchical states are developing to become functioning states, rather than intrastate order being in the process of degeneration. Fearon and Laitin posit that, in Europe and Latin America, the violence in the earlier period was 'integral to a state building process that actually caused a lower risk of armed conflict later on' (Fearon and Laitin, 2014, p. 3; see also Tilly, 1975). Thus, according to this theory, there is no increased urgency for international military actions – and, in addition to the positive rather than negative trend in state strength, nor are conflicts getting any deadlier for civilians. Melander and others have shown that the change in war trends, from interstate to intrastate and the greater suffering of civilians, started a long time before the end of the Cold War (Harbom, Melander and Wallensteen, 2008; Melander, Öberg and Hall, 2009). While Melander and others have examined conflict trends in all countries, Chapter 4 will examine them specifically in fragile states.

If conflicts are opportunistic and there is an urgency to react to them, and if reacting to them is morally acceptable, the remaining empirical question is whether the consequences of international intervention in conflicts in fragile states produce positive consequences. The answer of many scholars of new wars tends towards the positive. Political and scholarly justifications for interventionism often cite the cases of Bosnia and Rwanda as examples of how non-intervention results in tragedies (Kaldor, 1999, p. 3; Daalder, 1996; Clinton, 2000h, p. 974; Obama, 2011e). While moral cosmopolitanism does not make generalizations with regard to whether or not intervention can help the situation of civilians, but simply gives a moral justification to it in cases it does (Brick, 2009; Buchanan, 2004; Caney, 2005; Jones, 1999; Kant, 1999), and while some cosmopolitan scholars tend to emphasize the norm of non-interference despite their cosmopolitan commitment (Vincent, 1974), many cosmopolitan scholars of international relations who theorize about new wars are optimistic about the opportunities the international community may have in enforcing humanitarian norms (Buchanan and Keohane, 2015; Kaldor, 2012; Münkler, 2002). This book will mainly focus on the work of the latter category of cosmopolitan scholars as their ideas seem to interact with the political discourses of protection. These cosmopolitan scholars will be termed theorists of new wars.

Yet, this study will also focus on the theoretical perspectives where incomplete cosmopolitan commitment or incomplete understanding of the nature of new wars lead to outcomes that are worse than non-cosmopolitan outcomes. Chapter 6 of this book focuses on the phenomenon where a military operation is justified for international audiences by references to cosmopolitan justification, but which in domestic bureaucracy and for domestic audiences is justified by national priorities. The former justification makes operations possible in the international political realm, while the latter priorities shape the modalities of operations. Here cosmopolitan justification of nationally motivated and justified operations contributes to the failure of protection (if it can be called failure, as protection of global civilians may not have been the primary aim of the operation), and yet it would be difficult to claim that cosmopolitan ethics contributes to the suffering. After all, it was the lack of cosmopolitan commitment that was part of the explanation for the failure. This logic, in which cosmopolitan commitment suffices to justify but not motivate operations, is analysed theoretically by Falk. He opposes current ‘cosmopolitan operations’ because of the shallow commitment to cosmopolitan ethics. According to Falk:

> [a]t this stage in world politics any genuine humanitarian moves by states are likely to be underfunded and insufficient. In contrast, interventions backed by the requisite will and resources are likely to be strategic in motivation, and humanitarian only in rationalization; such interventionary violence will be illegal and anti-humanitarian. This is the meaning of Kosovo. (Falk, 2003, p. 325; for a relatively similar argument, see Gilmore, 2014)

The new war theory posits that, to tackle intrastate anarchy, one should intervene and suppress violent opportunities that could be exploited by conflict entrepreneurs, terrorists and dictators. According to Kaldor, '[t]he analysis of new wars suggests that what is needed is not peacekeeping but enforcement of cosmopolitan norms, i.e. enforcement of international humanitarian and human rights law' (Kaldor, 1999, pp. 124–5). Kaldor rejects an old British peacekeeping concept that assumes that minimal power should be used and instead subscribes explicitly to the Weinberger–Powell Doctrine: use of overwhelming force that creates an environment that negates opportunities for violence that exist in a weak system of governance in fragile states (ibid., pp. 128–9).

If new wars are a result of declining control and policing, then control and policing need to be introduced in fragile states to end violence. This logic can be found in the US rhetoric of cosmopolitan interventionism. The threat is opportunistic, so opportunities for violence need to be negated by the 'overwhelming force' of strong powers (Clinton, 1997, p. 1257). Victims need protection and the moral basis underlying protective missions is unchallengeable (Obama, 2012a, p. v). The common prescription of theorists of new wars is that cosmopolitan powers should have responsibility to protect in intrastate anarchies, resorting to force if needed, even if this means violating the sovereignty of states that are unable or unwilling to protect their citizens (Bellamy, 2002; Duffield, 2001; Habermas, 2000; Kaldor, 2003; Linklater, 2017; Mello, 2010; Münkler, 2002; Thakur, 2016). External force should be used to block violent opportunities and to introduce a setting like that in functioning states. This prescription for humanitarian intervention is central to the theory of new wars. For the sake of conceptual clarity, I will use the cosmopolitan theories of uncivil wars (Snow, 1996), degenerative wars (Shaw, 2003), and new wars (Duffield, 2001; Gilbert, 2003; Heupel and Zangl, 2010; Kaldor, 2012; Mello, 2010; Münkler, 2002) as a theoretical model for political humanitarian interventionist justification (although the mode of intervention is not necessarily exactly that described by the theory).

Yet, even if almost all theorists of new wars agree that an international military effort at protection could be successful, there are differing interpretations about the ways in which real-life protection wars have been conducted. While Habermas praised the international effort in Kosovo as a purely cosmopolitan effort (Habermas, 2000, p. 61), the way in which humanitarian law was enforced in Afghanistan, Iraq and thereafter has been explicitly criticized by many new war theorists (Kaldor, 1999, p. 159). While Kaldor, for example, accepts humanitarian interventions in principle, she criticizes the Western approach for the misunderstanding of the nature of the fragile states. In such states, according to Kaldor, the approach was old-fashioned, militaristic, Clausewitzian, and aimed simply at defeating the enemy or forcing one's own will on it. This is the logic of military combat in old wars; in new wars, the intervention must win the hearts of the people and help build the state structures that could then control violence (Kaldor, 2012, pp. 152–61). Chapter 8 of this book will develop this idea and look at the consequences of the power-centric approach that focuses on protection by defeating, coercing or bribing the agent who poses an intentional threat to global civilians, rather than doing something to protect people from unintentional threats (by offering humanitarian assistance), or by approaching threats by means of mutual self-restraint (by developing multilateral mechanisms of arms control), or by means that do not affect the agent of threat (by accepting refugees). There the focus is in the discourse strand on protection, but the analysis makes a difference between power-oriented and non-power-oriented approaches to it.

The question of whether humanitarian interventions to protect civilians are useful or not also depends on the agency of protection, not just on the approach adopted. Chapter 7 of this book will focus on the question of agency and ownership of protection and norms that protective operations enforce. New war theorists claim that there is no need for cosmopolitan agency (global agency that is also 'owned' by the targets of cosmopolitan norm enforcement). Nor do they see any need for complete unanimity regarding operations of protection (Kaldor, 1999, p. 126). These theories can be seen as the theoretical foundation for unilateralist humanitarian interventionism by the US. Still, the success or failure of Western humanitarian interventions cannot be completely traced back to the presumptions of the theory, since the way in which interventions have been conducted does not completely correspond to the theory of new wars.

Some of the rationalist scholars and post-colonial theory disagree with this analysis. Fearon and Laitin (and Tilly) claim that great power rule in the Third World has generally created rather than solved problems. While in Europe, where state development took place without external interference, the creation of states led to order, 'Asia, Africa, and the Middle East. . .[which] experienced colonial and imperial wars before 1945, especially in the 19th century, were more likely to experience civil wars post-independence' (Fearon and Laitin, 2014, p. 3; see also Tilly, 1975). This is also the claim of post-colonial theory. While pre-colonial Africa and Asia had prosperous states even with some institutions of popular sovereignty, the slave trade and colonial intervention reversed this development. Instead, extractive rather than democratic institutions emerged. The difficulty of post-colonial state formation has been related to the growing power of elites within civil society (Mamdani, 2010) and the fact that new leaders of independent post-colonial states had no interest in changing the extractive state institutions into institutions that could serve people. Consequently, the fragile part of the world is not uncontrolled chaos; it is a well-managed disorder that produces benefits to its users and designers. Such disorder is a consequence of the legacy of colonialism and a result of extractive colonial state institutions (Chabal and Daloz, 1999).

Furthermore, Posen suggests that the US grand strategy should be based on restraint, and that the 'US has to give up some objectives. The coercive reform and political reorganization of other countries has proven expensive and "success" has proven elusive' (Posen, 2014, p. 169). Fearon and Laitin describe this conclusion as typically realist, and one that President George W. Bush supported before the terrorist attack on 11 September 2001 (Fearon and Laitin, 2004). Similar rationalist realism could be detected in the speeches by President Donald Trump, especially until the aerial operation against the Syrian Air Force base in April 2017 (Trump, 2017b).

Post-colonial theory suggests a diagnosis that leans more towards Posen, Fearon and Laitin than to the new war theories. According to Ayoob 'disorder is primarily the product of the early state of state-making during which, as the earlier European example demonstrates, violence and conflict are inevitable' (Ayoob, 1995, p. 13). The problem of anarchical states is not something new, but rather one that relates to the early phase of state-making. The Third World state is not disintegrating; it has never existed (Chabal and Daloz, 1999). Ayoob contends that states must be allowed to develop without external interference even if this means some violent and authoritarian phases. Yet, post-colonialist theory does admit that the collapse of the communist states of the Soviet Union and Yugoslavia contributed to the expansion of zones of disorder: 'The dismemberment of the SU and Yugoslavia at the end of the Cold War also has led to the geographical expansion of the Third World, which now embraces Central Asia, the Caucasus, and the Balkans' (Ayoob, 1995, p. 15).

Post-colonial theory also disagrees with the theory of new wars on the effect of external powers on state fragility. Ayoob is even more extreme in his conclusions about this than Posen and the rationalists. Ayoob maintains that Cold War great powers did not seek to control violence in developing countries:

> [S]uperpower involvement in Third World conflicts in supportive and other roles did not commit the two dominant global powers to ensure the security of their local clients and allies under any circumstances or to confront each other directly to ensure security for their allies. . .[the] Third World became the zone where East/West competition could be waged with minimal apparent danger of uncontrolled escalation. (Ayoob, 1995, p. 14)

Thus, the ending of superpower interest in the Third World was a blessing rather than a curse to developing countries.

So, according to theorists on post-colonial security, Western interference has never served the purpose of the developing world. Thus, avoiding such interference cannot be a problem, even though post-colonial theory recognizes state fragility as central to conflict problems (Ayoob, 2005, p. 959). According to the post colonial theory of security, security in the Third World is often challenged by intrastate threats related to lack of cohesion between people, lack of legitimacy and poor performance of the government. Building aid mechanisms outside the state and the government may address the immediate problems of the state, but only sidelines the vital state-building project, which, in the long run, is crucial to the people's security (Azar and Moon, 1988c).

According to Ayoob, the problem of humanitarian intervention in fragile states is related to the perceived illegitimacy of great power agency in the Third World. While Kaldor sees the source of legitimacy of such intervention in the quality of the operation (Kaldor, 1999, p. 159), Ayoob sees the lack of Third World authorship and ownership as the source of the problem. Even if the intervention is meant for the protection of civilians, the people who are objects of this protection tend to resist it because of this perception (Ayoob, 2001).

The reason post-colonial and new war theorists have a very different idea of the degree of ownership among the people that are being protected in fragile states is partly related to the difference in the focus in the study of cosmopolitan protection. The struggle against the authoritarian leaders of communist autocrats at the end of the Cold War is the favourite focus of the new war theorists. New war theorists suggest that there was a transcontinental movement of citizens (Burke, 2004), which gave rise to the emergence of a global civil society (Kaldor, 2003, p. vii). This global civil society has managed to advocate and sell the idea of a set of basic humanitarian norms, and a set of norms pertaining to their enforcement (Kaldor, 2003). Thakur suggests that the spreading of the international legal consensus can be identified in the introduction of a number of international conventions and agreements that a number of states have formally committed to and implemented (Thakur, 2016).

While this global civil society acts as one in areas related to fundamental human rights, against dictators, terrorists and human rights violators, it needs coercive institutions that can exercise overwhelming power to control and prevent the opportunities for the most extreme types of violations of the international humanitarian law (Kaldor, 1999, pp. 128–9). The world cannot wait for a world state to emerge (ibid., p. 126). Instead, global civil society must work with transnational institutions, such as the Western

European Union (WEU), Partnership for Peace, NATO Coordination Council (NACC), and with cosmopolitan countries (Kaldor, 2012, p. 188). Kaldor considers these forces that act for the security of global citizens, not for their national interests, as cosmopolitan countries, or cosmopolitan powers (powers that 'constitute an intensification of transnationalization in the military sphere') (ibid., 2012, p. 139).

However, when interventions are studied from the perspective of the Third World, the question of ownership changes. Even if East European civil society felt togetherness with their Western supporters, this is not necessarily the case with Iraqi victims of the Saddam Hussein's authoritarian violence. NATO or NACC, let alone the different coalitions of the willing or international security forces that NATO has control over or forces that consist of former colonial rulers, might not represent the victims of violence in fragile countries, and this, according to Ayoob, could be the reason conflicts may escalate with Western interventions (Ayoob, 2001). While Kaldorian optimism related to the feasibility of international intervention clearly interacts with interventionist political discourse, the question of whether intervention protects or not, and whether the question of agency of protection has consequences, are empirical questions that this study can and will address.

HOW CAN THE FAILURE TO PROTECT BE STUDIED?

This book represents constructivist pragmatist scholarship. The reason it is useful to study the success and failure of cosmopolitan protection is practical. If we continue to assume that whatever the Global North does to the developing world has only positive consequences, then we cannot make informed decisions on whether and how to interfere in violent unfairness in the Global South.

The reason the focus is on the success of a strategy or an orientation, and the knowledge behind such an orientation rather than on exogenous causal conditions of conflict fatalities, is practical too. If it is assumed that reality is exogenously constituted rather than something that strategies of genuine agency can create, we must abandon ontologies that could allow our purposive action to change things in a way that would minimize conflict fatalities. If the focus is only on exogenous causation, and if we feel that conflicts can only be explained through the degree of exogenous causal conditions (explanatory power of a model), we will be writing off the agency that we would need to use our knowledge to make peace and reduce violence (Heidegger, 1962). Therefore, it is also practical to try to understand social processes from within the purposes of agents, as Hollis and Smith (1990) suggest. Yet, while this study will begin from premises that do not write off agency, it will also not assume that social developments simply follow our intentions. Otherwise it would be difficult to understand why the willingness to protect civilians can lead to the escalation that eventually kills the civilians we wanted to protect. Agency interacts with social and material realities, just as, for example, Wendt and Wight suggest (Wendt, 1987; Wight, 2006), and the process of this interaction sometimes leads us in directions we did not intend to take. Thus, the interactive process where agency interacts with social and material structures requires our attention so that our agency could be more successful in achieving things we want to achieve.

However, the pragmatism of this study is not of the classical kind. Because classical pragmatists focused on the materially constituted realities, they could see the function of knowledge as instrumental. Whichever knowledge can help us deal with the reality around us is pragmatic in an instrumental sense. However, if the reality is constituted by our collective interpretations we cannot just consider instrumental pragmatism. We cannot just consider what tools knowledge offers for the fixing of a material condition, but instead we must think about what kind of realities our shared knowledge constitutes. A paradigm of race purity in a racist state can have instrumental value for the management of something we understand as races, but the very 'knowledge' of races already creates social agency of these races. Instead of just thinking whether theories of race purity can be used for something practical, we must also consider whether the existence of races as political actors that the theory and its concepts construct, is a positive, pragmatic reality. When classical pragmatism only considers instrumentally what we can do with certain knowledge or a certain paradigm, constructivist pragmatism that this study represents also considers what that knowledge does to us and our social realities. A constructivist pragmatist must also consider theories and concepts for the usefulness of the entity they constitute, as without our knowledge, theories and understanding (and convention) of many ideative entities, such as states as actors of international relations or money as an instrument of economic exchange, such realities would not exist. Thus, we must extend our use of the pragmatist criteria in our assessment of the practical value of theories from considerations of their instrumental value to the practicality of realities they constitute (Kivimäki, 2016, p. 18).

In addition to agency, a practical approach to protection would require the recognition of interaction between agency and elements of social structures such as roles, norms and identities that in causal models are often seen as problematic due to their partly endogenous relationship with behaviour. We cannot 'explain' in the classical positivist sense violence or non-violence by referring to norms, roles or identities, as none of these 'independent variables' are analytically separate from the 'dependent variable': one cannot claim the existence of a norm if everyone demonstrates a complete lack of that norm, or the identity of a fighter if the actor never fights. Yet, norms, roles and identities are relevant to and not just tautologies of violent or non-violent behaviour. By offering positive identities, it is possible to entice a conflicting party towards more cooperative behaviour, while by accepting norms, a community can alter the behaviour of its members.

To incorporate agency, socially constructed realities, partly endogenous social realities, and yet also recognize material realities, we will not be able to use all the methods that are used in causal modelling of behaviour. For the investigation of effects of cosmopolitan protection, we can start with correlative relationships between an approach (cosmopolitan protection) and consequences of that approach (in terms of fatalities and state fragility). However, due to agency and the fluidity of social structures, we cannot assume that what we can observe happening is something that had to happen. Instead, we must accept the possibility of alternative futures: things could have gone differently. Even the starting point of our analysis – the discussion of the consequences of protection – must be analysed with counterfactual realities in mind. The study of processes that enabled politically feasible use of violence must necessarily focus on the development of the interaction between agency, the emergence of social structures and the realities of material structures.

Analysis of the Consequences of Protection

The investigation of the extent to which military protection of global civilians has failed or succeeded will need a slightly different research strategy than the question of why the practice of protection has produced these outcomes. The first task related to the assessment of failure or success will require counterfactual analysis on the relationship between intervention on the one hand and fatalities and fragility on the other.

Doing this does not require very elaborate quantitative tools – we do not want to test multi-causal models, but only focus on the effects of one policy that can be easily identified. Thus, simple calculations suffice. However, the main methodological problem in this study is related to the problem of counterfactual reasoning: it has been suggested that the cost of intervention is easy to measure, while it is not possible to document the effect of intervention in preventing atrocities whenever such intervention is successful, since the evidence in these cases is missing (Paris, 2014, p. 574). To demonstrate that an intervention has failed one needs to claim two things:

(1) that in conflicts that were intervened, the level of fatalities and state fragility would generally have been lower had there not been an intervention; (2) that in conflicts that were not intervened, the level of fatalities and state fragility would generally have been higher had there been an intervention. Counterfactuals may be difficult to prove in individual cases, but an empirical observation of development in conflict fatalities in a historical era in countries and conflicts where interventionist policies are practised is possible. Comparisons in similar times, between similar fragile countries and between similar conflicts, make counterfactual analysis possible if we then compare cases of intervention and cases of non-intervention.

Analysis of the Path to Failure

The second part of this study (Chapter 5 onwards) focuses on discourses. The starting point of this analysis is the idea of treating text as data (Wilkerson and Casas, 2017). Textual analysis will be used to reveal how discourses interact with material and social structures and constitute social structures and how these structures interact with political agency. This investigation will follow the path of failure to protect by starting from the fact of the failure that has been established in Chapter 4, and by moving down that path backwards first to the counter-discourses of US protection. There the textual evidence is based on the translated speeches by Muammar Gaddafi (15 speeches and letters in 2001), Bashar al-Assad[4] (ten speeches after the beginning of the Syrian war in 2011), Saddam Hussein (five speeches, letters or interviews with Americans), Slobodan Milošević (nine speeches and letters 1998–2001) and the documents by the main terrorist enemies, ISIS (Islamic State administrative documents with 285 documents plus the so-called ISIS masterplan[5]) and Al Qaeda (24 translated documents related to the US or mobilization, from the CIA depository: Bin Laden's Bookshelf[6]). Because Sierra Leone is the main case of successful protection, it has received special attention in the textual analysis. There the focus is on texts by the group associated with the Revolutionary United Front (RUF) – the Armed Forces Revolutionary Council (25 press releases) – and the RUF itself (comments related to peace negotiations). The Sierra Leonean case has also been strengthened by interview material among UK officials involved in the intervention in 2000.

This textual evidence was investigated for the rationales of enemies of the West in their legitimation and justification (and mobilization) of violence. The focus was on how the Western practices and discourses helped these violent actors find perceived legitimacy for their violence. The method of analysis of the 'counter-discourse' is based on the coding of texts for their references to 'struggl',[7] 'bomb', 'attack', 'protect', 'defen', 'kill', 'revol', 'rebel', 'fight' and 'take up arms' (in all tenses) that refer to violent acts of the actors themselves in an approving manner. The qualitative analysis of the justifications of counter-cosmopolitan violence by terrorists, criminals and dictators has identified both identitive and activity-related justifications, of which the following were most prominent and frequent in the documents of enemies of the West:

- Identity of the opponent justifies violence if the identity is:
  - imperial (anti-imperialist justification);
  - colonial (anti-colonialist justification);
  - criminal (legalist justification).
- Action of the opponent justifies violence if the action is:
  - power-centric;
  - violent to people (reference to atrocities, threat to peace);
  - tribalist;
  - anti-democratic;
  - oppressive (reference to limitation of freedom);
  - impoverishing/exploitative;
  - threatening to state security;
  - in violation of an agreement/law.

Trends and cross-country/conflict differences in the strategies of legitimation of violence by enemies of the West were then established using NVivo.

With these tools and with more traditional content analysis of all the selected translated texts of enemies of Western cosmopolitan interventions I have then established three clusters of rationales in Western interventions that are being used by enemies for the constitution of legitimacy of their own violence. These three clusters are selfishness, unilateralism and militarism. Legitimations of enemy violence that draw from what is seen as the Western imperial justification, from the perceived breach of the international law on sovereignty, from the rhetoric of defence of the state against external aggression, internationally anti-democratic (powerful countries bullying weak countries), and from the rhetoric of oppression and limitation of sovereign freedom, have been lumped together in the cluster of unilateralism. Legitimations of enemy violence that draw from the rhetoric of colonial exploitation and impoverishment by the West, or selfish imperial power motives have been lumped together in the cluster of selfishness, while justifications that draw from the logic in which the enemy's violence is vindicated by the violence and military handling of the West are lumped together in the cluster of anti-militaristic justifications.

While the analysis of discourses does not imply a belief that justification of action is the only thing that is needed for a violent action, it commits to the idea that texts reveal more than just justifications, and that justifications too are needed as necessary conditions for political action that requires mobilization of forces and resources. While it is politically difficult to take into account the information that enemy propaganda can offer, it seems that conflicts escalate in interactive processes in which the discourses and approaches of one side constitute the legitimacy of discourses and practices of the other. Thus, even if the West should not be manipulated by the lies of terrorist discourse, such discourse contains information that can help avoid the escalation of conflicts.

Texts, even propaganda, can be studied as evidence if we focus on things it creates rather than on things it describes or refers to. Propaganda that emphasizes a norm, for instance, commits the speaker to it as it elevates the costs for him or her of violating it (Glanville, 2018). Yet, a propagandistic description of the realities on the ground cannot be used as evidence of realities on the ground.

This difference between the utility of studying realities that speech creates and the utility of studying a reality a speech describes on the basis of the speech is often misunderstood in political reality. According to President Bush Jr, for example:

> Usama bin Laden[8] used Somalia as an excuse for people to join his jihadist movement. In the past, they used the Israeli–Palestinian conflict. It was a convenient way to try to recruit people to their jihadist movement. They've used all kinds of excuses. This Government is going to do whatever it takes to protect this homeland. We're not going to let their excuses stop us from staying on the offense. The best way to protect America is defeat these killers overseas so we do not have to face them here at home. We're not going to let lies and propaganda by the enemy dictate how we win this war. (G.W. Bush, 2007e, p. 1703)

Here Bush assumes he can ignore the way in which bin Laden creates normative realities in his speech, simply by rejecting them. Yet, Bush seems to admit the failure of his approach when he admits that US operations and staying on the offensive increased anti-US terrorist mobilization. Even if Bush does not accept bin Laden's and anti-US militants' rationales against the US, they are still a reality if they increase anti-American mobilization. Yet, he claims it is the 'best way to protect America'. While public statements tend to manipulate the reality in a way that helps the speaker's bargaining leverage (by exaggerating one's commitment and determination, and by exaggerating signals of division among one's enemies), the construction of legitimate strategies creates realities itself, and is therefore a reality to be studied, not just a propagandistic picture of some objective reality.

Based on the clusters of rationales that enemies of Western interventions constitute in their texts I will then go further backwards along the path of failure to protect by examining how selfishness, unilateralism and militarism emerge in the Western discourse strand on protection. The purpose of the analysis of Western and anti-Western discourses is to reveal the interactive process in which both sides legitimize their violence by reference to the violence of their enemies. This way, textual analysis reveals the mutual constitution of legitimate violence in a process of escalation. The analysis of the counter-discourse reveals three sources from which enemies of the West tend to derive the perceived justification and legitimacy for their violence:

- the selfish nature of Western military action;
- the unilateralist approach of that action; and
- the militarism and power-centricity in the way Western 'protection' is conducted.

From enemy discourses, this study moves another step backwards by looking at how elements that enemies of the West in protection wars perceive as selfishness, unilateralism and militarism emerge in Western practice and discourse. Due to the central role of the US in military operations to protect global civilians, and due to the central role of the US's president in American foreign policy, I have selected the US government's *Public Papers of the Presidents of the United States* (US Government Printing Office, various years) as my primary data (Kivimäki, 2019b, forthcoming) for analysis of Western protection discourse. I have studied the entire period of the emergence of the discourse strand on protection starting from the last days of the Cold War until the last published electronic versions of the compilation of the presidential papers (1989–2012),[9] almost 30 million words.

Using this data, I will substantiate my claims on discourses in a more transparent, rigorous and convincing manner than by simply selecting sentences from various sources. Even if one does not assume that measurable material realities are the only reality, it is possible to avoid 'fantasy theories' (as Schweller, 1999, calls them), by treating texts in a methodical manner so that their interpretations may be verified or rejected.

However, instead of treating text as something that describes reality as the authors see it, this study is committed to a different ontology and thus a different method than most computerized textual analyses. It is based on the idea that world politics is not dictated by exogenous, material realities. Thus, my research on the social realities of protection must start from the discourses that are, on the one hand, a product of human activity, but which also facilitate and constrain the imagination and opportunities of human agency on the other. The interaction between agency, social realities and material realities cannot be revealed by a causal analysis that seeks explanations of developments based on exogenous material causes, nor can it be revealed by an analysis that does not recognize the importance of interpretations and discourses as social reality. Thus, such an analysis needs to look at meanings revealed in the texts. It must examine their relation to material, non-discursive events and structures as well as to purposive agency.

To make sense of frameworks that legitimize and justify killing in a military operation for an audience, one needs to analyse the texts that the actor presents to this audience. In this way, one can understand the ontological and normative foundations and the ways in which these foundations are mobilized and associated with projects such as military intervention. One needs dispositive analysis to reveal the knowledge behind the actions and practices of cosmopolitan protection (Foucault, 1974). However, when investigating apparently conflicting discourses, as is the case when one looks, on the one hand, at protection that tends to kill the ones it intends to protect, and on the other, at how selfish interests enter altruistic discourse strands on protection, one will probably not find a coherent set of texts within which all these contradictions make sense. Instead, one needs to analyse the historically specific processes in which the discourse strands of different issue areas meet and where compromises are needed and made within systems of decision-making. Different audiences can then be convinced by references to different types of normative and ontological premises in which dramatic events affect interpretations (Jäger, 2001).

We need to study the specific histories of interaction between action and social structures, in which actions are constituted by existing social structures and social structures are constituted by interpretative actions (Wendt, 1987). If we look at ideational constructs such as humanitarian norms, as well as human, group or national and international pursuits to rescue civilians anywhere in the world, we can see that these discourses and pursuits were born and they developed and created the institutions that they needed to succeed through specific historical processes. In these processes, social and material realities enabled and obstructed, directed and focused purposes and norms of civilian protection. Other norms and structures that political norms created affected the path from ideas to outcomes. Studying this path will require 'discursive process tracing', in which the focus is on texts that reflect and create discursive events, such as changing types of arguments, norms and interpretations, rather than merely material events. Quite as Justin Rosenberg has suggested, such analysis of path-dependent historically specific processes and changes requires methods that are grounded in historical and social analysis, rather than methods that assume ahistorical regularities (Rosenberg, 1994; see also Tickner, 2001, p. 9). It is focused on historically specific discursive events. These events naturally interact with changes in material realities, but they are not dictated by unchanging material regularities. Also, this interaction is well documented in texts related to political strategies on protection of civilians.

When tracing the processes of discourse development there are junctures at which deviations in the original intent behind a policy discourse enter the scene. Such junctures could be found in the following:

- Within the internal logic of the discourse strand that deals with protection of civilians: how certain types of arguments are allowed while others are not, depending on the normative and ontological premises of the discourse and pre-agreed-upon premises for argumentation on which the discourse strand is based. This part of the analysis uses the lessons of so-called dispositive analysis, aimed at reconstructing and revealing the knowledge lying behind discursive and non-discursive practices and reconstructing non-discursive practices that have led to the manifestations/materializations and the knowledge contained therein (Jäger, 2001, p. 47).
- In the entanglements of discourse strands (ibid., pp. 47–8) on protection and other interrelated issues. These entanglements are meaningful for the development of the normative and ontological premises of the discursive strand of protection. How, for example, the discourse strand on victimhood is used to depoliticize protection in the entanglements that expose discussion on protection to the ontologies and ethics of debates on victimhood (or criminality, or security threats, or democracy) affects the way in which the ownership of protection is shared.
- In the interaction of the text with audiences as part of the discourse context of protection (ibid., p. 48). It is clear that, domestic and international audiences, and rural national voters vs international diplomats have very different ethical and ontological expectations of the US president. Thus, texts produced for these two audiences affect the development of the discourse strand. The requirements imposed on the president or another decision-maker in US foreign politics based on a situation presented to a domestic or international audience affects US policy in varying ways, since consistency in the statements and knowledge revealed in texts and actions is necessary for credibility. Sometimes, interpretations of the realities of world politics are created to solve problems created by the need for consistency. US presidents, for example, tend to favour worldviews in which national interests can be reconciled with international responsibilities, and sometimes the need for consistency pushes them towards

interpretations that are not optimal in terms of credibility, or ones that can only be sustained by hiding the evidence against them.

- In the interaction of the discourse with the institutional settings to which they belong. The question of differing audiences is closely linked with the question of the structure of decision-making (ibid., pp. 47–9). The president primarily needs to persuade Congress to obtain funding for foreign operations, and the nation's voters to maintain the mandate and decision-making power on foreign operations. When the knowledge behind domestic and international audiences clashes, it is understandable that compromises need to be made, primarily at the expense of global ontologies and ethics.
- In events and discourse histories (ibid., p. 49). Crises in Rwanda, Somalia and Bosnia are often cited as the most important historical discourse contexts that affect the development of a discourse strand. The globalist ontologies of the immediate post-Cold War period were difficult to reconcile with the well-published events in Mogadishu in March 1993, when 18 US soldiers were killed. At the same time, the experienced consequences of the failure to react forcefully in Bosnia and Rwanda have served to boost interventionist arguments.

Despite dealing with interpretative reality and social constructs, in my investigation I have refused to make a random selection of what is important or to put forth loose claims about the representative quality of particular constructs. Instead, I have mapped discursive developments using computer-assisted textual analysis. For this I have used the NVivo text analysis program.

First, I selected proxy words for different discourse strands and used word frequency analyses to reveal how different discourse strands are related to each other and how this relationship develops. Second, I coded[10] clauses that deal with protection (selecting them by searching for the world 'protect' in its different forms) for the types of threats against which protection is needed. I ruled out instances covering protection of Americans and US institutions against non-external (for example, protection of American children against crime, decadence or tobacco and the like),[11] non-life-threatening threats (protection of US tobacco farmers, economic protectionism, etc.) and unintentional threats to the US and Americans (pandemics, environmental degradation,[12] securing of international traffic against technical dangers). Any other threats have been included in my further analysis.

The next phase of relational textual analysis focuses on the referent object of protection – that is, who is being protected. When possible, I have done this technically by looking at the grammatical reference of the word 'protect'. In some cases, though, the referent object of protection needs to be followed further in the paragraph and the speech/letter/interview. In this way, all clauses with the word 'protect' were included in this relational coding, which classified the referent objects into three categories: (1) protection of the US state and its people and institutions from intentional external danger; (2) protection of allies from comparable danger; and (3) protection crucial to their survival and well-being of people and institutions other than allied states from internal and external, intentional and non-intentional threats (that is to say, genuine cosmopolitan protection, such as protection of citizens in developing countries from terror, dictators and criminals, but also from developmental problems).[13] I call protection in the last category cosmopolitan because it cannot be seen as directly useful to US self-interest.

For the cosmopolitan type of protection, I also investigated the agency. I identified five types of agencies: (1) US agency; (2) allied agency; (3) US-led unrepresentative ad hoc coalition agency; (4) bilateral agency – where the US works with a developing country that is not in alliance with the US to protect that country and its citizens; and (5) representative international agency (United Nations, International Criminal Court, arms control regimes and agencies, and other actors that offer protection within countries that are members of the agency).

While the three first types of agency are clearly unrepresentative – there, somebody is protecting somebody else – the last category is undoubtedly representative. The bilateral/other agency is more difficult to interpret. This is a category of sentences in which cosmopolitan protection takes place in a country or is exercised for citizens of a country that is not allied with the US, but where some of the actors of protection, to varying degrees, are practising the protection themselves. These range from US drone programmes where sentences suggest the participation or acceptance of the local leader, to sentences of protection where the main actor is the country itself, but with US encouragement. Most sentences in this category deal with situations in which the US military is training and guiding the Afghan and Iraqi government, army and police in the protection of their own citizens.

Finally, I also coded those clauses where the referent object of protection was cosmopolitan (global civilian) according to the method of protection. Driven by the power of militarist responses in motivating and legitimizing violence of the anti-US camp (discourse analysis of Saddam Hussein's, Bashar al-Assad's and Al Qaeda's texts), I made a distinction between power-biased protection and protection that was not power biased.

When studying power bias – the preference for power strategies over power-neutral or power-negative strategies – I have selected the following

criteria for clauses in texts that determine whether they constitute power-centric realities for cosmopolitan protection:
A clause is power biased if the means of protection:

- prevents the acts of someone harming or threatening the people to be protected;
- deters someone from harming or threatening the people to be protected;
- rewards someone for not harming the people to be protected;
- destroys or weakens someone who is harming or threatening the people to be protected.

It is not power biased if protection is conducted:

- by action that does not affect the threatening agent (offering asylum etc.);
- against non-intentional threat (poverty, disease, etc.);
- by means of self-restraint: protecting democracy by the leaders in an agreement that concerns the protector (here agreements like the Helsinki Declaration signed by 35 nations in 1975 could be considered self-restraining, whilst democracy promotion in another country would be power biased as it deals with the behaviour of others).

This computerized textual analysis made it possible to show trends and developments in a transparent way. Coding was focused on the elements of the Western discourse that were revealed in the analysis of the texts of US enemies (actors that the US needed to protect its global civilians from) as elements that justified violence by dictators, criminals and terrorists. In addition to aiding a test of aspects of qualitative discourse analysis, a computerized textual analysis also directed the qualitative analysis to texts that are central and representative of various discursive changes or characteristics of the discourse strand.

The coding on NVivo of the presidential papers and the quantitative data on word and relational frequencies (Kivimäki, 2019b, forthcoming) are openly available in NVivo and Stata formats from the replication data depository of the University of Bath, Research Data Archive at doi:10.15125/BATH-00535.

NOTES

1. The expansion of security communities is not just geographic and quantitative, but also a qualitative phenomenon. Qualitative expansions of units of security governance (security communities), such as gradual democratization (inclusion of civilians in the group of protected, and the inclusion of security agency/protectors) and the inclusion of minorities in the security community have also reduced violence (Pinker, 2011, pp. 295–480).
2. Optimally, I would study the entire period from the crumbling of the Cold War order at the end of the 1980s until today, but as reliable data on state fragility are only available from 1995 and since reliable data on conflict fatalities end in 2016, this forces me to restrict the analysis of the consequences of protection to this time period.
3. There is an exception to the cosmopolitan neglect of the analysis of agency, see Pattison, 2010.
4. In this book, and in the bibliography I use the full name so spelled. When referring to the president in the main text I use, simply, Assad.
5. See the Aymenn Jawad Al-Tamimi website at http://www.aymennjawad.org/.
6. See https://www.dni.gov/index.php/features/bin-laden-s-bookshelf.
7. To catch all clauses with these words in all their variations, I make my searches using only the root of the words.
8. Also spelled Usama bin Ladin and Osama bin Laden. In this book I retain the spelling as used in quotations but use Osama bin Laden in my text.
9. Year 2012 is, so far, the latest year for which the USGPO compilation of presidential papers is available in NVivo-compatible format.
10. For help with the development of the nodes and testing the unambiguity of the coding rules, I am grateful to Riccardo Boscherini, Thomas Brewis, Maddy Holley and Astrid Vikström.
11. Since the threat of terrorism in US discourse is clearly externalized, even when the perpetrators are US citizens, I ruled all terrorist threats as external even though in the 1990s these were often seen as criminal threats rather than international political conspiratorial threats.
12. I coded protection of the environment as a separate category in the openly available dataset, but in this chapter it is conflated with 'other protection'.
13. I classified the protection of terrorists by rogue states in the category of protection that I have ruled out in the beginning to maintain the normative relevance of this category of protection.

2. State fragility and intervention, new wars and protection wars

DEFINITIONS

Warfare and conflict[1] fatalities have for the past few decades been a matter for fragile states. In strong states the system delivers well-being to citizens and thus people do not need to resort to violence or tribal affinities. Furthermore, in strong states, the police, the legitimate rules that citizens have ownership of, the strong feeling of togetherness and the common identity of citizens make conflicts unimaginable. In conflict literature, state fragility has been described as the lack of unity/integration of people and lack of competence and legitimacy of the state governance. This is the core condition that this study starts from: both new wars and protection wars take place in fragile states. However, before we can really make comparisons between new wars and protection wars, and study the impact of protective intervention, we must define state fragility and make it measurable. This will be the first task of this chapter. Only then will I move on to the operationalization of intervention so that we can make the necessary distinction between new wars (with no intervention) and protection wars (with protective intervention).

The focus of this book is on military interventions with warfighting (rather than peacekeeping) operations engendering fatalities, either using forces stationed in the country of operation or by air operations (manned or unmanned) from another country. Since much of the language of Al Qaeda and dictators like Saddam Hussein or Bashar al-Assad refers to the militarism, selfishness and unilateralism of Western interventions as a justification for 'Third World resistance' to Western actions, it seems clear that selfish, unilateral and militaristic approaches have a different impact on conflicts than restricted, globally owned peacekeeping operations of the United Nations. Therefore, the two types of protection must be studied in two different studies. In this book I will study only Western military operations.

Humanitarian interventions (= military protection) are those where the international declaratory justification of intervention is related to the protection of ordinary people on a global level (i.e., outside both national and allied countries' borders). New wars, again, are wars prior to protective interventions and conflicts where such interventions never take place. Protection wars are conflicts that began as intrastate conflicts within fragile states, but where humanitarian operations intervene. Therefore, perhaps simplistically, we can say that the violence left behind by non-interference in conflicts in fragile states is of the type called new wars by some cosmopolitan theorists, while the violence the liberal interventionism causes is in the form of protection wars.

When discussing protective operations, we are not talking about the geo-political strategic operations of the Cold War or the limited peacekeeping operations of the 1990s. Instead, we are talking about the interventions that began with the Kosovo operation in 1999. There are only three countries that have led such operations: the United States, France and the United Kingdom. Of these, the UK has conducted one operation (Sierra Leone, 2000) in which the US did not participate, while France has conducted two such operations (Central African Republic, 2006 and Mauritania, 2010).

For the operationalization of new wars, we will first need to look at state fragility and match existing analysis and definitions of new wars with the existing data on state fragility, so that we can integrate this study and contribute to the existing scholarship (on new wars and post-colonial interventions) rather than speaking past each other by using the same terms but meaning entirely different things.

I will integrate my investigation to rationalist, cosmopolitan new war theories, and post-colonial theories of intervention. For the original testing of these theories, I modify the existing data on state fragility. I use the State Fragility Index (Marshall and Elzinga-Marshall, 2017), relating the index's main components to the theories of new wars. I use selectively the indicators of fragility of the index to the extent they match with the definitions of the context of intrastate anarchy of new wars. To avoid tautological arguments, I also remove such components of the index that are analytically linked with conflict. Then I define a fragility threshold that matches the theories of new wars.

Subsequently, I link the index with the existing Uppsala University datasets on conflict (Allansson, Melander and Themnér, 2017; Gleditsch et al., 2002), one-sided conflict (Eck and Hultman, 2007) and non-state conflict (Melander, Pettersson and Themnér, 2016; Sundberg, Eck and Kreutz, 2012). Thus, I can measure the level of anarchy, and relate it to conflict and humanitarian intervention. To link this data to alternative, post-colonial explanations of new wars (Ayoob, 1991, 2001; Azar and Moon, 1988b), as well as to the rationalist research on causes of conflict in fragile states (Fearon and Laitin, 2014) this study will also produce a dummy variable that reveals whether a host of conflicts have a colonial history within the past 100 years.

OPERATIONALIZATION OF STATE FRAGILITY

The context of 'intrastate anarchy' is clearly the context in which new wars occur: 'new barbarism. . .is usually unleashed when overarching political or economic systems are either weakened or collapsed' (Duffield, 2001, p. 110). 'The new wars arise in the context of the erosion of the autonomy of the state and, in some extreme cases, the disintegration of the state' (Kaldor, 1999, p. 5). Thus, it is possible to accurately reconstruct the context of new wars as an intrastate context of fragile or failing states. This is also the context to which US cosmopolitan interventionism reacts. Thus, the starting point of both new wars and protection wars is intrastate conflict in a fragile country.

To answer the question of how protective interventions and the lack thereof affect state fragility, I need to consult statistics on state fragility. Monty G. Marshall and Gabrielle Elzinga-Marshall have produced such data since 1995, called the State Fragility Index (Marshall and Elzinga-Marshall, 2017). This index has been widely used and is considered reliable. Unfortunately, these data do not necessarily correspond to the definitions of state fragility of the theories of new wars and post-colonial conflicts. An additional complication is that they tend to be analytically and conceptually linked to elements of conflict. Thus, using such statistics will produce tautological conclusions: fragility is linked to conflict simply because conflict is in the definition of some of the statistics of state fragility. Consequently, before correlating existing statistics of intervention and conflict, I need to modify the data on the State Fragility Index. By doing this I create a 'New Wars State Fragility Index', which corresponds to the definitions of fragility of new war theorists and which does not have elements that are conceptually linked to elements of conflict.

New war theorists do not claim that fragility causes conflict in a linear manner. There must be something to fight for, as the most fragile states do not necessarily attract opportunistic groups if there is a complete lack of resources. Thus, the weakest states are not necessarily the ones with most conflict. Yet, opportunistic conflict entrepreneurs need state fragility for their opportunities to gain from violent conflict. The definition of a threshold for the condition of fragility is therefore needed so that the theorists of new wars consider it a relevant context for conflict. This threshold will be created so that it corresponds to the analysis of the context that gives rise to state new wars.

State fragility may be constructed by immaterial, unobservable interpretations and meanings that people give to ethnicity, religion and other sub-state identitive markers. It may, for example, be a state of affairs in which citizens do not recognize that they somehow belong to the nation.

Alternatively, their ethnic identities are dominant at the expense of their national identities. Even though such a situation is real, we cannot see, hear, taste or smell it. Yet, such discursive realities do interact with observable realities, and thus effects of these discursive realities that constitute state fragility can be observed. If it was possible to link existing indicators of state fragility to this aspect of the definition of new wars, it would be possible to identify such conflicts in a way that could allow the measurement of the development of new wars. I investigate whether the premises of the State Fragility Index (Marshall and Elzinga-Marshall, 2017), or some of its elements, can be used to define which of the contexts of conflict could fulfil the criteria that new war theorists set for new wars. This index measures state fragility on a cardinal scale from 0 to 24, and considers all states with values over 0 as at least somewhat fragile.

In fragile states, new wars often start when identitive (often ethnic) communities take up arms and protect their community when the state has shown itself to be unwilling to provide, or incapable of providing, security to all citizens (Fearon, 1995). Furthermore, economic realities within global capitalism require harsh measures against own populations, which often leads to conflicts in a state that has not developed institutional mechanisms for the regulation of capitalist competition (Azar and Moon, 1988c, p. 10). Duffield discusses predatory national institutions that fail to secure people, instead looking after elite interests or new war predatory agents (Duffield, 2001, p. 2). The security efficiency component of the State Fragility Index addresses this element of state fragility. Participation in wars, an element in the State Fragility Index (Marshall and Elzinga-Marshall, 2017, p. 52), can clearly be a proxy indicator of the security aspect of state fragility under discussion by new war theorists. Yet, using this indicator in an argument about the relationships between war and fragility creates tautologies we would like to avoid, so we will not use this element in the State Fragility Index. We are not necessarily looking for causal connections between fragility and conflict (which, per Hume's rules would require analytical independence of the dependent and independent variable; Hume, 2000). In its place we seek to look at the context of conflict. Yet, we still cannot use conflict indicators, as otherwise our claims of the prominence of the intrastate anarchy as a context of conflict would lose meaning: conflict cannot be a context of conflict.

The lack of security legitimacy of a state is one of the three key elements of the context of state fragility according to post-colonial theory (Azar and Moon, 1988a). It is also a crucial component of the context of new wars according to Münkler, Duffield and Kaldor (Duffield, 2002, p. 1051; Kaldor, 2012, p. 5; Münkler, 2002, p. 7). This lack of legitimacy and the need to use coercion is measured on the State Fragility Index (Marshall and Elzinga-Marshall, 2017, p. 52) by focusing on the persistence of coercive practices. Using a contextual definition of new wars and protection wars that is related to state terror and repression, which is also often reciprocated by armed groups, would again be tautological. Of course, the share of global fatalities of authoritarian violence and conflict between elites and the repressed people is greatest in fragile states if fragile states are already defined as those states that have these violent features. Thus, security legitimacy, too, needs to be ignored in our operationalization of state fragility. Due to these two limitations, the original 0–24 fragility scale has been reduced to 0–19.

State fragility in the State Fragility Index also has a political element. Political efficiency in this index is associated by regime durability and the lack of attempted coups. Part of the definitional dysfunctionality of states as instruments of the people is the opportunistic competition for state power motivated by partisan group interests, or the lack of integration as post-colonial theory would put it (Ayoob, 1991; Azar and Moon, 1988c). According to rationalist theory, this competition takes place between sub-state units, which, in the absence of a functioning state, take care of many of the security needs of citizens (Fearon, 1995; Poulton and Youssouf, 1998). Where new wars happen, this could be measured by the unwillingness of 'weak' and 'predatory' state leaders to give up power (regardless of the will of the people). What should also be considered is the willingness of alternative elites to capture that power by means other than those that the constitution or democratic principles define (Duffield, 2001, p. 16). Thus, elite competitions and clinging to state power are therefore non-tautological features of state fragility that new war theorists, as well as rationalist and theorists of post-colonial security, talk about. Fortunately, both features are measured as part of political efficiency of states in the Fragile States Index. The index borrows from the Polity IV data (Marshall and Jaggers, 2000) on regime stability, Leadership Durability data (Bienen and Van de Walle, 1991) and the Coup d'États Events Dataset (Marshall and Ramsey Marshall, 2016) and creates indicators with values between 0 and 3 (both included) based on the:

- country regime durability (Polity IV variable 'durable') in which one fragility point is given to states with a regime change within the past ten years;
- leaders' time in office, where the country gets a fragility point if the leaders have been in office for more than 12 years; and
- coups, in which one fragility point is given to countries that have experienced one or two coups, and two fragility points to countries that have had more than two coups.

Political legitimacy in this index is a function of democratic institutions and the lack of discrimination in the political system or policies (Marshall and Elzinga-Marshall, 2017, pp. 52–3). Lack of democracy is not just a feature of state fragility, but a definitional part of new war problématique (Kaldor, 2012, p. 152). In a new war context, the state is often not an instrument of the entire people but an institution of criminal exploitation. Fragility implies that the society is fragmented and factional, as there is no equality of citizens (Azar and Moon, 1988a). In the absence of a functioning state apparatus that serves all, the largest ethnic groups often take the role of the state in the production of security and public goods for its members (Castells, 1996, p. 135; this same explanation can be seen in the rationalist theory by Fearon, 1995). Therefore, the interests of sub-state groups motivate new wars, that is, identity politics (claim to power based on identity), rather than geopolitics or ideology as in old wars (Kaldor, 1999, p. 6). The primacy of sub-state identities also motivates the ruling class who will use the state apparatus for the protection and well-being of their specific ethnic group at the expense of other groups. Duffield (2001, p. 16) describes its institutions as 'weak and predatory' and its ruling ideology as often openly discriminatory. Private and public interests of politicians 'are mixed together in new wars, what is done with economic and political interest cannot be separated anymore' (Kaldor, 1999, p. 2).

The State Fragility Index borrows its political legitimacy score from the Polity IV data and the updated Minorities at Risk Discrimination (Gurr, 1993) and Elite Leadership Characteristics data (Marshall and Elzinga-Marshall, 2017). It measures political discrimination based on five indicators:

- Factionalism (which in Polity IV is the '2parcomp' indicator);
- Ethnic Group Political Discrimination against 5 per cent or more of the population (which is from the Minorities at Risk indicator 'poldis');
- Political Salience of Elite Ethnicity (from Elite Leadership Characteristics indicator 'eleth');
- Polity Fragmentation (Polity IV's indicator 'fragment');
- Exclusionary Ideology of Ruling Elite (from Elite Leadership Characteristics dataset's indicator 'eliti').

All these indicators are clearly in line with the definition of the post-colonial and new war context of state fragility and thus this element of the State Fragility Index can be used to operationalize new wars.

New war theorists also talk about the efficiency of economic production of livelihoods as a relatively stable observable indicator of state strength, and the lack of such efficiency as an indicator of state fragility (Duffield, 2001, pp. 15–16). This way, development or lack thereof becomes explicitly a security issue, and thus underdevelopment as a feature of fragile states becomes an important context of new wars: 'The threat of an excluded South fomenting international instability through conflict, criminal activity and terrorism is now part of a new security framework. Within this framework, underdevelopment has become dangerous' (ibid., p. 2). While some elements of this dangerous underdevelopment are closer to a phenomenon that can be measured with human development rather than macroeconomic indicators, the debate is varied, and it often also refers to the most basic income issues. New war theorists do consider a level of macroeconomic development as a relevant factor in the definition of the economic fragility of a state where wars would then be defined as new wars (Castells, 1996, p. 135; Duffield, 2001, p. 5).

The element of economic policy capacity in the definition of post-colonial state fragility has this same feature as one of the three defining factors of state fragility (Azar and Moon, 1988a). The rationalist theory that emphasizes the inability of states to offer services that ethnic units can offer to their members comes close to the definition of economic efficiency as part of state fragility and thus context of wars.

The State Fragility Index borrows from the World Bank's *World Development Reports*' per capita income values in its operationalization of economic efficiency (Marshall and Elzinga-Marshall, 2017, p. 53). Together with the political legitimacy data on non-discriminatory policies, the per capita income indicator is less controversial than this index used alone (as in many other studies). Furthermore, since the index's social efficiency is based on Human Development Indicators (United Nations Development Programme, various years), with the same scale of 0–3 as for economic efficiency, the socio-economic definition of state fragility comes very close to the definition of the state fragility concept in the new wars theory. Most of the theories on new wars operate in the conceptual context of human development and human security. It views the criminal economies of fragile states as instruments of such development and security (see, for example, Kaldor, 2013).

The social legitimacy in the State Fragility Index uses infant mortality as its criterion and uses data from the US Census Bureau (US Census Bureau, n.d.). This is something that could come close to the indicators of human development that are used in new war theories' characterizations of state fragility. There are specific mentions in the key sources of several theories of new wars about infant mortality. The suffering of innocent children is often cited in defining and contextualizing state fragility in new war states. In some cases, survival and rights of children are explicitly cited in the prescriptions to the international community related to the enforcement of humanitarian values (Duffield, 2001, pp. 32, 62, 123, 207). Thus, this element of the State Fragility Index should also be included in the operationalization of the fragility element of the new war context.

It is still necessary to decide the threshold in the New Wars State Fragility Index that enables us to define the context of new wars. This can be defined by looking at the levels of new war fragility in cases that theorists define as ripe for new wars. By then defining all countries over that threshold as fragile, we can move from random examples to a systematic study of all new war conflicts.

The condition of fragility in Bosnia and Herzegovina is perhaps the most used case of conditions that fuel opportunistic violence. At the time the conflict ended, our own modified fragility index gives the country a fragility level of 8. Thus, conflicts in a country with a fragility score of 8 must be new wars, if the country is not internationalized by great powers. Kosovo is another iconic case of conditions that new war theorists identify as fragile. The fact that the international community finally acted against violence of new wars in Kosovo has often been seen as a turning point in the development of new wars (Duffield, 2001, p. 41; Münkler, 2002, p. 125). Jürgen Habermas saw the international enforcement of humanitarian norms in Kosovo as a sign of a future cosmopolitan state (Habermas, 2000, p. 61). At the time of the Serbian repression in Kosovo in 1998–99, Serbia's fragility value in our scale that considers the political, economic and social indicators of the State Fragility Index was 7.

The Colombian and Chechnyan criminal economies have been used as examples of economic conditions of fragility (Kaldor, 2012, pp. 108–9). Thus, the context of those Chechen wars needs to be seen as that of state fragility. During the intensive phase of the Russo-Chechen war, until the end of 1999, the fragility value of Russia in our revised index was 7. In 2000 it was 6.

During the most chaotic phase of the Colombian war against the Revolutionary Armed Forces of Colombia (FARC) in 2002–05, the fragility level of Colombia was at 6. For this reason, the operationalization of this characteristic of new wars must take six fragility points in our revised State Fragility Index as the threshold. All those intrastate conflicts that take place in countries with fragility level 6, or above, will pass the fragility criterion of new war theorists. With this threshold, the iconic cases of fragility that new war theorists talk about can all be classified as having taken place in fragile states.

OPERATIONALIZATION OF PROTECTIVE INTERVENTION

To identify interventions, I need to use Uppsala Conflict Data Program (UCDP, Allansson et al., 2017) data on external involvement in intrastate conflicts and intrastate one-sided violence and non-state violence (UCDP, 2012). Not only conflict violence as defined in the Uppsala data, but also violence against unarmed civilians and conflict not involving states (non-state violence) must be considered, because the chaos of fragile states offers opportunities for gainful violence for both states and non-state groups against unarmed civilians or between non-state groups. These types of violence (for example, violence against women or ethnic warfare) are central to the description and definition of new wars (Heathcote, 2017; Münkler, 2002, pp. 128–9).

To operationalize the sort of external involvement that counts as protective intervention, I must take a closer look at the key concepts in the theory of new wars and post-colonial security. Since the definitions of these theories do not match all the definitions used in existing databases, I must add a dummy variable to existing Uppsala University datasets to indicate whether a fragile country has experienced military intervention.

Finally, to operationalize and identify which interventions by which countries can be seen as protective, I must make a closer analysis of definitions of intervention in new war theories and of official documents and speeches from potential countries that justify their military action by referring to cosmopolitan protection.

The theory of new wars claims that these wars are a product of disinterest by great powers during intrastate anarchy. Thus, we must define intervention as the difference between otherwise similar categories of protection wars and new wars. The former are intrastate conflicts in fragile countries in which a great power has intervened to protect people, while the latter are those in which great powers have not intervened. Between these two lies a category of conflicts in which great powers – for example, Russia – intervene, but without a cosmopolitan interest in protection. These conflicts are neither new wars (because in these wars, violence is controlled by a great power), nor protection wars (because of the lacking cosmopolitan justification). The first task for operationalization is thus to operationalize the type of great power intervention separating new wars from protection wars.

It is possible to begin operationalizing intervention by looking at intrastate conflicts (in fragile states) with a supporting great power presence. UCDP data code secondary participation in conflicts and assume that such participation requires military presence in the battle location. Coding of intervention in Uppsala datasets, however, is not based on a definition made by new war theorists. The description of international control in intrastate violence seems to make clear that the definition set by new war theorists (military intervention in intrastate violence in a fragile state) sets a lower threshold for fragility than the UCDP coding of internationalized intrastate conflicts.

Many interventions are based on air power without a ground force presence in the battle location. New war theorists consider these interventions are considered as military involvement in a conflict, although UCDP does not code them as secondary conflicting party involvements. Kaldor, for example, calls such warfare 'spectacle warfare' (Kaldor, 2003, p. 133; 2012, p. 163) and since this has been regarded in new war theory as external interference in intrastate conflicts, it must be included in our operationalization of interference – given that we have assumed that US interventionism follows the logic of the cosmopolitan theory of new wars. We need to consider those conflicts where external ground force or aerial operations have been used – by manned or unmanned (drones) aircraft – as internationalized wars rather than pure intrastate conflicts.

Theorists of new wars do not consider just any interference as a remedy for intrastate conflicts in fragile states. We cannot call an internationalized new war a cosmopolitan protection war unless it is justified by the interest of protecting civilians globally. Thus, some justification for interference is necessary for investigating the effects of protective intervention on fatalities. American interventions are clearly of the type that justify calling an internationalized intrastate conflict in a fragile state a cosmopolitan war of protection. Yet, we cannot classify US-controlled conflicts as the only protection wars. As a remedy for new wars, Kaldor called for international organizations and 'multilateral states' ('states that see their primary interest as a multilateral framework of rules, a system of global governance') to enforce humanitarian norms (cosmopolitan law enforcement) amid new war violence (Kaldor, 2003, p. 137; 2012, pp. 198–201). Kaldor and Duffield explicitly considered the North Atlantic Treaty Organization (NATO) to be an instrument for the enforcement of humanitarian norms and the control of violence in new wars: 'multinational peacekeeping, arms control agreements involving mutual inspection teams, joint exercises, new or renewed organizations like the Western European Union (WEU), Partnership for Peace, NATO Coordination Council (NACC) – which constitute an intensification of trans-nationalization in the military sphere' (Kaldor, 2012, p. 188; see also Duffield, 2001, p. 58). Thus, those conflicts in fragile states controlled by NATO or NATO countries should not be considered new wars; here, opportunistic violence is controlled by the international community for the benefit of global civilians.

A rhetorical commitment to the type of protection that new war theorists prescribe is also quite clear in the justification of conflict involvement made by NATO members. Then US President George W. Bush revealed his rhetorical commitment to the cosmopolitan ideals of new war theorists when launching his campaign against Iraq: 'As our coalition takes away their power, we will deliver the food and medicine you need. We will tear down the apparatus of terror and we will help you to build a new Iraq that is prosperous and free' (G.W. Bush, 2003c). The new war theorists' idea of the existence of an international humanitarian law that must be enforced by the international community is also clear in Bush's speeches: 'The UN must fulfil its mission of peace by keeping outlaw states to account, by aiding the rise of stable democracies, and by encouraging development and hope as alternatives of stagnation and bitterness' (G.W. Bush, 2005b, p. 1221). More recently, US counter-insurgency and counter-terrorism strategy have been explicitly guided by an effort to protect civilians (logical enough, given that the very concept of terrorism is defined by its threat to civilians). It introduces the idea of 'population-centrism' (as opposed to 'enemy-centrism') and focuses on the well-being of civilians as an objective (US Government Interagency Counterinsurgency Initiative, 2009, p. 14).

When intervening in Iraqi violence, then UK Prime Minister Tony Blair said:

> The Iraqi people deserve to be lifted from tyranny and allowed to determine the future of their country for themselves. We pledge to work with the international community to ensure that the Iraqi people can exploit their country's resources for their own benefit, and contribute to their own reconstruction, with international support where needed. We wish to help the Iraqi people restore their country to its proper dignity and place in the community of nations. (Blair, 2003)

Prime Minister David Cameron repeated this cosmopolitan logic in connection with the operation in Libya:

> [T]here are people suffering terribly under Qadhafi's[2] rule. Our message to them is this: there are better days ahead for Libya. Just as we continue to act to help protect the Libyan people from the brutality of Qadhafi's regime so we will support and stand by them as they seek to take control of their destiny. (Cameron, 2011)

The French rhetorical commitment in Libya to the cosmopolitan values of new war theorists is equally clear:

> Today, we are intervening in Libya, under a mandate of the United Nations Security Council, with our partners and in particular our Arab partners. We are

> doing so to protect civilians from the murderous madness of a regime which, in killing its own people, has lost all legitimacy. We are intervening to enable the Libyan people to choose their own destiny. (Sarkozy, 2011)

Among other great powers, Russia was the only one to initiate interventions in intrastate conflicts in a fragile state after the Cold War. Kaldor explained the new war context with reference to the collapse of the Soviet Union (Kaldor, 1999, p. 3), stating that if Russia were to participate in a conflict (Tajikistan, 1995–96, Georgia, 2008 and Ukraine, 2014), it should not be considered a new war, since the overwhelming power of the Russian military would change the very nature of the warfare. Russian interference in Tajikistan, Georgia and the Ukraine cannot be classified as cosmopolitan protection either. Russia used its own type of protection rhetoric and even the concept of 'Responsibility to Protect' for its military operations in Georgia and the Ukraine. However, in both cases the right to protect was based on an ethnic rather than cosmopolitan concept. Russia felt it had the right to protect ethnic Russians and people – outside its boundaries – who had Russian citizenship. This is not the same cosmopolitan concept of protection that new war theorists represent. Therefore, Russian intervention in Tajikistani, Ukrainian and Georgian intrastate conflicts will not be viewed as cosmopolitan law enforcement, since it does not transform intrastate conflicts into cosmopolitan protection wars. These conflicts, however, should not be coded as new wars either. Russia did have an interest in controlling violence in these former Soviet States.

Our coding on international military interference in conflicts in fragile states will take its departure from the Uppsala conflict data coding of internationalized intrastate wars in fragile states (as operationalized in this book). These data disclose information on 62 years of internationalized intrastate conflicts in fragile states, with US intervention since 1995 (the data on new war state fragility start in 1995, but the first protection wars began in 1999). Thirty-three of these years relate to the US-led fight against Al Qaeda and the Taliban in Afghanistan and the vicinity since 2001. With one exception, Hezbi Islam, all domestic conflicts against the government during the continuing US military presence in the country have also been correctly listed as internationalized intrastate conflicts by the Uppsala data. These internationalized intrastate conflicts include the government's war – against the Taliban since 2003 and Al Qaeda since 2001. However, until 2006, the Pashtun Islamist group Hezbi Islam fought the Taliban without international involvement. Hezbi Islam has not been listed as a party in conflict with the US in the Uppsala data, even though their activity was listed as intrastate conflict. This coding has been retained in this book's coding of internationalized conflicts: there is no evidence of direct

US–Hezbi Islam fighting until 2008, and the US state department's list of terrorist organizations did not include Hezbi Islam before 2007 (Associated Press, 2013; Briggs, 2014; Bureau of Investigative Journalism, 2015).

Eleven years of intervention relate to the fight against various Islamist groups (the Kurdish Ansar al-Islam, Reformation and Jihad Front, Mahdi Army and Islamic State), mostly in Iraq since 2003 (Dodge, 2013; Goldberg, 2018; Hoffman, 2004; US Department of Defense, 2008).

Six years of intervention relate to the US battle in Yemen against Al Qaeda on the Arabian Peninsula (AQAP) since 2009 and Ansar Allah (or Ansarallah, as it is called in the Uppsala data and Houthis, as they are called in the media), at least since 2016. There was only one operation against Al Qaeda in 2002, and only three against AQAP in 2009, but many more after that (Hudson, Owens and Callen, 2012; Bureau of Investigative Journalism, 2016).

Five humanitarian interventions were related to the French-initiated operations in Mali. In Mali, in 2013–16, the groups that the French/US coalition fought were: Ansar Dine, Signed-in-Blood Battalion, Movement for Unity and Jihad in West Africa (MUJAO), al-Murabitun and Al Qaeda in Maghreb (but not the Tuareg ethnic challenger to the government in the south, the MNLA, before its association with Islamist militias in 2015) (Chivvis, 2015).

The remaining seven years of intervention include: US intervention in support of the Somali government against Al Shabaab since 2015; continued US intervention in Libya against IS since 2016; the coalition effort in Kosovo in 1999; the British operation in Sierra Leone in 2000; and the French operations in the Central African Republic in 2006 and in Mauritania in 2010.

However, new war theorists have defined military interference using a lower threshold than that in the UCDP data on internationalized intra-state conflicts. At the same time, Uppsala data on 'secondary support' in wars use a threshold so low that it does not correspond with the implicit definitions of new war theory regarding the international enforcement of humanitarian norms in new wars. According to Uppsala definitions:

> [A] secondary supporting party provides support to a primary party that somehow affects the development of the conflict. . . The support given can be of several types, for instance, financial, military (short of regular troops), logistic etc. . .actively given to strengthen the party in the particular conflict. (Uppsala University, Department of Peace and Conflict Research, n.d.)

This is why this study has had to create a new variable that follows a different definition of the word 'internationalization', one referring to military operations by outside powers, not with ground forces alone, but also using air and naval forces, and not limited to intrastate conflicts, but also including non-state conflicts or one-sided violence.

This new definition of intervention adds 26 new years of conflict to the 62 years of conflict involving US intervention, years in which such intervention is conducted using air power alone. The Uppsala data do not consider these as military involvement, but they must be counted as interventions if we follow the definitions introduced by new war theory. Furthermore, one conflict started as a one-sided conflict; thus, its internationalization did not constitute an interstate conflict in the view of new war theorists but was an internationalization of an existing intrastate conflict. Finally, there is one conflict that has simply been coded incorrectly in the UCDP data.

These 26 years of interventionist conflicts that are not coded in the UCDP data, but which must be coded when following the definitions made by new war theories, are the following:

- US manned and unmanned air warfare against Al Shabaab and Al Qaeda in support of the government of Somalia since 2007. In 2007, the UCDP data attribute fatalities to the conflict with the Islamic Courts Union (ICU) (Bureau of Investigative Journalism, 2017b).
- US aerial operations (and covert operations on the ground) in support of the Government of Pakistan in its fight:
    against the TTP (Tehrik-i-Taliban Pakistan = Pakistani Taliban and its splinter group since 2014, Jamaat-ul-Ahar), and Laskar-e-Islam 2007–16;
    - against Islamic State in 2016;
    - against IMU (Islamic Movement of Uzbekistan) in 2014 (this conflict is lumped together with US warfare against the TTP in the UCDP data).

US aerial operations in Pakistan had already started in 2004, but due to political sensitivities no official data exist on the fatalities they caused. Pakistan's fight against its challenges in Baluchistan has not been coded as warfare with developed country involvement, as the Baluch groups have so far managed to avoid US drone strikes (Amnesty International and Human Rights Watch, 2013; Aslam, 2015; Williams, 2010). UCDP data do not record US participation in warfare in Pakistan, since it was conducted without stationing troops there. However, nor do they record any fatalities from warfare between the Pakistani government and militant Islamists (except for those between the government and the militants of Baluchistan), even though the Bureau of Investigative Journalism can name 94 victims of US drone warfare alone in 2006 (Bureau of

Investigative Journalism, 2017a; Thompson, 2009). Since this book uses UCDP data, these victims go unrecorded here too.

- US-led operations against Islamic State, enemy of the Syrian government within Syria since 2014. These operations have been mainly airborne – and thus not listed in the UCDP data. In 2013, there were secret US-led operations and support for anti-government militias, which could be coded as internationalization of the conflict, but since the extent of operations cannot be verified and we do not know whether or not there were US combat troops on the ground, this has not been included in this book. The year 2013 witnessed a major escalation of conflict in Syria, and the decision not to code this conflict as internationalized that year undermines the costs of intervention (Farmer, 2013; House of Commons and Foreign Affairs Committee, 2015; Miller, 2013; Rubin and Barnard, 2015; Teimouri, 2015).
- The international operation against Gaddafi in Libya in 2011, which is listed as an intrastate conflict with no external involvement because international intervention was conducted with use of air power only (Kuperman, 2013).
- The US attack on Houthi rebels/the government in Yemen in 2016, which was limited to indirect support and a single direct military operation (Rosenberg and Mazzetti, 2016; *New York Times*, 2016). Since it was an air operation this could not have been counted in the UCDP data as US involvement in the conflict, but it is included in our data (Kivimäki, 2019b, forthcoming).
- The conflict in Iraq in 2003, which was classified as an interstate conflict by the UCDP because it was not preceded by intrastate conflict. However, the definition of new wars includes one-sided violence and non-state conflicts as new wars, and since such situations preceded Western intervention in Iraq (Eck and Hultman, 2007), the 2003 conflict against Saddam Hussein's government must also be considered a protection war. Kaldor was very explicit in labelling Iraq (before the allied intervention) as a new war, and accused the US of not understanding the nature of new wars – as a result, the international response to this war failed (Kaldor, 2012, p. 152).
- US intervention in the conflict between the Taliban state and the Northern Alliance (UIFSA) in Afghanistan in 2001. Here, it seems the UCDP is simply mistaken in its ruling. This fight was clearly intervened in by US forces (and not just by Iran) against the Taliban government (*USA Today*, 2001; Williams, 2010), thus, the US internationalization of the conflict must be acknowledged. While the UCDP rules it a conflict that only Iran (with no commitment

to cosmopolitan justifications of intervention) internationalized, it should be seen as a protection war because of US intervention in the intrastate conflict between the Northern Alliance and the Taliban state of Afghanistan. The ruling on this does not seriously affect the conclusions of this study, but the correction is made for the sake of completeness of the list of protection wars.

The main borderline case here is Yemen, where US involvement started with a very minor presence. The US war against Al Qaeda in Yemen witnessed an aerial operation already in 2002. Again in 2009, the US had three confirmed aerial operations with fatalities in conflict, producing more than 25 annual conflict fatalities. Following the rulings of Uppsala data, the conflict in Yemen can be classified here as protection in 2009, but not in 2002. In 2016, the US also became directly involved in the conflict between the Houthi government and the government of President Abd Rabbuh Mansur Hadi, as US air operations targeted Houthis in addition to Al Qaeda on the Arabian Peninsula. In most other countries, the beginning of US involvement is more robust and will not be difficult to classify.

The case of the Al-Qa'ida in the Land of the Islamic Maghreb (AQLIM) or Al Qaeda in the Islamic Maghreb (AQIM) in Algeria is also an interesting borderline case. This organization and its predecessor, the Salafist Group for Preaching and Combat, were listed as terrorist organizations and were considered a threat, especially to European civilians. France and the US certainly helped the Algerian government to defeat this organization, but there was never the kind of direct military effort with fatalities caused by Western forces as in the above-mentioned cases. Thus, in the absence of direct, military operations, the Algerian struggle against its Islamist enemy is not coded here (or in Uppsala data) as a case of internationalized conflict in a fragile state. Instead, it is still seen as a new war without such international involvement.

Another border case is Operation Desert Fox in 1998 in Iraq, which involved aerial activities by the US and the UK. However, since protection wars are defined as deadly (involving fatalities) this operation cannot be counted as a protection war; it targeted arms manufacturing facilities rather than defining an enemy that needed to be destroyed. Therefore, Uppsala data do not classify this military operation as a conflict, and thus this study will not define it as a protection war. The same is also true for the peacekeeping operations of the 1990s, which are not coded as internationalized intrastate conflicts in fragile states (protection wars) in this study or in the Uppsala data.

In sum, interventions led by the US and its cosmopolitan allies, Britain and France, are presented in Table 2.1. The updated protective military

Table 2.1 Protection wars

Main Fragile Country and/or Location of Battle, Years of Intervention	Leading Actor in Humanitarian Intervention	Main Target of Intervention
Serbia/Kosovo, 1999	United States	Serbian government
Sierra Leone, 2000	United Kingdom	RUF and Sierra Leone soldiers turned rebels
Afghanistan, 2001–	United States	Al Qaeda, Taliban
Pakistan, 2004–	United States	Taliban and Islamist groups
Iraq, 2003– (excluding 2012 and 2013)	United States	Al Qaeda, IS and other Islamist groups
Central African Republic, 2006	France	Union of Democratic Forces for Unity
Somalia, 2007–	United States	Al-Shabaab (2007: ICU)
Mauritania, 2010	France	AQIM
Libya, 2011, 2016–	United States, United Kingdom and France	Government of Libya (2011), IS (2016)
Yemen, 2009–	United States	AQIM (and, in 2016, the Houthi government)
Mali, 2013–	France, United States	AQIM
Syria, 2014– (2017–)	United States	IS (and covertly, the Syrian government)

intervention data are openly available in Stata and Excel formats from the University of Bath Research Data Archive at doi:10.15125/BATH-00535 (Kivimäki, 2019b, forthcoming).

NOTES

1. In standard conflict literature, wars are defined as conflicts that claim at least 1000 fatalities per annum, whereas conflicts can be classified militarized disputes with the minimum of 25 fatalities per annum. Even though this book assumes the Uppsala Conflict Data Program (UCDP) definition of conflicts and battle deaths (conflict fatalities), it will not make a distinction between conflict and war. Instead, it may refer to conflicts with less than 1000 fatalities as wars, and it will use the words war and conflict as synonyms. This is because the new war literature does not make a distinction between conflicts and wars, and thus to use the concept of new war in the way it is used in the literature, I will also need to disregard the standard distinction between the two terms.
2. In this book I retain the spellings as used in quotations but use Gaddafi so spelled in my text.

3. The nature and rationale of protection wars

THE BEGINNING: KOSOVO

In the conflict in Kosovo, an ethnically distinct part of the state of Serbia (then Serbia-Montenegro) fought for separation from the rest of the country, and a violent Serbian repression of this effort targeted ethnic Kosovars (Kosovo Albanians). Because of the violence of the central government, the international intervention in 1999 was legitimized as an effort to protect Kosovo. This conflict is often seen as the first conflict in which the West was acting, not in its own geopolitical, ideological or national self-interest, but in the global cosmopolitan interest. According to UK Prime Minister, Tony Blair (1999), 'the Kosovo war marked the beginning of the new age of human rights enforcement'. Tony Blair also expressed a much wider perception that this was a war fought not for self-interest but 'over the values of civilization' (ibid.). While some cosmopolitan scholars sympathized with this view and felt that this Western action helped anticipate the future cosmopolitan state that they promote (Habermas, 2000, p. 61; 2001; Wheeler, 2003), others pointed to the incompleteness of cosmopolitan commitment. According to Falk (2003), one of the problems is that pure cosmopolitan action tends to be under-resourced and therefore its consequences fall shorter than anticipated. The UN's under-resourced effort to protect people in Srebrenica during the Srebrenica Massacre of July 1995 could be taken as an example of this. For Falk, Kosovo is an example of where cosmopolitanism is just in rationale and justification, while its motives are strategic and selfish. As in Kosovo, interventions backed by the requisite will and resources are likely to be strategic in motivation, humanitarian only in rationalization, and such interventionary violence will be illegal and anti-humanitarian (Falk, 2003).

The Western effort in the protection of Kosovo was justified by:

- referring to the brutality of Serb violence and to the suffering of Kosovo Albanians;
- framing the violence as criminal in motive (Clinton, 2000d, p. 2146); and

- pointing to the defiance of the Serbian state regarding resolutions of the United Nations against the Serb violence (Clinton, 1999b, p. 1760).

Western forces' justifications for their own role as agents of protection were:

- the emergency caused by Serb violence;
- the UN resolutions that the UN alone was unable to enforce; and
- the implicit UN legitimation of NATO and US action and implicit global identity of the US and NATO-led troops.

According to Clinton '50,000 people (in Kosovo) are facing freezing or starvation this winter because the same person who caused the problems in Bosnia, Mr. Milosevic, refuses to abide by United Nations resolutions' (Clinton, 1999b, p. 1760). While the conclusion of this diagnosis focused on the need to do something, it did not focus on who should be doing something, and what that something was. Even though Serbia was in violation of UN principles, it had to be the US, not the UN, who took the lead in the action. And instead of offering blankets to the freezing, or food for the starving Kosovars, the 'something' that needed to be done was a military operation.

Serbia's leader, Slobodan Milošević, in turn, promoted in his interpretation of the situation a dissociation of ethnicity from politics and claimed that the problem was not related to the former: 'We do not have a problem with any national community, and there is 26 of them, except with a part of [the] Albanian national community in Kosovo, those who are engaged in a separatist movement'. He claimed that the conflict was about separatism: 'Disintegration of Serbia. No one in Serbia can agree with secession of any part of its country' (Milošević, 1998).[1]

Furthermore, Milošević and the Serb supporters, including Russia, saw the Western effort to divide Yugoslavia and then also Serbia-Montenegro as a geopolitical project, one that pushed forward the NATO alliance at the expense of the Russian sphere of influence (Milošević, 1999b, 1999d). Interestingly, Serbia also criminalized its opponents in the conflict, suggesting that 'Albanian narco-mafia gives money to foreign journalists and politicians for the media war against us' (Milošević, 1998; see also 1999d) and claimed that the Western forces were facilitating and collaborating with 'a pact with murderers, rapists, criminals and drug dealers' (Milošević, 1999a). And, according to Milošević, the Western training and arming of these groups was a violation of the UN Security Council resolution that prohibited arms deliveries (ibid.).

In addition to criminalizing them, Serbia also saw separatist movements as externally agitated and terroristic, and thus less legitimate than indigenous opposition (Milošević, 1999b). Milošević also justified his opposition to the 'separatist forces' (Milošević, 1999a) and the Western coalition by criticizing their militarism: 'USA believes it can resolve everything by force and that is the weakness of many great powers that perished in the past' (Milošević, 1998). At the same time, Milošević saw the violence that justified US military action as something caused by the paramilitary irregular forces (Milošević, 1999b).

From the need to protect the Kosovo Albanian victims of the conflict, the US rationale for protection concluded that the West had the right to intervene and protect. At first, UN resolutions were cited and the Serbian defiance of them were also to be part of the reason for Western protection of Kosovo. Then, following the defiance of Milošević, the rationalization focused on the responsibility of the US, NATO, and nations that the US invited to join the 'International Security Force' (Clinton, 1999b, p. 1760).

Yet, the international protection force was not entirely separate from the UN, even though Clinton, especially in his domestic rhetoric, tried to frame it as such. In his attempt to invite Russia to participate in the International Security Force, Clinton admitted that 'the international force ideally should be endorsed by the United Nations' (Clinton, 2000e, p. 760) and, in reality, the US/NATO-led force was mandated by the UN Security Council Resolution 1244 of June 10, 1999 that authorized, for an initial period of 12 months, member states to establish an international security presence in Kosovo and it operated together with the UN Interim Administration Mission in Kosovo (UNMIK) by providing security and control of the borders there. It was, however, important for Clinton to be able to claim that these 'forces are under NATO command and control and rules of engagement' (Clinton, 2000a, p. 2304). The legitimacy of such NATO leadership of a cosmopolitan operation was based, just as Kaldorian theory suggests, on the quality of action rather than on its agency. Crucial here was the fact that the international force could also protect the Serb minority in Kosovo after it had pushed the national Serbian police and security personnel out of the area (Clinton, 2000c, p. 603).

Milošević's anti-cosmopolitan framing of world politics emphasized agency more than the US framing. Legitimacy of governance in the world system was based on the role of nation-states. All nations had the right to emphasize their own national self-interest and the norm of non-interference in their governance of their own citizens: 'My duty is to protect the interest of my people and my country. If anyone has a problem with that, I can only tell you that I am proud of my role in defending and protecting the interests of my country and of my people' (Milošević, 1998). In this framing, the focus of legitimacy of protection is not only on the type of action but also on the agency of action. Milošević saw US/NATO-led protection as imperial (Milošević, 2000b) and colonial (Milošević, 2000a) and demanded that cosmopolitan action should be led by a cosmopolitan agent, the United Nations.[2] After the beginning of the conflict, Milošević wanted UN rather than US agency of protection, and insisted on the leadership of the UN with the absence of the countries directly involved in the fighting (i.e., Serbia and the US coalition; Milošević, 1999a). The question of agency of protection was central in Milošević's critique of the NATO action: Serbia wanted to have:

> [. . .]returned the United Nations to the world stage as it was not functioning since before the start of the aggression 80 days ago. This is our contribution to the efforts of the entire freedom-loving world, to the tendencies to create a multi-polar world, and not accept the creation of a world which will be ruled by the dictate of a single power from one center. (Milošević, 1999c)

After the US bombing of the Chinese Embassy in Belgrade, Milošević tried but failed to establish an international alliance with China, Russia, India, the Arab world, South America and Africa against the Western intervention by referring to the principle of state sovereignty (Milošević, 1999d). At the time, Russia was very weak, and China felt economic integration with the West was more important than the promotion of the Westphalian framing of world politics.

In justification of the military intervention in Kosovo, US rhetoric created Kosovo as a natural entity, which without intervention would have looked much less legitimate. Clinton talked about an area where 'roughly 40,000 Serbian troops and police are massing in and around Kosovo'. However, this area was part of Serbia, and thus without the articulation of Kosovo as a separate entity, it would have been difficult to visualize the 'massing in and around' of the national police there. Thus, the creation of the unnaturalness of Serbian police in Kosovo made it possible to argue that '[o]ur firmness is the only thing standing between them [Serbian forces] and countless more villages like Racak, full of people without protection, even though they have now chosen peace' (Clinton, 2000f, p. 410). For Milošević, the existence of the Serbian police force in Serbia was a natural thing, and the Western involvement and alleged mobilization of the Kosovo separatists was another reason for such presence. In the presidential address to the nation in 1999, NATO violence against the national security forces was explicitly declared as a reason for an increased Serbian effort to punish the intruders: '[S]ince March 24 until today, 462 members of the Yugoslav Army and 114 members of the police of the Republic of Serbia were killed in the 11-week war. We will never be able to repay them for this. We must do what we can and what is our duty' (Milošević, 1999c).

Clearly, in this way, legitimate violence is constituted in the Kosovo conflict in the violent interaction between conflicting parties. The US side failed to see the symmetry in the legitimation of their and their opponent's violence, as they point to the genocidal, anti-cosmopolitan practices of Serbia and see them as something that defines Serbia and Milošević (Clinton, 1999b, p. 1760). However, these practices, Milošević claims, were carried out by self-appointed paramilitary leaders that the government resisted and condemned to long prison sentences (Milošević, 1999a, 2001a). Furthermore, the lack of democracy in Serbia was seen as a reason why US violence and Serbian violence could not be seen in a symmetrical setting by the US (Clinton, 1999b, p. 1760). And Milošević again failed to see the symmetry because of the anti-cosmopolitan framing of state-centric world politics:

> When our soldiers die, they know what they are dying for – for their homeland, for their fatherland. And [what] are your soldiers dying for, 5,000 miles away from their homes. They are killing children in their sleep, they are killing women, young girls, peaceful citizens, they are destroying everything we have built up in the five decades since World War II. (Milošević, 1999a)

Both sides saw each other's violence as unprovoked, and their own violence as a reaction to it.

The conflict in Kosovo was among the least-failed protection wars, because, first, it did not last very long, and second, the political dispute became less heated within the decade. Intervention was associated with an increased number of fatalities, but also with the ending of conflict fatalities after a short period of internationalized intrastate warfare. The fragility of the Serbian state increased with the international intervention, but after the de-escalation of the political dispute and after the independence of Kosovo, state structures were strengthened and the opportunities for violence were curbed. Figure 3.1 shows the development of fatalities and conflict fragility. The number of fatalities and the New War State Fragility Index have been standardized between 0 and 1 to allow the treatment of the two sides of the problem of protection wars simultaneously.

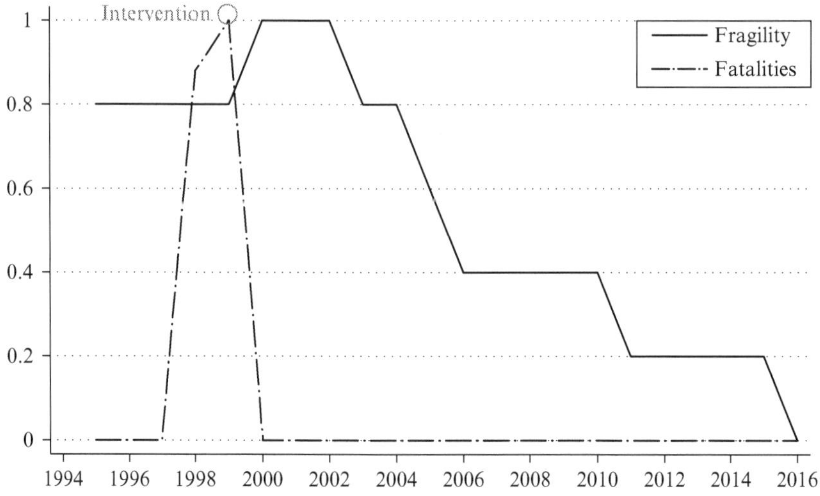

Figure 3.1 Standardized fatalities in Serbia/Kosovo

WAR ON TERROR IN DICTATORSHIPS: AFGHANISTAN, IRAQ, LIBYA AND SYRIA

The deadliest protection failures – Syria, Iraq and Afghanistan – and the Libya intervention, which President Obama considered his greatest mistake, were all cases where civilians were threatened both by a brutal, authoritarian state and widespread terrorism. In Iraq and in Libya this terror entered the country after the defeat of the authoritarian states, while in Afghanistan and Syria terror was already the main problem at the time of the intervention. In Afghanistan, Iraq and Libya, Western forces managed to remove the autocrat from his rule at the beginning of the conflict, while in Syria they managed to weaken the administration with their support of opposition militias and their occupation of parts of the country. Nevertheless, the destruction and weakening of the authoritarian states and the delay of better state structures gave opportunities to violent non-state groups (Kaldor, 2012, p. 161). At the same time, the extended foreign occupation without 'concerted international agreement for intervention' provided motives and perceived legitimacy for these terrorist organizations, as it was impossible to gain 'any consent or support from the state or the local population concerned' (British Army, 2009, p. CS7-1). Finally, the poor handling of the integration of the old authoritarian state administrations into new democratic state structures contributed to the mobilization of old state elite into terror (Coles and Parker, 2015; Watt,

2015). All this can be seen from the fatalities and fragility statistics as an initial success in the reduction of fatalities of authoritarian violence and the original violence against the autocrat, followed by mobilization and a fresh increase in the number of fatalities.

While the motives of these interventions may have been diverse (including the resistance of weapons of mass destruction, WMDs, in the hands of dictators, and the need to defend Western nations from terror), their justification was also clearly cosmopolitan: 'The lives of Iraqi citizens would improve dramatically if Saddam Hussein were no longer in power, just as the lives of Afghanistan's citizens improved after the Taliban. The dictator of Iraq is a student of Stalin, using murder as a tool' (G.W. Bush, 2003a, p. 1756). Also, the rhetoric of Libyan conflict and the aerial strike on the Syrian Air Force was clearly referring to cosmopolitan morale. According to President Obama (2012f, p. 289), 'unless he [Gaddafi] is willing to step down, there are still going to be potential threats towards the Libyan people. And we will continue to support the efforts to protect the Libyan people'. And, according to President Trump:

> Using a deadly nerve agent, Assad choked out the lives of helpless men, women and children. It was a slow and brutal death for so many. Even beautiful babies were cruelly murdered in this very barbaric attack. No child of God should ever suffer such horror. Tonight I ordered a targeted military strike on the airfield in Syria from where the chemical attack was launched. (Trump, 2017c)

Even if WMDs and terrorist activities have implications for national defence, they are still both, by definition, technologies and groups that threaten and target civilians; thus, even the justifications related to terror and WMDs were cosmopolitan.

State fragility and fatalities statistics suggest that, in 2002, Bush was still right about improvement of the lives of Afghans (G.W. Bush, 2003a, p. 1756) as the terrorist attack on September 11, 2001 had given some legitimacy for the US operation against Al Qaeda in Afghanistan, and mobilization against the occupying force had not yet begun. As can be seen from Figure 3.2, development in Afghanistan seemed relatively optimistic until 2004 and the strength of state institutions as well as the functionality of state in Afghanistan improved better than could be assumed from the media. The same can be seen in studies that take their evidence from grassroots level (Böhnke, Koehler and Zürcher, 2017).

The situation in Iraq was rather similar (Figure 3.3), with initial success in the reduction of fatalities until the mobilization of the old forces, which led the country into disarray. In Iraq, the reduction of conflict fatalities was positive for a longer time, but development of indigenous state structures took longer than in Afghanistan.

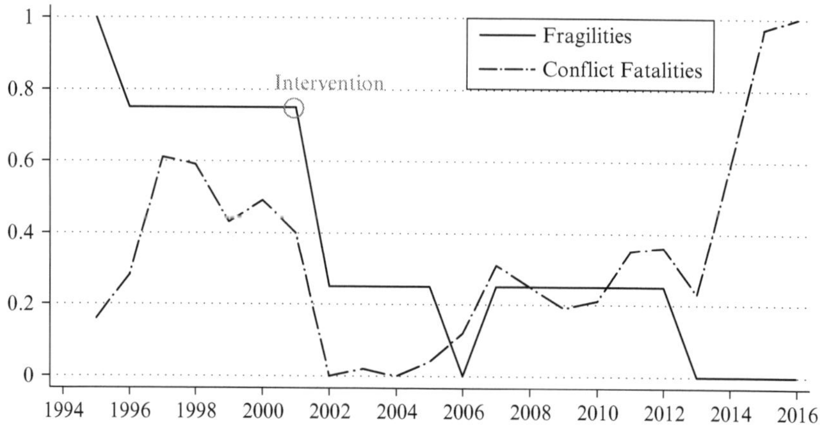

Figure 3.2 Standardized fatalities and fragilities in Afghanistan

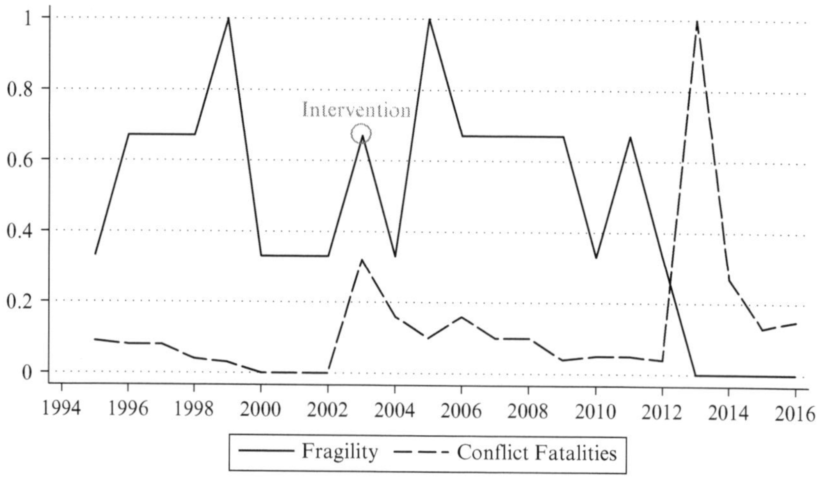

Figure 3.3 Standardized fatalities and fragilities in Iraq

US presidential documents reveal that the US wanted to fight the old forces and terrorists by offering better governance (G.W. Bush, 2009b, p. 1231). However, much of the counter-discourse of both authoritarian rulers in Iraq and Afghanistan, as well as the terrorist groups, was based on the critique of the identity, rather than on the policy, of the foreign occupier. The majority of Iraqis resented the fact that they were ruled by foreigners, not just the way foreigners ruled them (Hussain, 2016; Rayment, 2005).

Although US rhetoric on Iraq and Afghanistan emphasized the fact that the US did not intend to rule these countries forever, nor was it willing to accept just any terms of peace and independence. Thus, the existing terms of peace in the state seem to be stable only with extensive foreign presence, and this presence again creates political problems of violence and resistance. This is something President Obama realized, yet he was not willing to allow the type of state formation and terms of domestic peace that could have enabled domestic political stability (on the terms of the Taliban) without the external presence of military force (Obama, 2011c, p. 1845).

While emphasizing that the US was not an imperial force that wanted to rule over Iraq, Afghanistan or any of the intervened countries, there were limits to where self-determination could lead. On the one hand, it could not lead to a situation that was detrimental to the US defence against terror: 'Our goal in Iraq is victory. Our goal is to have a country that can govern itself, sustain itself, and defend itself and be an ally in the war on terror' (G.W. Bush, 2007c, p. 2007). This was already a limitation to self-rule as it meant that these countries had to allow US drone warfare against terrorist organizations within their territories. For the opposition to this proviso, this meant that death sentences in Afghanistan, Iraq and elsewhere were issued in Washington, DC.

Furthermore, the US was not prepared to accept terms of peace that constituted its humiliation. The return of Gaddafi, the Taliban or the 'Saddamists' in power in Libya, Afghanistan or Iraq would have constituted such a humiliation. At the same time, it was not easy for the 'champion of democracy' to justify ruling out these political forces from the democratic process. Therefore, it is interesting to see how, suddenly, at the time of the first general election both in Iraq and Afghanistan, ideology entered the political discourse as something that was inherently related to terrorism. Terrorism was no longer just a tactic, as it was first defined, but also a political objective: terrorist ideologies (Islamism of the Taliban) and authoritarianism (Saddamists) had to be ruled out of democratic ideological competition as these ideologies were the root of terrorism. According to Bush:

> We're fighting an enemy that knows no rules. They're inhumane. They are evil people who have taken the religion and kill in the name of that religion to achieve geopolitical objectives. They're bound by a common ideology. They want to establish a caliphate that ranges from Indonesia to Spain. I'm not making this up. I'm simply repeating that which we have learned about the enemy from their own words. (G.W. Bush, 2007b, p. 1746)

Here Bush is not talking about the violent, terroristic tactics of achieving a caliphate, but the goal itself. A caliphate was terroristic, even if it was achieved democratically without violence. In addition to associating Islamist (Taliban) political objectives with terror, Bush and Obama also associated authoritarian (Saddamist) objectives with terror:

> [T]he best way to protect America and to keep the peace is to change the conditions that give rise to hopelessness and extremism. And the best way to do that is to spread freedom around the world. I don't believe freedom is America's gift to the world. I believe freedom is the Almighty God's gift to each man and woman in this world. (G.W. Bush, 2006b, p. 616)

Even though democracy is normally associated with the freedom of political competition, the return of Saddamists and Islamists in Iraq and Afghanistan would have constituted a US humiliation. This could not be accepted and thus both political ideologies needed to be excluded from political competition as something that was necessary both for security from terror and for the security of democracy: 'Victory will be achieved by meeting certain objectives: When the terrorists and Saddamists can no longer threaten Iraq's democracy' (G.W. Bush, 2006e, p. 1855).

The argument of freedom as a domestic ideology that the US needed to promote for the sake of security and for the defeat of terrorism emerged a year after 9/11 and was repeated nine times that year (never in 1999 or 2000), 39 times in 2004, and, suddenly, 178 times in 2005, during the year of Iraqi and Afghanistan elections. After the elections the argument was repeated occasionally (17 times in 2006 and three times in 2007). The securitization of ideology during the Iraqi and Afghan election campaigns and during the development of the political party structure can be seen in the frequency of ideological terms in US presidential papers at the time of these developments (Figure 3.4).

This interference in the selection of political preferences and ideologies that were acceptable for the US was among the main accelerators of opposition and resistance of the US forces in Iraq. Support for terroristic and authoritarian political positions also became a way to articulate against US power in the protected former autocracies. According to a journalist with plenty of contacts in radical areas of Iraq and Syria, the support of ISIS had to be related to the identity of the organization as an enemy of the US. On its own, the violent identity of the organization could not have mobilized support for the organization (Mahmood, 2014).

The US rationale in Libya was perhaps the most purely related to the protection of the global civilian. Libya had been a useful ally in Western counter-terrorism, and thus power politics would have spoken against military operations against Muammar Gaddafi's regime. The protective operation in Libya was also tied closer to the UN mandate than in any of the previous or forthcoming operations. The operation was seen as

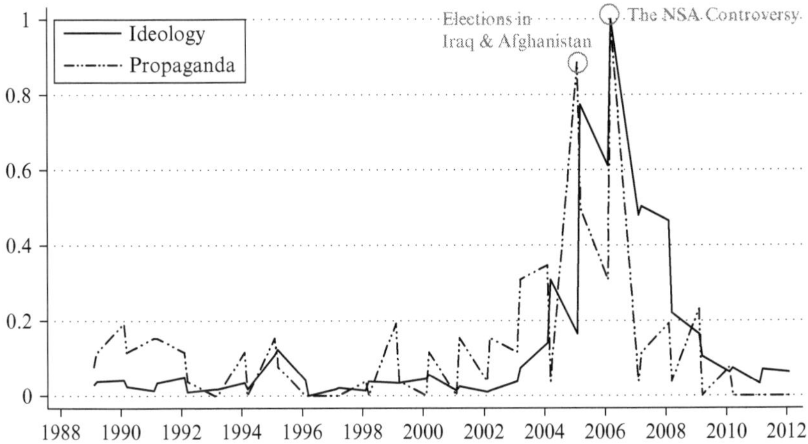

Note: The NSA controversy was the debate on the Terrorist Surveillance Program where the National Security Agency, NSA, was authorized to monitor, without obtaining a court warrant, the phone calls, Internet activity, text messages and other communications involving any party believed by the NSA to be outside the US, even if the other end of the communication lay within the US. This was often argued against as ideological control and argued for as control of the process of anti-US radicalization.

Figure 3.4 Standardized frequencies (per 1000) of 'propaganda' and 'ideology'

mandated by the UN as it was based on UN Security Council Resolution 1973 of March 17, 2011. There was a clear humanitarian justification for the operation, yet regime change was not written into the UN mandate, it was resisted by two veto powers of the UN Security Council, and the US decision that the UN mandate could not be fulfilled without a regime change was made in a meeting with NATO allies and not in the UN:

> The Libyan Government's continued violation of human rights, brutalization of its people, and outrageous threats have rightly drawn the strong and broad condemnation of the international community. By any measure, Muammar al-Qadhafi's Government has violated international norms and common decency and must be held accountable.
>
> Left unchecked, we have every reason to believe that Qadhafi would commit atrocities against his people. Many thousands could die. A humanitarian crisis would ensue. (Obama, 2012e, p. 155; 2012d, p. 247)

For domestic and alliance management-related reasons, President Obama also had to claim credit and ownership for the protective operation in Libya for NATO,[3] and this ambiguity gave opportunities for discursive strategies that framed the conflict in a way that justified Gaddafi's violence. The Gaddafi government considered the international military intervention as a NATO operation, rather than something the world organization, the UN, had justified. As a result, it saw it as an operation to establish the rule of colonial and corporate elites in Libya (Gaddafi, 2014).

The strategy of US protection was slightly different in Syria than it had been in previous conflicts. This difference was undoubtedly partly due to the near collapse of the state in Libya following the ousting of Gaddafi and the subsequent rise of Islamist terrorism in the country. In Syria, the US supported anti-government forces, sometimes to the extent that compromised its commitment to the fight against terror. Yet, until April 2017, there were no direct confrontations with government forces. In contrast, in Iraq, Afghanistan and Libya, the change of regime had been the first move in the US counter-terrorism and protection strategy.

In Syria, the US was fighting on two fronts: covertly against the authoritarian rule of President Bashar al-Assad, and overtly against the Islamic State of Iraq and Syria, ISIS. This setting was particularly complicated because the latter was, as the name reveals, mainly challenging the rule of Assad.[4] The alliances in the war in Syria with Turkey and its Kurdish militia enemies added to the complication, as did the occasional contradictions between motives and justifications. The attack on the Syrian Air Force in April 2017 was clearly justified on cosmopolitan grounds: violence against innocent civilians (see Trump's speech, 2017c, above). However, in the same speech, the operation was also justified by references to the identity of global cosmopolitan and national interests:

> It is in this vital national security interest of the United States to prevent and deter the spread and use of deadly chemical weapons. There can be no dispute that Syria used banned chemical weapons, violated its obligations under the Chemical Weapons Convention and ignored the urging of the U.N. Security Council. (Trump, 2017c)

The difference between the discursive battle in Syria and Libya and that in Iraq and Afghanistan was that in Libya and Syria the government could use the discourse on terrorism to defend their rule and externalize their enemies. Both President Bashar al-Assad and Chairman Muammar Gaddafi used the terrorism discourse and:

- associated the opposition with terrorists;
- associated the defence of the nation and stability with the defence of the regime (against foreigners and terrorists); and
- associated the opposition with aggression from foreign forces.

According to Assad, against terrorists there was no space for 'mildness' (al-Assad, 2014b) and therefore there was perceived legitimacy for the authoritarian violence against his opponents. The cooperation of Western intelligence agencies with Gaddafi's security forces in exchanging information about 'terrorists', only months before turning against the Gaddafi government and switching from the terminology of 'terrorists' to that of 'democratic opposition' (Elster, 2011), made it easy for Gaddafi to frame domestic opposition as an illegal, immoral, external terroristic threat.

The association between the regime and the country was revealed most clearly in the inauguration speech of Assad after the 2014 elections, where the president thanked his voters for having 'been steadfast and committed to your homeland' as if choosing in favour of this regime's leader was a more steadfast commitment to the homeland than voting another person to the country's leadership (al-Assad, 2014a). For Gaddafi, the association between the regime and the nation was based on the theory that the opposition was, in reality, mobilized by foreign powers and not the people of Libya:

> The NTC [National Transitional Council],[5] who gave them legitimacy? How did they obtain legitimacy? Did the Libyan people elect them? Did the Libyan people appoint them? And if only the power of NATO bombs and fleets grant legitimacy, then let all the rulers in the Third World beware for the same fate awaits you! (Gaddafi, 2011h)

Gaddafi felt that the CIA had machinated the opposition to his rule. According to Gaddafi, a leading figure among the rebel military leadership, Khalifa Haftar, who became the commander of the Libyan Armed Forces after the collapse of the Gaddafi regime, was affiliated with the CIA. Haftar lived in the US for nearly 20 years and only returned to Libya after the February 2011 rebellion against Gaddafi. Gaddafi loyalists claimed that he had been a member of the CIA-Muslim Brotherhood's National Front for the Salvation of Libya (NFSL) and its military wing, the Libyan National Army (LNA) since 1988. In this way, violence against domestic groups opposed to Gaddafi was justified as national defence, as the forces that fought the government were framed as foreign. The rebellion was seen as an American war and defence against it was seen as defence of sovereignty and (the Libyan type of social and economic) freedom from US and corporate rule:

> The Libyan people must not permit themselves to be subjugated under foreign rule and they must remember the sacrifices of the martyrs who have fought and died for our freedom. Do not let their sacrifice be in vain. I call on the people of Libya to continue the resistance and fight any foreign aggressor that moves against Libya, today, tomorrow and forever. (Gaddafi, 2011i)

The US support for Assad's enemies was also associated with colonialism, and it also externalized the domestic enemy, and dissociated the militant opposition from 'internal opposition':

> The President said that our war with terrorism is a war of destiny and existence where there is *no space for any mildness*, adding that we are today determined, more than any time before, to *resist projects of division and colonial sedition* which target Syria and the whole region. (al-Assad, 2014b; my emphasis)

The language of anti-colonialism was also mobilized to justify the fight of Gaddafi, who felt that he had 'stood up to the West and its colonialist ambitions' (Gaddafi, 2014).

Because of the association between the opposition and terrorism, and the opposition and Western military action, both Gaddafi and Assad also associate US action with terrorism. Gaddafi's reference in his justification of his fight against the US explicitly used the killing of a civilian (his adopted daughter) as justification for his demonization of the US and his own violence (Gaddafi, 2014), while Assad felt that the West used terrorists to subject independent-minded countries to their rule: 'The opposition linked to foreign countries and the terrorists have but one master; they are members of one body, one master mind as [sic] to blackmail Syria and transform it to a satellite country or [sic] they would continue to destroy Syria' (al-Assad, 2015).

While the authoritarian rulers of Iraq and Syria could utilize the global discourse on terror for the justification of violence against their oppositions, the terrorist organizations could utilize the Western discourse on democracy against their autocratic opponents. According to the so-called ISIS master plan, the need to establish an Islamic state was partially motivated by the authoritarian culture of personal cult, that is, idolization of Assad and others in his government, which, according the ISIS beliefs was '*haram*' or sinful (ISIS, 2015e). Furthermore, ISIS's 'Public call for citizens of the IS' emphasizes oppression as something that justifies resistance, which within the Islamic state is regulated by the Islamic courts, but which outside the 'just order of the Islamic state' has to be fought by other means (ISIS, 2015a).

At the same time, ISIS could use the nationalistic rhetoric of authoritarian leaders on colonialism and foreign domination. When designing the order of the caliphate, ISIS emphasized as its first principle that all international agreements with foreign powers by the caliphate will have to respect the 'internal sovereignty of the Islamic State and not allowing for other states to intervene in matters of Islamic rule or the general politics of the Islamic State' (ISIS, 2015e). The focus of ISIS resistance of foreign domination was not on the type of rules foreigners represented but on the agency of rule: an alien agency in the Islamic state was the reason for resistance, and the fact that such an alien agency could help fight autocracy was not a sufficient reason for allowing such influence. The fight against the autocrats of Libya, Iraq and Syria was therefore partly justified in the minds of the ISIS leaders by the need to resist autocracy, while the fight against the US coalition was related to resistance to foreign domination – that is, agency of foreigners, regardless of the type and content of the foreign rule. The exploitative nature of foreign influence was cited later in the principles of foreign relations of the Islamic state, but this was clearly subordinate to the principal objection of foreign authorship of politics within Islamic lands.

While the number of fatalities and the level of state fragility rose as the Western intervention became more prominent in Syria, and the rise was instant in Libya, the immediate development after the intervention was more complicated. As can be seen in Figures 3.5 and 3.6, the development in the year following the military intervention was positive, and only once the Western opposing forces remobilized in these countries, and once warfare began to take the form of primarily air operations, did violence and state fragility start to rise. By June 5, 2017, the US had conducted 8772 air operations in Syria and 8786 in Iraq (https://airwars.org/data/). Even though the evidence on fatalities was not complete for 2017 and 2018 at the time of writing, by the time this book is published, it is likely that fatalities and especially fatalities due to US operations will have continued to increase in Iraq, Syria and Afghanistan, although perhaps not in Libya.

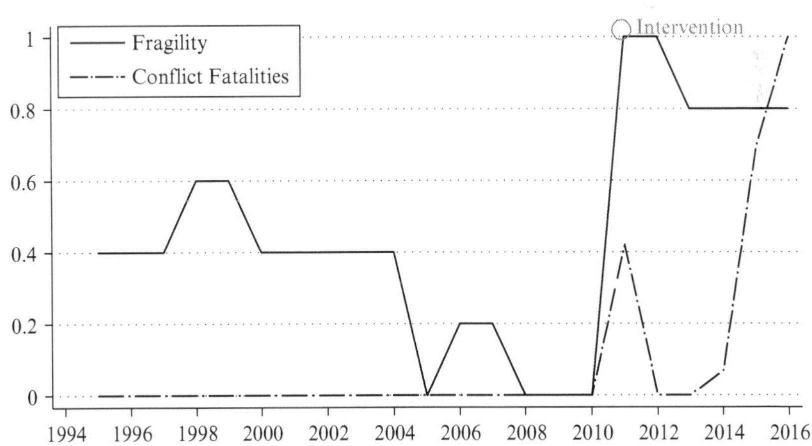

Figure 3.5 Standardized fatalities and fragilities in Libya

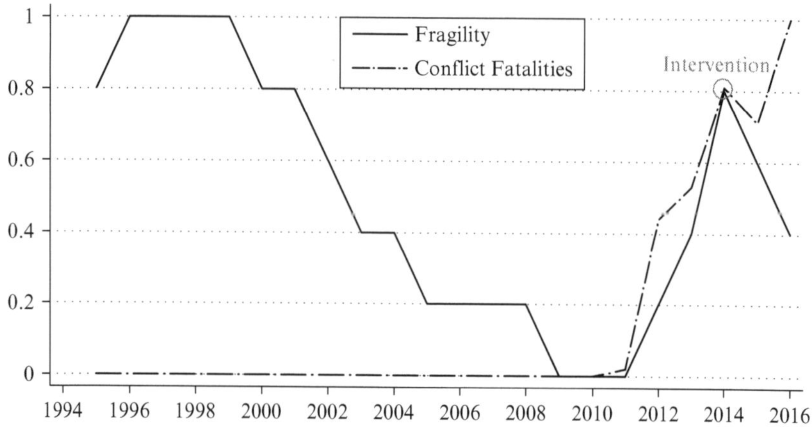

Figure 3.6 Standardized fatalities and fragilities in Syria

WAR ON TERROR IN ANARCHIES: SOMALIA, PAKISTAN AND YEMEN

The context of protection of civilians against terrorists in collapsed or extremely fragile anarchic states was slightly different from the context in which the Western coalition also needed to counter an authoritarian elite. In the latter, for example, the US and Western fight against the tyrant might have consolidated the power of a terrorist rebel movement. This had been the danger especially in Libya, Iraq and Syria. In failed states, however, the West only had one enemy, the terrorists. Second, due to the lack of publicity, there was a relative lack of any public moral hazard, as warfare could be kept almost completely secret. During the preparation for the intervention in 2008 and 2009, US presidents mentioned Yemen only once besides citing it in a list of other countries, and even then, the word Yemen was related to the attack on the US embassy in Yemen, and not the country itself. Information on these conflicts is very difficult to verify. Finally, if we look at the numbers of fatalities in these conflicts and compare them with state fragility we realize that, unlike in the case of autocracies, in anarchic states, fatalities and fragility do not positively correlate. In the case of Somalia and Pakistan, for example, intervention seems to be associated with strengthening of the state but an increase in conflict fatalities, while in Yemen, state fragility increases but fatalities fluctuate considerably. States do not seem to be instruments of security in these countries, perhaps especially when they are built by external intervention (Figures 3.7, 3.8 and 3.9).

In Somalia, US military and paramilitary activity has lasted longest.

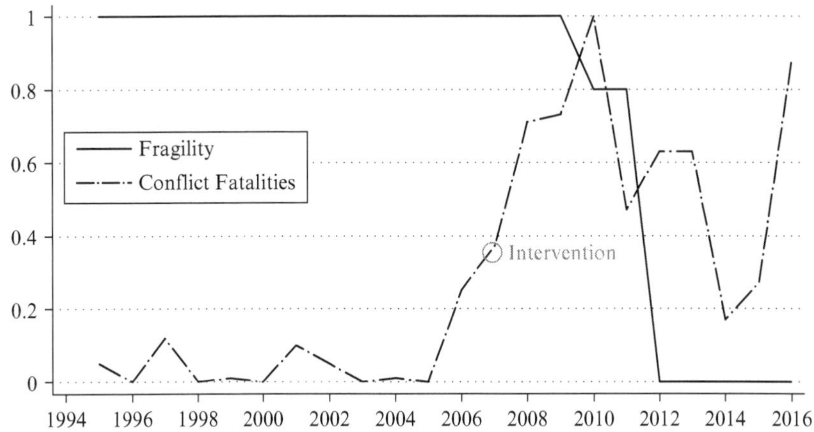

Figure 3.7 Standardized fatalities and fragilities in Somalia

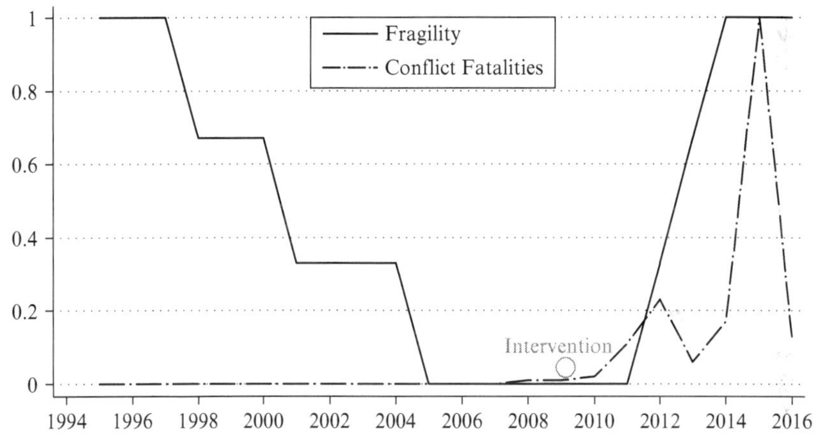

Figure 3.8 Standardized fatalities and fragilities in Yemen

Like in Pakistan (Obama, 2010a, p. 366) and Yemen (G.H.W. Bush, 2009, p. 1329) the US legitimation of military interest in Somalia has always been somewhat humanitarian and cosmopolitan. Already, President Clinton defended his police action in 1993 as:

> [. . .]essential to send a clear message to the armed gangs, to protect the vast majority of Somalis who long for peace, to enhance the security of our forces still in Somalia, to hasten the day when they can safely return home, and to strengthen the effectiveness and the credibility of U.N. peacekeeping in Somalia and around the world. (Clinton, 1994e, p. 840)

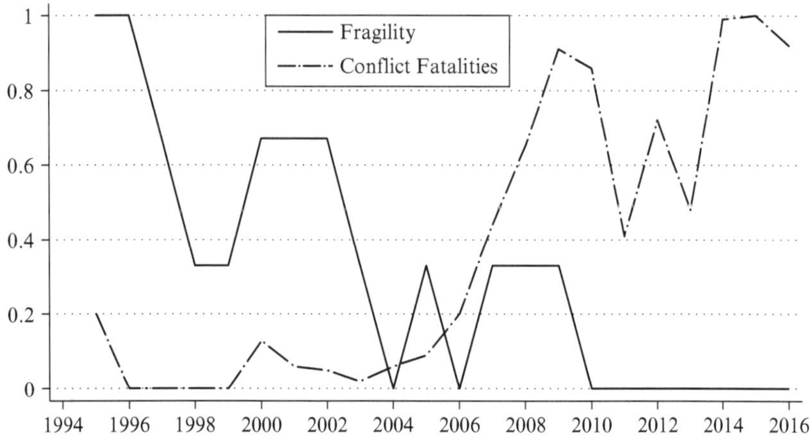

Figure 3.9 Standardized fatalities and fragilities in Pakistan

Again, despite the cosmopolitan justification, the security of US troops was also important.

The interesting difference between Somalia and the other two cases of anarchic counter-terrorism, Yemen and Pakistan, is that in the beginning of US military operations in Somalia in the 1990s (operations that did not, however, add up to a full intervention) the American administration was committed to allowing the United Nations to lead, whereas in Pakistan and in Yemen as well as in Somalia in the new millennium, the military operations were very much a unilateral US affair. Clinton's (and Bush Sr's) approach in the beginning of the 1990s, before the UN failures to protect civilians in Rwanda and in Srebrenica, was very appreciative of the idea that cosmopolitan action requires cosmopolitan agency if the international system was to develop towards global democracy (Clinton, 1994b, p. 970). Clinton was wary of the danger of being perceived as unilateral, imperial or colonial, and these were the labels he wanted to avoid until the end of the 1990s, when he started to portray US and NATO operations as somehow international and global:

> [E]very peacekeeping mission or every humanitarian mission has to have a date certain when it's over, and you have to in the end turn the affairs of the country back over to the people who live there. We were not asked to go to Somalia to establish a protectorate or a trust relationship or to run the country. That's not what we went for. (Clinton, 1994a, p. 1624; see also Clinton, 1994f, p. 1742)

The problem President Clinton had with his peacekeeping operation in Somalia was that his electorate was in the US, and the US public, according to the study by Mueller, valued US lives much more than Somali lives, and thus an approach that could have maximized the protection of lives equally was out of the question (Mueller, 1996). This pushed Clinton to a greater nationalist justification of action. In Somalia, this meant withdrawal and military restraint.

When the US operation in Somalia continued, this time not as an operation against criminals in a failed state, but as one against an Al Qaeda-linked terrorist organization, Al-Shabaab in 2007, the operation was already very similar to the one that had started three years earlier in Pakistan and the one that had started in 2002 and continued in 2009 in Yemen. In all these operations the US military had relative freedom to operate, even though both Yemen and Pakistan, despite their relative lack of control of their conflict areas, both reacted occasionally to the extensive independence the US military exercised inside their territories. Yet, after the terrorist attack on the US on September 11, 2001, US victimhood tended to justify global warfare on terror, and this was difficult to reconcile with a strict respect for the sovereignty of chaotic states that did not have control over their own territories. Furthermore, there was a strange, logical error in President Bush's thinking with regard to offensive warfare. The idea that Bush kept on repeating was that, '[w]e're striking our enemies before they can strike us again'. Thus, the reason why Bush went into the areas of Islamist terrorists was that they had come to America on September 11, 2001, yet he believed that staying on the offensive would not provoke them to come back to America, but instead, Bush's logic suggested, when they had to fight the war in their own countries they would not have time to plan an attack in the US. Thus, the assumption was that what provoked the US to go on the offensive would *prevent* the terrorists from doing the same. According to Bush:

> [. . .]wars are won on the offensive, and our friends and America are staying on the offensive. We're finding them. We're on the hunt. We're rolling back the terrorist threats, not on the fringes of its influence but at the heart of its power. We're making good progress. We're hunting the Al Qaida terrorists wherever they hide, from Pakistan to the Philippines to the Horn of Africa to Iraq. (G.W. Bush, 2004a, p. 1277)

Unsurprisingly, ISIS and Al Qaeda texts suggest that terrorist fighters were recruited by reference to the fatalities and disrespect for the sovereignty of Muslim lands: ISIS is explicit about the justification of violence against Christians and their allies in the Crusade in 'Muslim lands' (ISIS, n.d.), while Osama bin Laden made the provocation effect even more explicit:

> I say to you that security is an indispensable pillar of human life and that free men do not forfeit their security, contrary to Bush's claim that we hate freedom.

> If so, then let him explain to us why we don't strike for example – Sweden? And we know that freedom-haters don't possess defiant spirits like those of the 19 – may Allah have mercy on them. No, we fight because we are free men who don't sleep under oppression. We want to restore freedom to our nation, *just as you lay waste to our nation. So shall we lay waste to yours.* (Bin Laden, 2004; emphasis added)

Here, of course, the terrorist argument is contradictory as it refers to Bush as the enemy and then legitimizes violence against civilians. This is where the logic of escalation in interactive conflict processes lies: punishment is often disproportionate and interactively broadens the targeted group of people.

The fact that the US needed to support governments that allowed the Western counter-terrorism, created problems for state-building in these countries. Since drone attacks and targeting of terrorists was decided upon by the US, this created a situation where the state had to be constructed around a regime that accepted handing over the definition and identification of terrorists to a foreign country and allowed the execution of US-designated terrorists inside their own territories. Due to obvious nationalistic sensitivities, this made it difficult to build democratic states around regimes that were willing to allow such an infringement to their sovereignty. Therefore, with regard to Yemen, Pakistan and Somalia, the US has to decide between democracy and alliance if it wants to consolidate state apparatus in these countries. It cannot have a government that is both democratic and pro-alliance with the US.

Protective operations in Yemen, Pakistan and Somalia intended to avoid US fatalities in these areas of relative anarchy, and they were therefore based on air warfare. The limited access to human intelligence on the ground made estimates of fatalities very unreliable, however, while estimates of which of the fatalities were civilian and which were military were even more speculative (Knuckey et al., 2017). Until the beginning of the Trump presidency, and the entry of ground troops into Somalia and Syria, the US admitted only 200 civilian deaths in all its air operations in the protection wars. At the same time, Airwars, the non-governmental organization (NGO) that collects data on US admitted airstrikes and on the ground, has suggested that there might be up to 10 000 civilian fatalities of US air warfare in all protection wars (Woods, 2017). Even higher figures are available from leaked US documents – according to classified documents on the so-called Haymark Operation in Northern Afghanistan, from February 2012 to March 2013 nearly 90 per cent of those killed by drones were not the intended targets. In Somalia and Yemen, the US intel capability was far lower, meaning that the ratio there could be even worse (Scahill, 2015, p. 22).

UK AND FRENCH OPERATIONS: MALI, MAURITANIA, CENTRAL AFRICAN REPUBLIC (CAR) AND SIERRA LEONE

The difference between UK and French operations and US operations was that military war fighting phases of the former were generally very short, while presence continued at the level of politics, peacekeeping, state-building and development cooperation. Only the operation in Mali has not been progressed from its military phase, even though there the cooperation has moved from national unilateral towards more genuinely international UN-led operations with the main focus on state-building, rather than defeating the enemy. Furthermore, except for Sierra Leone, these conflicts were very small, killing only a small fraction (tens of people in Mauritania, and an annual maximum of 200 in Mali and CAR) of the number of fatalities in conflicts that the US intervened in.

The US also saw all these operations as humanitarian with the objective of protecting civilians from terrorists and criminal rebels (terrorists in Mali, Mauritania, and criminals in Central African Republic and Sierra Leone; for Obama's humanitarian justifications on CAR, see Obama, 2012b, p. 1278; for his humanitarian justifications on Mali, see Obama, 2015; for Mauritania, see Obama, 2014). Unlike US interventions in general, where the enemy of the US had managed to hide its violence behind national or religious rhetoric, in Central African Republic and in Sierra Leone, rebel forces were often openly opportunistic and lacking any credible justifications for their actions. This, together with the population's frustration with rebel violence and the shortness of the military operation, made it easier to avoid framing the intervention as a foreign occupation. Rebellion and terrorist violence in all these countries was also associated with the motives of neighbouring countries, making it more difficult for the rebels and terrorists to marginalize Western big power influence as 'foreign'. All these differences, especially between the Sierra Leone intervention and the main failures of protection, will be contrasted in Chapter 4, which identifies the elements of cosmopolitan interventions that provoked anti-cosmopolitan challengers of the West.

In general, Sierra Leone could be considered as a relatively successful case of protective intervention. There the military operation intended to block violent opportunities for economic gain, and then quickly took on an assisting role in state-building. As can be seen in Figure 3.10, the UK intervention was instantly associated with lowering the numbers of fatalities, while the development in the strengthening of the state could be seen only six years after the intervention due to the continuing political and economic aid work.

While in Mali the escalation of conflict associated with the French

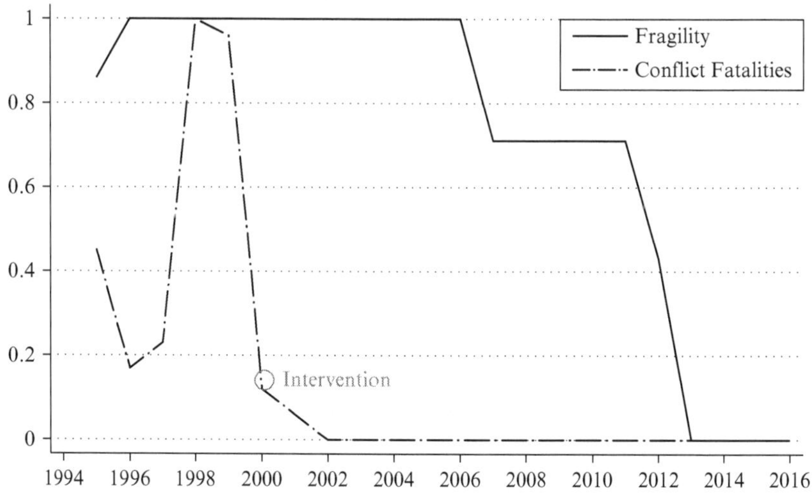

Figure 3.10 Standardized fatalities and fragilities in Sierra Leone

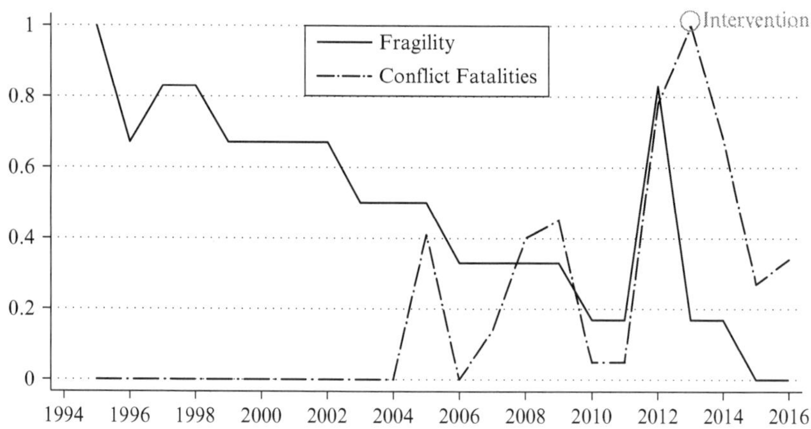

Figure 3.11 Standardized fatalities and fragilities in Mali

intervention dramatically increased the number of fatalities and weakened the state, the effect was short-lived, and the number of fatalities and the problem of state fragility both started to decline soon after the initial military phase of the French operation (Figure 3.11).

The French operation in Mauritania was a minor operation in a miniscule conflict and was associated with a minor, short-lived increase in conflict fatalities, but also a failure to strengthen state structures (Figure 3.12).

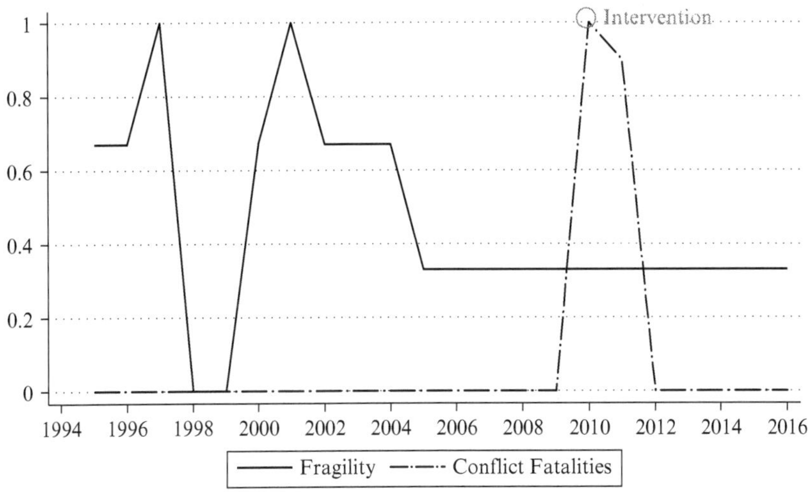

Figure 3.12 Standardized fatalities and fragilities in Mauritania

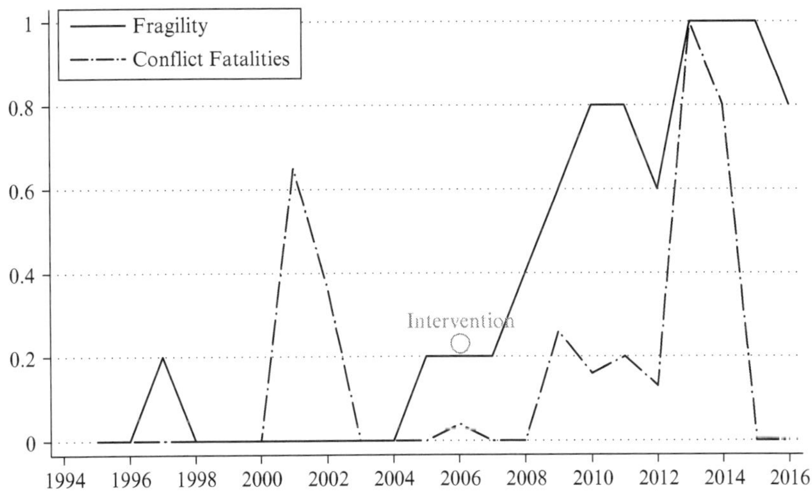

Figure 3.13 Standardized fatalities and fragilities in CAR

The French involvement in 2006 in the Central African 'Bush War' also failed to help state-building, and as a result, new rebel groups emerged after the 2006 conflict and conflict fatalities increased, even if not necessarily in the conflict that the French forces had participated in (Figure 3.13).

NOTES

1. Yet, when the audience is his own party, Milošević is much more 'ethnic' in his formulations: 'If the Socialist Party of Serbia and Serbia did all they could for the Serbs outside Serbia in war and peace-time in the territory of the former Yugoslavia, for the Serbs, who at the very beginning of the winds of war and throughout, sought refuge in Serbia, the Socialist Party of Serbia and Serbia did more than they could' (Milošević, 2000a).
2. Yet, of course Milošević did not recognize the mandate of the International Criminal Tribunal for the Former Yugoslavia created by the UN Security Council (Milošević, 2001b).
3. Obama said, for example, that '[w]e stood with the Libyan people as they rose up and demanded their rights. A coalition that included the United States, NATO, and Arab nations persevered through the summer to protect civilians' (Obama, 2012a, p. v).
4. The so-called 'ISIS master plan' mentions Nusayris first as enemies of ISIS. Nusayris is a derogatory term for the Alawites, the ethnic/religious sect of President Bashar al-Assad (ISIS, 2015e).
5. The National Transitional Council consisted of groups in armed opposition to the regime of Muammar Gaddafi. The Council declared itself the only representative of the people of Libya in March 2011.

4. The consequences of humanitarian interventions

INTRODUCTION

Now that we have defined and operationalized state fragility and intervention and identified new wars and protection wars, we can study the consequences of protective interventions by comparing the two types of conflict. We can make three kinds of comparisons that each say something about the effects of interventions.

First, I will use UCDP (Allansson et al., 2017) and Peace Research Institute Oslo (PRIO) conflict data (Lacina, 2009) to show that protective interventions were largely absent in the 1990s until Kosovo in 1999, but that after Kosovo such interventions have become quite common. The two contexts, one with no interventions and the other with frequent interventions, will then be correlated with the development of global conflict fatalities and general state fragility in the world. This comparison makes sense, as one might imagine that the era of intervention could also impact states that have not been intervened in. Thus, to obtain the broadest picture of the global effects of interventions, one needs to know what happens to global conflict fatalities, and the state fragility that provides the context for such fatalities, before, during and after these interventions.

In addition to global comparison, which is vulnerable to many kinds of historically specific intervening conditions, one needs to make comparisons between states. On this level, I will look at the development of fatalities and state fragility in countries where protective interventions take place and in countries where no intervention has taken place but where chaotic violence and new wars are left to continue without robust military interference.

Third, I will look at specific intrastate conflicts in which protective interventions have been conducted and compare them with such conflicts where no interventions took place. This is the narrowest and most specific perspective from which it is possible to follow the impact of intervention not just on a country but also specifically on the conflict that has been intervened in. This perspective offers new information as some countries have endured many conflicts, some of which have been intervened in and some have not. To see how great a threat to human life non-intervened intrastate conflicts in fragile states are in comparison with those conflicts in which external countries do intervene, I will look at the development in the number of fatalities in conflicts in both categories of warfare.

STATE FRAGILITY AND FATALITIES

Before moving on to the effects of interventions on state fragility, we take a quick look at the relationship between fragility and fatalities. First, using Uppsala Battle Deaths data (Allansson et al., 2017; Gleditsch et al., 2002), it is possible to calculate that up to 84 per cent of all conflict fatalities have taken place originally in domestic conflicts inside fragile states. If we also include fatalities of interstate conflict in which at least one side of the conflict has been a fragile state (such as the one between Ethiopia and Eritrea), we can see that such conflicts have caused 98 per cent of conflict fatalities in the world. This is significant given that, according to the definition adopted here, almost half (47 per cent) of the world's countries are currently not defined as fragile.[1]

Since Uppsala Conflict Data Program (UCDP) statistics of conflict fatalities define conflicts as something that the state participates in and that are between at least two armed groups, we will must broaden our analysis to both one-sided violence (Allansson et al., 2017; Eck and Hultman, 2007) and non-state conflicts (Allansson et al., 2017; Sundberg et al., 2012).

One-sided violence takes place between an armed group or government and an unarmed group of people. New war theorists consider violence against civilians as very typical of the asymmetry of new wars. Almost all analyses of violence in new wars cite violence against unarmed women. For Mello and Münkler, violence against unarmed groups such as women is a defining factor in the strategies of new wars: 'Violence against women in war has historical precedents, but in contrast to "old wars", where sexual violence on enemy territory had been largely dysfunctional, a resexualization of violence can be observed in "new wars"' (Mello, 2010, p. 299; see also Münkler, 2002, pp. 142–53; Duffield, 2001, pp. 212, 226; and Burke, 2013, p. 18). Furthermore, violence against unarmed ethnic groups is typical of new wars, for instance, the democidal violence by ethnic Serb militias against ethnic Bosniak civilians. Duffield also views violence against children (Duffield, 2001, pp. 32, 226) in Bosnia as new war violence, even though children are not a group with armed representatives.

Non-state conflicts are those where the government is not involved. These too need to be included in our investigation of new wars, since one of the main issues in new wars is the inability of the state to prevent and control violence inside fragile states (Kaldor, 1999, p. 4). Such violence that excludes state participation should also be considered as new war violence, not just conflict violence.

Thus, in addition to statistics on conflict deaths, we must examine fatalities during one-sided violence and non-state conflicts in fragile states. Over 97 per cent of all one-sided violence that UCDP data list (Allansson et al., 2017; Eck and Hultman, 2007) takes place in fragile states. Data on non-state conflict (Allansson et al., 2017; Sundberg et al., 2012) further suggest that 87 per cent of fatalities of non-state conflict also takes place in fragile states.

Thus, the claim of new war theorists, rationalists and post-colonial theorists, that post-Cold War conflicts are associated with fragility of states, seems very plausible. Conflict theory that was obsessed with great power wars and interstate wars can be criticized from the perspective of the study of new wars. We have been obsessed about the wrong anarchy, the one *between* states, while we should have been focused on the anarchy *within* fragile states. Conflicts have moved to fragile states and thus it is justified for conflict theorists to define the type of warfare we now see developing in fragile states as new wars. That the new war explanation also corresponds to the realist explanation of anarchy as the permissive mechanism of conflict, makes the theories of new wars more attractive. However, this does not mean that the fragile context of current warfare is necessarily something new and there seems to be some evidence suggesting that it is not (Melander et al., 2009).

To test the new wars claim that the neglect of fragile states by cosmopolitan powers has led to increased conflict fatalities and the weakening of order in these states, one should first define which era constitutes the period of decline in great power interest in violence in intrastate anarchies and which periods do not.

PERIODS OF INTERVENTION AND NON-INTERVENTION

It is now possible to use the UCDP data (Allansson et al., 2017; Gleditsch et al., 2002) with the amendments made to it in Chapter 2 for the study of the patterns of US, UK and French patterns of intervention over time. Two more revisions are required by the theoretical context of new wars, however. Both the Korean War and the Vietnam War are coded in UCDP data as interstate conflicts. However, both originally centred on a domestic dispute related to the political system of the state. Both involved one-sided violence seen by new war theorists as conflict. Thus, participation in these wars by the US (and other Western powers) must be coded as intervention in intrastate conflicts.

Theorists of new wars have regretted that after the conclusion of the Cold War, intervention by developed countries in intrastate conflicts within Third World states also ended (Daalder, 1996; Kaldor, 1999, p. 3). There were plenty of interventions in such conflicts, but until the Western intervention in the 1999 conflict in Kosovo, the interference that took place was not of the sort that could be seen as 'international control' of gainful violence in a fragile state. Opportunistic forces from neighbouring fragile states that interfere in the gainful use of violence in a fragile state cannot be seen as controlling violence or enforcing humanitarian law. On the contrary, Kaldor and others claim this is typical of new wars. In the new war context, fragile countries are vulnerable to violence and exploitation by various criminal and opportunistic forces from neighbouring fragile states (Duffield, 2001, p. 106; Kaldor, 1999, p. 3; Shaw, 2003, p. 2). Moreover, intervention by a neighbouring developing country could not bring with it the overwhelming force required to control violent opportunists (Weinberger and Powell recommendations).[2] Thus, intrastate conflicts that are internationalized by other neighbouring fragile countries can still be considered new wars.

According to the Uppsala data (Figure 4.1) (Allansson et al., 2017; Gleditsch et al., 2002), as adjusted for the new trends in air-based intervention, the cosmopolitan great powers – the United States, France and the United Kingdom – were not involved in internationalized intrastate conflicts after the end of the Cold War until the cosmopolitan involvement in Serbia (in support of the repressed people of Kosovo in 1999).[3]

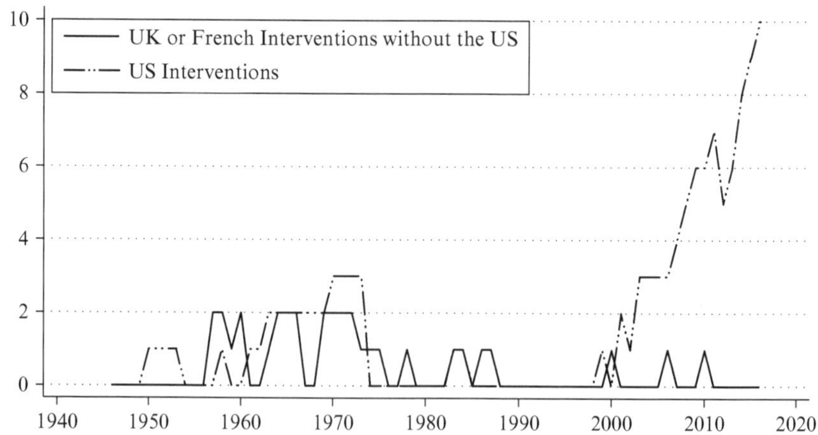

Figure 4.1 US and Western interventions in intrastate conflicts

US interference in domestic conflicts in fragile states did not always define the context of the Cold War. After withdrawal from Vietnam, the US was hesitant to interfere, even when there were strategic Cold War priorities at stake. The type of Cold War context spoken of by new war theorists, when both superpowers interfered in conflicts in fragile states, only existed between 1961 and 1973, when US, Chinese and Soviet involvement was extensive, especially in the Indo-China region. Even without continuous intervention, potentially violent, opportunistic actors did not dare shake the stability of US (or Soviet) client states for fear of retaliation. This changed after the Cold War, as the US lost its rationale and the Soviet Union its existence. This lack of interference is a relatively new occurrence. It could provide a basis for the new war theorists' claim of novelty in the context of new wars – by and large, Western great powers, the US, the UK and France, abandoned developing countries and did not intervene militarily with a mandate for warfighting in violence in these Third World fragile states between 1989 and 1999.

We can see that the post-Cold War period up until 1999 was one in which the world lived under non-interference, while after 1999 the large number of cases of interference in intrastate conflicts suggests that the world began witnessing a more interventionist period.

FATALITIES AND FRAGILITY IN THE ERA OF NON-INTERFERENCE AND IN THE ERA OF INTERVENTION

Using the above operationalization of protection wars (88 conflict years) and new wars (665 conflict years) since 1995 (see also Table 4.3), it is now possible to use UCDP data on fatalities to see how the two different periods, that of non-interference until 1999 and the interventionist period from then on, compare in terms of conflict-related fatalities (Figure 4.2).

When great powers neglected involvement in fragile states, this decreased rather than increased conflict fatalities. This is a common trend in the 1990s, as UCDP data show (Allansson et al., 2017), not just as something limited to the latter half of the decade, nor to fragile states. Throughout the era of new wars in the 1990s, there is a tendency towards a decline in conflict fatalities. Moreover, battle deaths only started to rise some years after the great powers began attempts to control such violence, particularly after the intervention in Iraq in 2003 and especially after the internationalization of the intrastate war in Syria in 2013 (see Figure 4.2). The lack of a positive correlative relationship between disengagement from violence of the great powers in fragile states and a rise in battle deaths after the

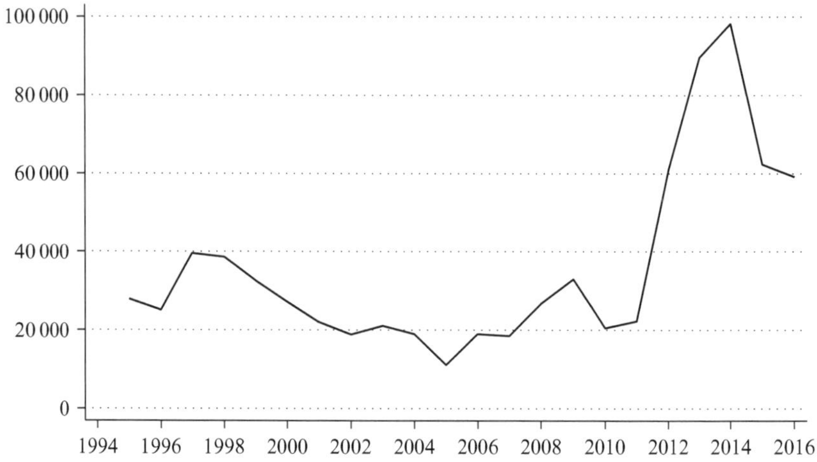

Figure 4.2 Fatalities in intrastate conflicts in fragile states: protection wars and new wars

number of interventions by protective great powers seriously challenges the premises of cosmopolitan interventionist policies.

If we then match this development in international involvement in conflicts in fragile states (Figure 4.3) with the New Wars State Fragility Index, we can see that the relationship between neglect and fragility is not what the theory of new wars claims. New wars theorists have suggested that big power abandonment of Third World state fragility is a deteriorating problem. This, together with the alleged increase in fatalities within new wars, is cited as the main reason for pleading urgency in favour of international action (Kaldor, 1999, p. 3). Yet, as Melander and others have shown, there was no increase in the suffering of civilians after the Cold War (Melander et al., 2009) and the above figures suggest that the abandonment of fragile states by the great powers in the 1990s was actually a positive rather than a negative thing.

A simple calculation of annual averages of global state fragility also casts serious uncertainty on the new wars theory. There is a clear decline in state fragility in the 1990s, at the time when new war theorists were alerting the world to a new threat caused by it (Figure 4.3). It seems clear that the claims of increasing fragility in the post-Cold War world, and that this is due to the abandonment of fragile areas by great powers, are both myths.

State fragility does not seem to have emerged only recently; state-building has progressed differently in different places. It also seems, as suggested

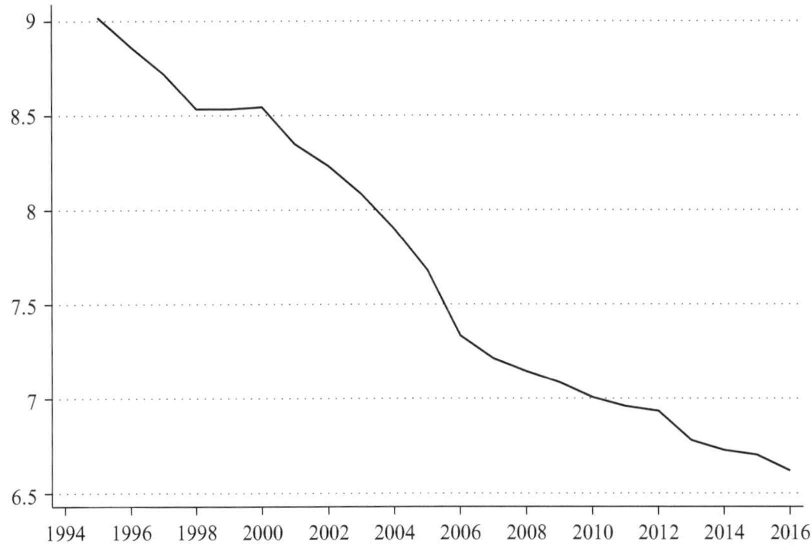

Figure 4.3 Development of state fragility in the world

by the post-colonialist research of Ayoob, Moon and Azar, that the Third World has never had a stable state structure (Ayoob, 1991, 2001, 2004; Azar and Moon, 1988a, 1988c). As colonialism and Western interventionism have prolonged its development, the Third World generally consists of fragile states. The Euro-/West-centric focus of the analyses of the process of state-building has created the misperception by new war theorists of state degeneration. When Kaldor discusses the process of 'internal pacification', she refers to developments in Europe (Kaldor, 2012, pp. 1–20; see also, Giddens, 1985, pp. 181–91). Yet, when she talks about state degeneration she refers to European peripheries (Bosnia, Kosovo) or to the Third World. Here she is guilty of overgeneralizing the European experience, something that is very common and is criticized by the scholars of post-colonial security. If the developing world was considered by itself, it would be possible to see how the historical contexts and path dependencies affect political developments. While Europe and the West are ready for cosmopolitan protection, the fact that the developing world is not even ready for national security governance makes the Western project of cosmopolitan protection difficult.

A look at the countries that are late-comers to state-building lends support to an even more extreme statement. If we correlate fragility and historical colonialism – the West's effort to protect and impose moral order in the Third World – we can see that interference in state-building has not contributed to internal pacification. On the contrary, countries with a colonial past within the last 100 years have an average fragility score of almost 11. On the other hand, those who have not experienced colonialism within the last 100 years score less than 5. Up to 84 per cent of former colonies are fragile, while only 40 per cent of those countries without a recent colonial past are fragile. Naturally, here we are conflating different types of external interference humanitarian and colonial. They are arguably very different, one greedy and exploitative and the other now seen as more altruistic. Yet, the ongoing protective military operations are only partly justified by altruistic interests, while colonialism, at the time, was also largely justified as a civilizing and Christianizing, altruistic mission.

Furthermore, it seems clear that the instability that caused the collapse of communist countries, such as Yugoslavia and the Soviet Union, led to much less serious fragility than colonialism. This too, goes against the intuition of the various theorists of new wars, who tend to consider the conflict in Bosnia as the archetype of new wars. Countries 'colonized' by communist powers, such as Kosovo, Bosnia or the Warsaw Pact countries, tend to manage their state-building much better than former colonial countries. Afghanistan was weakened after Soviet withdrawal, but simultaneously the level of violence reduced drastically, according to PRIO data. Therefore, it seems clear that the focus post-colonial theorists place on intrastate anarchy leads to better conclusions and prescriptions than new war theorists' focus. Intrastate anarchy is a serious conflict problem, as Heupel posits (Heupel and Zangl, 2010), but one that has not been brought about by the abandonment of fragile states by great powers.

FATALITIES AND STATE FRAGILITY IN PROTECTED AND UNPROTECTED CONFLICT COUNTRIES

To produce more sophisticated results, we will now compare countries where humanitarian intervention took place to countries where new wars were allowed to continue.

Based on the assumption that external intervention in a fragile state affects all conflicts of a particular country, it is possible to compare developments in levels of violence between fragile states where intervention occurred and those where conflict continued without intervention (protection wars and new wars). Furthermore, I will also compare violence before, during and after protective intervention. To defend this perspective, it could be argued that in countries like Iraq or Afghanistan, where the former security establishment was entirely wiped out by an international military operation, the government's ability to fight opponents was fundamentally affected (regardless of whether or not the cosmopolitan international community was involved in all conflicts). It could also be supported in the case of Syria, where Western direct international military interference and indirect support of enemies of the state weakened the state.

It is now possible to calculate the development in fatalities once the international community decides to intervene in new war violence in a fragile state. This association between protection and fatalities is established in Table 4.1 by calculating the average number of fatalities for three years before the protection started and comparing it with the average number of fatalities during the entire protective operation. Since most of these operations are ongoing, it is not possible to include the period after protective operations in the comparison. For those countries in which military operations have ended, an average of the three post-operation years has been presented in Table 4.1. The case of a two-year non-intervention period in Iraq in 2012 and 2013 is an exception. There, the two years of non-intervention are seen as the post-intervention period for the first intervention and the pre-intervention period for the second intervention.

The calculation of fatalities is based on the UCDP data, while the

Table 4.1 Fatalities and protection

Main Fragile Country and/or Location of Battle, Years of Intervention	Number of Fatalities Before Intervention	Number of Fatalities During International Involvement	Number of Fatalities After the International Operation
Serbia/Kosovo, 1999	412	1404	0
Sierra Leone, 2000	2396	382	480
Afghanistan, 2001–	5373	4232	n/a
Pakistan, 2004–	374	5585	
Iraq, 2003–11	64	3005	12845
Iraq, 2014–	12845	4624	n/a
CAR, 2006	0	45	88
Somalia, 2007–	100	1191	n/a
Mauritania, 2010	0	15	4
Libya, 2011	0	1930	107
Libya, 2015–	107	3859	n/a
Yemen, 2009–	97	1481	n/a
Mali, 2013–	82	243	n/a
Syria, 2014–	14550	36892	n/a
Total	36400	64888	n/a

operationalization and identification of new wars and protection wars come from the analysis above. As is common, I have divided the number of fatalities with the number of battle locations when calculating fatalities in a specific fragile state in cases where a conflict has occurred in several locations.

Based on Table 4.1, it seems clear that protective interventionism has not succeeded in reducing violence. All other cases except Sierra Leone – and perhaps Afghanistan – can be considered relative failures. In Afghanistan, the number of fatalities varied for a number of years so that the average number of fatalities during the still ongoing involvement in aerial operations is lower now than it was before international involvement began. Yet, there does not seem to be an end to violence and the number of fatalities is still very high.

The case of Iraq is more difficult to assess due to the drastic escalation of conflict between the two US-led operations (2012 and 2013, with no US presence and an increase in fatalities). There the first operation seems to have been a failure, whereas the second has finally helped the situation – in comparison with the two years between the interventions. Taken together as one development, the intervention in Iraq can only be seen as an overall failure to protect.

Looking at all cases together, we can see that fatalities almost doubled (an increase of 80 per cent) once protection started. Only Sierra Leone was clearly left better off after an international military operation in 2000. While a study of how the operation in Sierra Leone was different from all the other protective operations would be important, one should also remember that this country did not become a model state. On the contrary, Sierra Leone is still very much a fragile state.

Even if the number of conflict fatalities appears to increase with protective interventions, one might argue that, in the long run, the destruction of terrorist cells, brutal dictators and conflict entrepreneurs by means of great power intervention might at times be useful – the removal of opportunistic conflict actors may clear the way for the development of state structures to control violence. Empirical evidence, however, seems to go against that assumption too.

It seems that the overall development of state fragility is not strongly associated with policing by great powers. State fragility seems to decline steadily during the period of great power neglect (1990–98) as well as during the time of cosmopolitan interventions (1999 onwards). Thus, it would not be possible to claim that humanitarian intervention has greatly improved the situation in intrastate anarchies in general, yet nor has it worsened.

However, a more targeted investigation on the violent fragile states where cosmopolitan powers have intervened could provide us with further

Table 4.2 Fragility, fatalities and protection

	New War Fragility		
	Before	During	After
Serbia-Montenegro, 1999	7.0	7.0	8.0
Sierra Leone, 2000	19.0	19.0	19.0
Afghanistan, 2001–	18.0	15.9	
Iraq, 2003–11	13.0	13.4	12.3
Iraq, 2014–	12.5	12.0	
Pakistan, 2004–	12.7	11.3	
Central African Republic, 2006	14.3	15.0	16.0
Somalia, 2007–	19.0	16.6	
Mauritania, 2010	15.0	15.0	15.0
Yemen, 2010–	13.0	14.5	
Libya, 2011	6.0	11.0	10.3
Mali, 2013–	15.3	14.0	
Syria, 2014–	9.0	11.5	
Average	13.4	13.6	

evidence on the relationship between cosmopolitan intervention and the problem of intrastate fragility. We can calculate the development of fragility once the international community decides to intervene in the new war violence of a fragile state. In Table 4.2, I have presented cases of US, UK or French intervention with military force (ground force or air force, including drones) in fragile states and the development of their state fragility in the process of international enforcement of order. This association (between humanitarian protection and fragility) is established by calculating the average fragility for three years before the protection started and comparing them with the average fragility during protective operations. As in the case of conflict fatalities, since most of these operations have not ended it is not be possible to bring the period after the operations into comparison. For those states in which military involvement has ended, an average of the three post-operation years has been presented in the table.

While, in general, states were becoming less fragile (see Figure 4.3), those states whose governance was 'supported' by cosmopolitan enforcement of humanitarian norms were not developing in the same direction. In fact, the average level of fragility of all those countries that were intervened in since 1999 has increased slightly. If we look at civil wars and internationalized civil wars that were not interfered in by cosmopolitan powers we can see that their state fragility did not generally deteriorate during the conflict. If we remove protection wars from the list and only examine conflicts by looking at the year immediately before interventionism started in 1999 and produced fatalities in at least two years, we can find 90 conflicts in fragile states until the end of our statistical investigation in 2016. In only ten of them has state fragility deteriorated after the first year of war, while in 33 of them fragility improved during the conflict (in 47 conflicts there was no change). On average, state fragility (measured by the New Wars State Fragility Index) was reduced by 4.1 points after the first year of conflict, from 13.1 to 12.7. This finding lends support to the post-colonial claim that state-building is violent, but which if not interfered in, it will yield results. Thus, it seems evident that humanitarian interventions have not, in general, been beneficial to the strength of states.

In protected states, the change in fragility was normally very small, except in the case of Syria and Libya. In these cases, protection was associated with a drastic decline in state strength. It would not be possible to say how these states would have developed absence an external intervention, but we can say that the external intervention has not managed to fix the problem of state fragility. In the cases of Libya, Central African Republic, Serbia (Kosovo), Mauritania and Sierra Leone, fragility can also be measured for a period (average of three years) after protection had ended. In none of these has fragility decreased after the ending of protection (as compared to the period before protection). Drone, or limited, warfare has had to continue in all other countries. In Afghanistan, Pakistan and Somalia, where protection has been associated with increased state strength, it must be supported with ever continuing violent protection from outside the state, with substantial numbers of annual fatalities. The fact that conflict continues in Afghanistan suggests that even this case cannot really be considered successful. It is necessary to conclude that armed interventions to protect humanitarian order have not produced the protection they were designed for, despite their public justification.

FATALITIES IN PROTECTION WARS AND IN NEW WARS

In addition to considering the effect of intervention from the point of view of global eras or fragile states, investigation can be made into the level of individual conflicts. We must, of course, keep in mind that international involvement in and of itself does not cause all escalation of intrastate conflict in fragile states. By introducing new means of violence, it might bring about some part of the expansion of violence and number of fatalities, but most of the escalation ensues from an interactive process in which one party's violence is seen to justify the opposing party's violence.

Table 4.3 Fatalities of new wars and protection wars

	Obs.	Mean	Std. Dev.	Min.	Max.
New war annual fatalities	665	800.56	3835.22	25	68 503
Protection war annual fatalities	88	2967.92	3894.51	29	16 581

For violent authoritarian rulers, external intervention often legitimizes greater violence in the name of national survival. Part of the reason for the increase in fatalities may stem from a locking of positions between those who enforce the norm of non-interference and sovereignty and those who enforce cosmopolitan humanitarian norms. Yet, it is possible to see from the Uppsala data on conflict fatalities and the data on new war state fragility (Kivimäki, 2019b, forthcoming) with the revised variable of protective intervention, how the intensity in the two types of conflict has developed.

The average annual number of fatalities in protection wars is 2968, while the average annual number of fatalities in new wars is 801 (Table 4.3).

Thus, there seems to be 3.7 times more fatalities in protection wars than in new wars. This may, of course, be related to a selection bias. Intervention is naturally more likely in serious and intensive conflicts than in less serious conflicts. Yet, if we interpret conflicts as interaction and as processes of mutual constitution (rather than as causal processes) we can see how intrastate violence attracts and legitimizes external intervention, which again invites and attracts increased intrastate violence.

To study the contribution to violence of external intervention (rather than observing the interactive process), however, we will have to look at the development within each conflict before and after the protective intervention. But then, a comparison between conflicts in which cosmopolitan great powers intervened and those in which they did not, is made difficult by the fact that in the case of the latter conflicts, it is difficult to define when it was that the great powers did NOT intervene. Furthermore, it can be suspected that the coding of the conflict ID in UCDP data changes when intervention changes the nature of the conflict. However, if one trusts the coding of the Uppsala data, it would be possible to make comparisons based on an assumption that great powers could have intervened after the first or second year of conflict.

In the period 1995–2016, there have been 193 conflicts[4] within fragile countries, 101 that lasted at least two consecutive years, and 60 that lasted for at least three years. It emerges that put together the number of fatalities in all of these new wars increased after the first year by 27 per cent (yet, we must remember that the first year is not a full year for most of the conflicts), 11 per cent on the third year, but then started to decline. If we then compare these with conflicts where there was an intervention, we can see a much greater increase in fatalities. There have been 19 protection wars, and in all but one: the conflict in which the French–US–UN coalition joined the Mali Government's battle against the Coordination of Azawad Movements in 2015. Yet, even in Mali, the success in this particular conflict was shadowed by the continuing fight against other terrorist movements, most notably Al Qaeda in the Islamic Maghreb. If we compare the combined number of fatalities during the first year of intervention and the previous year, we can see an increase of 720 per cent! In almost half the cases (9/19) Western great powers have intervened either before any conflict violence has occurred or within the same year such violence has started. If we look at the immediate effects of intervention in those conflicts that had started already before the year of intervention, we can see that still the increase of fatalities on the year of intervention is 501 per cent. Furthermore, there is a strong declining tendency (49 per cent) in fatalities in the year before intervention. Of the five cases of conflicts that had continued for at least two years before the intervention, in four the conflict intensity had declined in the year before the intervention. The only conflict in which the US intervention followed an intensification of conflict took place in Iraq in 2014, after an intensification of the conflict from 2012 to 2013. Thus, it seems that humanitarian interventions tend to respond to conflicts where conflict violence has already started to decline. This and the change brought by interventions seems to prove the complete failure of protection.

When all post-1994 new wars and protection wars are viewed in a stacked line graph, the former from their start and the latter three years from their internationalization, the impact of protective intervention in an intra-state conflict becomes clear (Figure 4.4).

Figure 4.5 on new wars shows a very different picture.

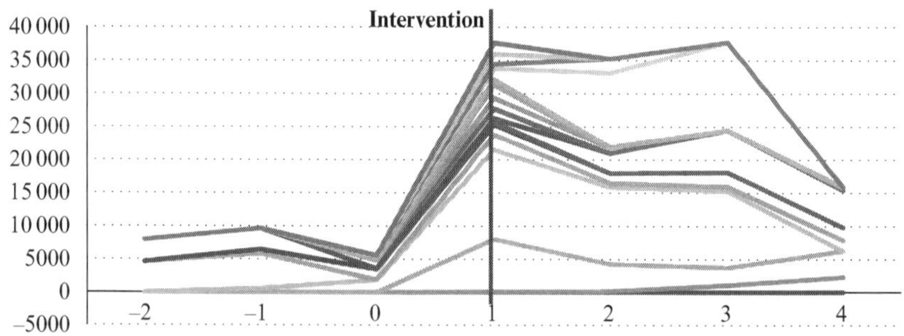

Figure 4.4 Development of fatalities in all protection wars (from three years before to four years after intervention)

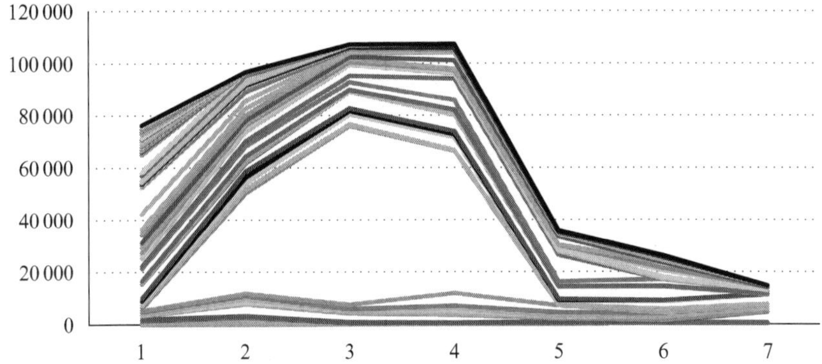

Figure 4.5 *Conflict fatalities during seven years after the onset of a new war*

The apparent dysfunctionality of interventionism cannot be explained away by suggesting that more intensive protection wars were then also shortened. The average duration in years of protection wars is longer than the average duration of new wars: 5.5 (std. dev. 4.9, n = 19) against 3.5 (std. dev. 4.6, n = 193).[5] Thus, if external intervention cannot be justified as something that deals with the problem of state fragility, as seems to be the case, nor can it be justified as something that tackles violence in state-building.

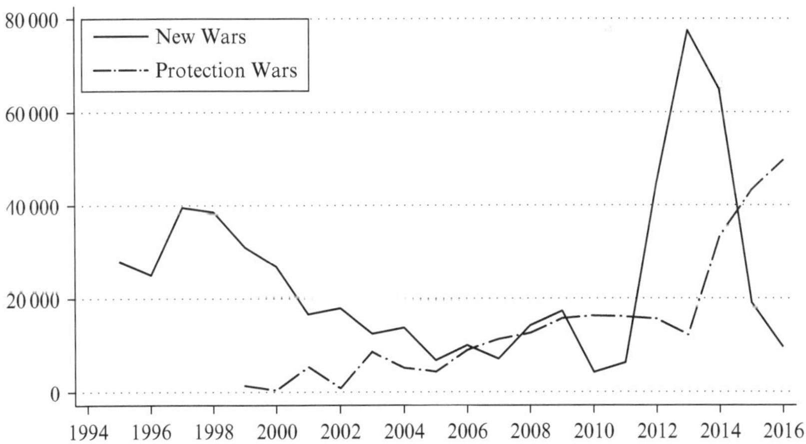

Figure 4.6 *Fatalities of intrastate conflicts in fragile states: contribution of new wars and protection wars*

If we then look at the development of conflict fatalities in both new wars and in protection wars, it seems that protection wars are set to become a greater source of fatalities than new wars (Figure 4.6).

Conflicts intended to protect civilians are becoming as much of a risk for people as those conflicts in which cosmopolitan great powers do not intervene.

CONCLUSIONS

It seems clear that the theories of new wars, post-colonial security and rational explanations of conflicts have opened an interesting debate on anarchy and conflict fatalities. They have shown that anarchy is still a permissive cause of political violence and results in violence. This chapter confirms these findings by showing that 98 per cent of conflict violence, 97 per cent of one-sided violence and 87 per cent of non-state violence take place in the type of intrastate anarchy discussed by theorists of new wars, post-colonial theory and rationalist explanations of conflict. These theories have also shown that mainstream conflict research has mistakenly concentrated on the wrong anarchy. While focusing on anarchy between states, the violence takes place primarily in intrastate anarchy. The use of the New Wars State Fragility Index, modified for this book from the State Fragility Index and the three different Uppsala University datasets, have made it possible to verify this.

Furthermore, the theories of new wars also drew a picture of worsening intrastate anarchy and a spiralling deterioration of the conflict situation. However, this chapter also added to the evidence presented by Melander et al. (2009) against this claim specific to fragile states. Not only was human suffering easing with the abandonment by great powers of new wars, it also seemed to have had an effect on state fragility. States were developing stronger controls over violence during the 1990s when great powers were ignoring violence in fragile states. In the new millennium, those states that cosmopolitan powers intervened in to create order often became more anarchical. At the same time, anarchy was generally reduced in those states where violence remained internal.

The record shown in this chapter on the development of violence when great powers intervene in violence in fragile states is no better than the record on the development of state fragility. Conflicts escalate, fatalities increase, states that are intervened in become deadlier, and the era of intervention has been associated with a global increase in conflict violence. All this testifies to the failure of military protection of civilians in fragile states. However, showing that protection wars do not actually protect civilians is not enough. The problem of violence against innocent civilians continues and something needs to be done about it. Yet, clearly, it is not sufficient just to 'do something' or signal disapproval when dictators kill their citizens and terrorists slaughter innocent civilians. We need to discover the 'something' that could actually help the situation rather than making it worse. Before finding ways forward, we must explain what, in the current policy of military protection, has gone wrong and only then can we find ways to create better policies.

The explanation of the path to failure of protection will begin in the next chapter. We identify and analyse the elements in the rationales, discourses and practices of Western protection that constitute the justifications for dictatorial, criminal and terrorist violence. The identification of these elements will continue with an analysis that explains how such elements have emerged in the discourses and practices of Western protection.

NOTES

1. Yet, 61 per cent of country-years during the period under our investigation were classified as fragile.
2. According to Weinberger and Powell, the enforcement of humanitarian order requires the use of overwhelming force, which creates an environment that negates opportunities for violence that exist in a weak system of governance in fragile states (Kaldor, 1999, pp. 128–9).
3. PRIO data (Gleditsch et al., 2002; Lacina, 2009) record one interference in conflict in the Central African Republic, in which France alone participated. UCDP data, which this study uses, record none.
4. Defined by UCDP conflict ID, fragility of the battle location and non-interference. Here, too, a conflict ceases to be the same conflict if there is a pause (at least one year of less than 25 fatalities) in hostilities.
5. Here also, one-year conflicts are included. If one-year conflicts are not included, protection wars are still clearly longer than new wars. The average number of years of duration of such conflicts after an intervention has been 6.3, while the average duration of such new wars is 5.7 years.

5. Counter-cosmopolitan discourse: what are the reasons for violence?

INTRODUCTION

This chapter will focus on the ways in which violence is justified in the discourses of those countries and groups that were, or are, enemies of Western protection wars. The starting point of this analysis is an assumption that conflict mobilization and the justification of violence can, at least partly, be understood as an interactive process. While part of the escalation of conflict may be understood by looking at the characteristics or non-interactive approaches of the enemy, part of the enemy constitution of legitimate violence depends on the input of and interaction with Western discourses. The claim that a violent interpretation of Islam may make some terrorist organizations hostile to non-Muslims is likely true, and this is something that the texts of Al Qaeda and ISIS also testify to. Yet, texts by the enemies of Western cosmopolitan protection also testify to the interactive nature of conflict mobilization, and justification of violence.

Based on the selection of texts in this chapter, it is not possible to define how much of the enemy action is informed by discourses that are born in interaction with the West. This is because the selection of texts has consciously attempted to tease out these interactive tendencies to reveal the sources of escalation in the Western rather than in the enemy's approaches. This focus, however, does not mean that one can trace all sources of failure of protection through Western discourse. There is no doubt that the illogic of the terrorist discourse in which violence against civilians of another country is a legitimate approach if the leaders of that country have subjected one's own civilians to violence, is at the core of the escalation of terrorist wars. Yet, when one focuses on Western interventions, it is possible to trace the discursive interaction between Western and its enemies' approaches to see what elements of the Western approach are least successful.

This does not mean going along with enemy propaganda. It does not mean accepting the enemy's articulations constituting legitimacy for their own violence. Yet, even without accepting enemy articulations, one needs to understand them as real on some level when they enable violent mobilization.

George W. Bush's rejection of Al Qaeda articulations could be considered as an example of a problematic logic where disapproval leads to refusal to recognize a social reality. He rejects bin Laden's construction of 'legitimate violence' by saying: 'We're not going to let lies and propaganda by the enemy dictate how we win this war' (G.W. Bush, 2007e, p. 1703). Yet, because bin Laden managed to mobilize people due to Bush's offensive, staying in the offensive was, indeed, not an optimal strategy for the safety of Americans. Furthermore, even though bin Laden's strategy of struggle was immoral, this did not make the offensive (which involved many more people than bin Laden) moral, or the grievances that bin Laden demonstrated irrelevant or immoral to take into account. Therefore, an analysis that investigates the interaction between enemy discourses can be strategic and ethical.

The enemy of the West's part of this interaction is the focus of this chapter. The following three chapters will then trace back to the emergence of those elements of the Western discourse that influence the main elements of the enemy discourse of legitimacy for what – in the Western discourse – are understood as terrorist, criminal and dictatorial violence.

Since the sample of enemy discourses is not as systematic as the case of US presidential discourse (which is selected by the presidential administration itself and maintained without censorship), there is a greater need for caution with regard to quantitative conclusions. Since the sources of Al Qaeda discourse are selectively declassified by the CIA, it is not possible to claim that the selection of texts that are openly available are a fair and representative sample of the Al Qaeda discourse.[1] The same problem exists with regard to all terrorist texts, but also, to some extent, with regard to texts of those dictators who have become enemies of the West. In countries like Iraq, where both the mainstream publication outlets (which are Western) and the domestic archives depend for their legitimacy on the selection and restriction of the availability of Saddam Hussein's texts, it is unlikely that the existing collections are a product of sufficient resources and freedom of archiving. Instead, compared to the analysis of the US discourse, the analysis of the enemy discourse manages to identify what kind of arguments exist, but cannot conclude quantitatively how different lines of argument compare to one another or how they have developed over time. It is possible, but not likely, that some of the arguments for violence that enemies of the West present are completely censored from the collection that is publicly available. This is not likely to be a major problem given than most of the arguments that counter-discourse produces need to be public and whatever has originally been presented publicly is unlikely to be completely censored by the West.

The main problem is that when declassifying documents that mobilize the enemy's own troops and fighters, some of the arguments that are not declassified might be pronounced more frequently in reality than in the CIA archives. Thus, despite the harvesting of data with NVivo by seeking words (in all forms) that refer to violence (attack, bomb, struggle, protect, defend, fight, kill, rebel and revolt) and by coding them into categories of rationales that justify violence, this chapter will not produce graphs on the development of the frequency of the 'imperialism rationale for violence', or compare the power of the 'militarism argument' and the 'infidel argument' with exact percentages. NVivo computer-assisted textual analysis is used to identify and classify arguments for violence, rather than for making claims on their representativeness or trends. Thus, this chapter will show what kind of arguments of violence exist, how they refer to the approaches and discourses of the West and the US, and what kind of logic and knowledge such arguments are based on. The method of this analysis is interpretative and more qualitative than in the case of the analysis of the US discourse.

EXISTING THEORETICAL LITERATURE ON REASONS FOR ANTI-COSMOPOLITAN VIOLENCE IN FRAGILE STATES

Much of the classical critical literature on interventions relies on the Marxist idea of the usefulness of taking the material power relationships of survival between capitalists and labourers as the starting point to explain the development of societies (Marx, 1990). To survive one needs to produce; and to produce one needs labour and capital (machinery). This sets the foundation of the power relationship of societies in which the 'bargaining power' of the capitalist, who has both labour and capital and who can survive longer without cooperation with labourers, is greater than that of the labourer. While different societies develop differently, the material setting after the invention of money has had this basic structure in common, and this has led to regularities that enable us to interpret developments on the level of political superstructures.

Since in the Marxist analysis the political superstructure of states, parties and other political institutions are mostly instruments of the capitalist, or at least based on the economic system, states tend to have an institutional preference for and inclination towards maximizing the benefit of the capitalist. Lenin and Luxemburg developed this idea to the analysis of conflicts (Bukharin and Luxemburg, 1925 [1972]; Lenin, 1999), which, on the one hand, revealed something empirically attractive – the assumption that states are partly driven by economic self-interest – but also something empirically less successful – the idea of inevitable conflict between capitalist states. The former assumption tends to be evident in almost all theoretical arguments critical of protective interventions – interventions tend to fail their purpose of protection because they become corrupted by selfish economic interests. How much if at all the 'ownership of the state by the capitalists' plays a role varies from theory to theory. While many dependency theorists (Cardoso and Faletto, 1971 [1979]; Wallerstein, 2004), and modern anti-neoliberal theorists (Chomsky, 2016) see the hand of global capitalists behind Western interventions, others view economic selfishness on the level of states and try to explain it as a phenomenon of liberal interstate relations (Kivimäki, 2013).

Critique of economic selfishness has penetrated cosmopolitan thinking too, and there are theorists who support the ethical position of cosmopolitan thinking, but view humanitarian interventions as impossible due to the structure of state-centric decision-making in world politics and due to the immaturity of cosmopolitan commitment among the people of the world (Falk, 2002, 2003; Kivimäki, 2019a, forthcoming). Regardless of the 'fundament' of economic selfishness, theories that assume national economic selfishness conclude that objects of protection will and should oppose protective interventions. Protective operations fail partly because of selfish implementation, which causes collateral damage. Partly they fail because of the resistance to such selfishness, which escalates conflict.

In all these theories, the focus of attention on the critique of humanitarian intervention is the motive behind it. Another type of theory suggests that the problem is not in the motives of the *agency* of protection, but on the *identity* of the protector that creates resistance to protection. In subaltern realist theories, the problem of Third World governance is the difficulty of state-building. Without states, the voice of the Third World cannot be heard in world politics. Yet, in a globalized world, it is seen as important for the people of the developing world to get their voice heard, otherwise it will be difficult for the Third World to feel ownership of the humanitarian order being imposed on it. While incompletely representative states represent in an incomplete manner, subaltern realists claim that they still do it better than outsiders. The development of indigenous state capacity, even at the risk of temporary problems with human rights, is important in the long-run work against violence. External interference in this process is seen by subaltern realists as a disturbance to the long-term goal of mature, democratic, peaceful state structures, given that the international slave trade, colonialism and capitalist dependence on the 'First World' have been reasons for the delay in state-building in the Third World in the first place (Ayoob, 1991; Azar and Moon, 1988a, 1988c). Thus, it is understandable that people in the protected areas easily feel that outsiders must be resisted, not due to their motives or what they do, but because of who they are. In this argument, the problem is not necessarily that protection as such does something negative, but that resistance to it – resistance that is understandable due to the requirements of state-building – escalates conflicts and makes military protection deadly. Unilateralism gives rise to resistance and legitimacy to dictatorial, criminal or terrorist violence and this explains the rise in fatalities each time (except in Sierra Leone) Western protection has begun.

Finally, there are also theories that suggest that resistance is legitimized by the ways in which protection is implemented. According to feminist scholarship, due to the overly militaristic, masculine ways in which security policies are conducted, there are more fatalities and resistance to protection (Enloe, 2000; Tickner, 1992, 2001). Dictators, criminals and terrorists obtain justification and support due to the heavy-handed approach of Western protection, and this, together with the protective militarism itself, adds to the number of fatalities of conflict.

In addition, instead of masculinity and militarism, some of the new war theorists blame the failure to win the hearts and minds of the protected people on the diagnosis of the situation, which leads to policies of protection that fail to be effective. According to Kaldor, the problem is that Western interventions of the past two decades have adopted old-type diagnoses of warfare. In these kinds of wars, they assume that destruction forces the enemy into submission. However, in new wars, the problem is structural and requires attention to the build-up of a structure that can control opportunistic violence – destruction cannot achieve that. The challenge has not been the enemy but the structure of weakness of institutions in control of violence – the context has been that of a new warfare – and as a result the task has been one of state-building rather than one of state destruction (Kaldor, 2012). According to both Kaldor (2012) and Tickner (1992, 2001), heavy-handed dealing with local people in the areas that need protection from authoritarian or criminal violence have actually strengthened the legitimacy of the violent local actors and helped them constitute narratives of legitimacy – violence has justified violence.

While the existing literature directs our investigation to possible mechanisms in which enemies of Western protection can react to Western approaches in a way that aims to legitimize their violence, the following sections will look more specifically at how ISIS, Al Qaeda, Muammar Gaddafi, Slobodan Milošević, Saddam Hussein, Bashar al-Assad and the Sierra Leonean rebels have articulated realities that they have tried to use for the legitimation of their own violence and how these social realities are related to the approaches and discourses of Western protection. The starting point is the assumption that Western protection can provoke violence due to its motives, agency and methods. Each of these will be analysed against the discourses of the enemies of Western protection.

HIDDEN, SELFISH MOTIVES AS A PROVOCATION

The question of whose values interventions protect and whose interests they serve is at the core of the debate on cosmopolitanism. In the political debate this has offered opportunities for the legitimation of violence against protection. There have been claims that protection is an approach where a big power operates outside its borders but promotes its own interests – interests that may be in contradiction with the interests of the protected nations. Such arguments have derived justifications from the discourse strands on colonialism and imperialism, or simply on the arrogance of power. 'Imperialist powers' have been accused of using the universalist concept of human rights for their imperial purposes (al-Assad, 2017), while dictators, criminals and terrorists have been accused of selfish marginalization of international humanitarian voices so they can benefit from the chaos of the state apparatus without international interference (Trump, 2017a). These positions are not far from the positions in the debate between subaltern realists (Ayoob, 1997) and solidarist supporters of the critical security studies perspective (Krause, 1998), with many of the enemies of protective operations drawing on the former position and protectors on the latter.

Almost all the 'victims/perpetrators' in Western protective action draw directly from the idea of economic exploitation of the Third World. Osama bin Laden talks about 'the despotism of Big Money and its role in the current wars between us' (bin Laden, 2015a) and asks his supporters to defend Muslim lands from the efforts of 'international and the regional powers to control our area and to take our oil unjustly' (bin Laden, 2016b). At times, Al Qaeda's diagnosis of US behaviour corresponds very strongly with the Marxist ideas of states as the instrument of capitalists (the theory of state monopoly capitalism). According to an Al Qaeda document:

> The course of the policies of the present administration in several areas clearly reveals that whoever enters the White House, even with good intentions to safeguard the people's interest, is no more than a train operator. His only task is to keep the train on the tracks that are laid down by the lobbyists in New York and Washington to serve their interests first, even if it is counter to your security and economy. Any president who tries to move the train from the lobbyist's tracks to a track for the American people's interests will confront very strong opposition and pressures from the lobbyists. Your president described the decision by the court in favor of corporations to intervene in the political arena as a victory, but it is not [a victory] for the American people except for the big corporations. (Bin Laden, 2015c)

Interestingly, one cannot see traces of similar Marxist concepts in ISIS discourse. Clearly, for ISIS, US imperialism means imposition of cultural approaches, and rejection of Islamic norms, and oppression of Muslims, rather than economic exploitation (ISIS, 2015a). Saddam Hussein's rhetoric is surprisingly similar[2] in this respect: resistance to oppression and cultural and political domination by the West motivates violent action, not economic exploitation (Hussein, 2001). However, according to Gaddafi, interventions are intended to force nations into a new colonial arrangement, again referring to selfish oil interests:

> This is a renewed effort to return Libya to what it was before the revolution[3] a property of Western companies and not the Libyan people, in order to enslave the Libyan people after they were rulers. To return Libya to its colonial days after it was free; post Al-Fatah revolution. (Gaddafi, 2011j)
>
> The easiest solution would be to invite colonial powers from the beginning, to come and take the oil from our people and stop the aggression. (Gaddafi, 2011k)

There is no doubt that Gaddafi used anti-imperialist rhetoric for the mobilization of violence against Western powers: 'Take back your resources. Do not be afraid of power. Possess it. It is your power, wealth and arms that the governments, banks and armies stole from you' (Gaddafi, 2011f).

Milošević, who could not claim that Western powers were interested in oil or other raw materials that Kosovo did not offer, framed the imperialism argument slightly differently. On the one hand, his diagnosis was in line with dependency theory. According to him, the result from protective intervention would be that the Serbian 'economy will be in the function of development of other countries'. For him, the Western aggression was also targeting Serbia's economic model that threatened liberal orthodoxy. For him, the defence of his country's own non-liberal, social-democratic mode of economy (with free education and social security) was clearly a rationale for violent resistance: 'Small Serbia and people in it have demonstrated that resistance is possible. Applied at a broader level, it was organized primarily as a moral and political rebellion against tyranny, hegemony, monopolism' (Milošević, 2000a).

Gaddafi's argument was very similar. According to him, Libya was offering an alternative economic model and the Western intervention wanted to take:

> [. . .]away the freedom of our country, to take away our free housing, our free medicine, our free education, our free food, and replace it with American style thievery called 'capitalism', but all of us in the Third World know what that means, it means corporations run the countries, run the world, and the people suffer. (Gaddafi, 2014)

Given that in the Libya operation one of the leading nations was Denmark with the very same economic freedoms as Gaddafi lists, this argument was not entirely convincing, yet, it may nevertheless have convinced some of the Libyan fighters.

ISIS and Al Qaeda applied similar, more cultural interpretations of the selfish imperial motives of Western protectors that justified violent resistance. Osama bin Laden talked about the cultural hegemony that Western protection of universal human rights represented and felt that a different Islamic human rights concept had to be defended from:

> [. . .]informational and educational subordination that changes the teaching of the religion suited to loyalty and submitting to the Infidels, and to other subordinations, their interests are the loss of religion and the absence of values, and the loss of identity, and these are huge losses, and another subordination in the foreign policy that commits the area's leaders to support America against the Muslims under the banner of fighting terrorism, as they claimed. (Bin Laden, 2016d)

Violence against humanitarian intervention and Western forces that opposed terrorism was clearly legitimized by exaggerating understandings of what would happen to the indigenous cultures if they did not resist the West: 'the submission of the area, and its falling behind and absolute following of the policies of the obscene infidel alliance in all axes, which means westernizing the region, and changing the face of the Arab Peninsula and enslaving it with what suits the Zionist American arrogance' (bin Laden, 2016b). To defend against such cultural imperialism ISIS needed to occupy areas where it could block the effects of the hegemonic Western media (ISIS, 2015d). Milošević mobilized resistance to NATO imperialist objectives that aimed at colonization in which Serbia's 'culture will be done away with, whose past will be wiped out who will be ruled by those bribed or blackmailed hoodlums' (Milošević, 2000a).

If we look at the narrative of selfish oppression as a justification for violent resistance of Western humanitarian interventions, it is possible to see the difference between the discourse of the Revolutionary United Front (RUF) rebel soldiers in Sierra Leone on the one hand, and the opponents of US intervention on the other – the RUF did not accuse the UK of selfish motives. With the exception of Kosovo, all US interventions were conducted in countries with raw materials that the US had economic interests in. The UK, at the same time, was not significantly involved in the diamond economy that was at the core of selfish interests in Sierra Leone, and thus the actor that conducted the protective intervention was never seriously accused of having imperial interests, despite its colonial history (Bendre, 2017;[4] Johnstone, 2017;[5] Keen, 2005; Richards, 1996; Thompson,

2017[6]). Furthermore, in Western Africa, the UK did not have allies that would mutilate civilians and steal diamonds (as the rebels did), and so enforcing order against such violent and criminal means did not provoke accusations of UK double standards. In the Middle East and Central and South Asia, the US had close allies that could be accused of similar atrocities that protective interventions opposed.

The fact that the rebels in Sierra Leone were so heavily involved in the diamond trade and self-enriching abductions, also made it very difficult for them to seriously accuse the UK (even though they could accuse their own government they also fought against) of economic selfishness. And, while it is true that the Sierra Leonean revolution was also driven by disappointment in the government (not the UK or the international community), the cause of the rebels was tarnished by selfish moves and ruthless violence. Nevertheless, although the media described the rebels and soldiers that supported them as 'thugs masquerading as armies', and as 'the closest to pure banditry' (McGreal, 2000), the Sierra Leonean revolution was not simply primordial barbarism, but instead had roots in grievances and social cleavages (Richards, 1996). The country was divided along ethnic lines, and the political discourse had made ethnicity relevant to political mobilization (Keen, 2005, pp. 14–15). Thus, elections had become little more than an ethnic census, as Zartman (2011) describes the situation when politics is structured along ethnic lines. While the rebels did have a programme for the improvement of the country's democracy (Revolutionary United Front of Sierra Leone, 1995), their greed in the process of revolution, and even in the process of peace[7] negotiations, ruled out their ability to credibly accuse the UK's protective 'Operation Pallister' of economic selfishness. Compared to groups that conducted suicide operations (who can hardly be accused of selfishness), or a leader who was willing to live in a tent, the RUF claim for moral high ground on the basis of selflessness was considerably less credible.

In addition to economic selfishness, the Sierra Leonean rhetoric of resistance was also unable to utilize claims of cultural imperialism in their constitution of legitimate violent resistance against the protective intervention. Unlike many of the Islamic or Slavic enemies of Western interventions, the Sierra Leonean rebels did not have an identity that could offer them cultural opposition to the UK. The RUF was not a religious movement and due to its opposition to the African regional efforts at resolution of the conflict, nor could it use the African, Third World or anti-colonial difference in its discursive resistance of the UK intervention.

While the UK was responsible for the humanitarian intervention, it seemed that when the rebels cited foreign interference, the main target was Nigeria (Armed Forces Revolutionary Council, 1997), who had much closer ties with the diamond economy; the United Nations also received its share of criticism as an agent with a partisan agenda (Revolutionary United Front of Sierra Leone, 2000; Sankoh, 2000). However, the UK did not attract as much criticism – its approaches and discourses of protection confused selfish and cosmopolitan justifications much less than would have been the case if it had had strong national economic interests and if it had seen a cultural/religious revival of the protected areas as a strategic threat.

FOREIGN AGENCY OF THE PROTECTOR AND THE LACK OF OWNERSHIP OF PROTECTION AS A JUSTIFICATION FOR ANTI-COSMOPOLITAN VIOLENCE

The question of who protects seems at least as equally important as the question of what values and whose interests are being protected. The two questions are naturally linked, as the perceived unilateral use of global power by the US, NATO and 'the West' has been seen as the reason for the selfishness in the selection of values to be protected. Unilateralism has been resisted by referring to various pre-agreed-upon premises for argumentation related to the discourse on imperialism, colonialism, international law/UN charter (sovereignty and non-interference, breach of contracts), national security (state security), democracy and power politics. It has been used as the reason for not feeling ownership of the global humanitarian norms that protective interventions promote, and a motive for their violent opposition. Analysis of the counter-cosmopolitan political discourses seems to suggest that the question of agency of protection has offered more than the question of selfishness of protection for the legitimation of counter-cosmopolitan violence.

The clear majority of articulations by anti-cosmopolitan dictators against 'foreign presence' used the pre-agreed-upon premises for argumentation related to the principles of sovereignty of states. Some of them came very close to the arguments of Ayoob (1997), according to which states were necessary instruments of security for people of the Third World and that external intervention hampers indigenous state-building. Statements were presented in which enemies of protective operations justify their violence and brutality by referring to Western willingness to interfere in and take charge of domestic affairs in Syria, Iraq, Libya, and other states. According to Bashar al-Assad, for example, 'The sectarian systems turn the people of a homeland to enemies, thereby colonialist countries introduce themselves as a protector to certain groups inside this homeland' (al-Assad, 2016b; see also the speech by bin Laden, 2004, in which he explains US operations in the Middle East by reference to their imperial interests). State-building and the defence of the 'homeland', for Assad, is threatened by foreign troops and insurgents and terrorists that foreigners support in the interest of gaining power and control over Syria. Assad's rhetoric is somewhat unclear and associates regime stability with the stability of the state, and the defence of the country and its people with the defence of the regime (al-Assad, 2014b). A very similar discourse on the defence of the state, confusing regime and state, can be found in the texts by Saddam Hussein (Hussein, 2003b) and Muammar Gaddafi: 'The people of Libya, the true Libyans, will never accept invasion and colonization' (Gaddafi, 2011h). As in Gaddafi's and Saddam Hussein's rhetoric, it is quite clear also in Milošević's rhetoric that the priorities of state security give legitimacy for violent resistance of Western protective operations: 'We Serbs are as one on this life and death issue of national honor and sovereignty' (Milošević, 1999b).

Gaddafi explicates the problem of foreign agency in Libya in his critique of the way in which the National Transitional Council[8] was considered representative of Libyans and generalizes it to all Third World countries: 'if only the power of NATO bombs and fleets grant legitimacy, then let all the rulers in the Third World beware for the same fate awaits you!' (Gaddafi, 2011h). In this way, Gaddafi's speech tries to construct common Third World agency against the imperial (humanitarian) powers.

Even though Al Qaeda were fighting legal governments in various Muslim countries, its rhetoric too occasionally emphasized the need to avoid foreign interference in the sovereignty of Muslim countries. According to bin Laden:

> The reality confirms that today there is no room for the small countries and small states in the midst of the savage imperialists and colonization and the large presence of parties that have the tendency to be attracted to them, either willingly or fearfully. Hence, the need for the revolution to remain in progress until the mujahidin of the east meet the mujahidin of the west and the entire nation's people would be liberated. (bin Laden, 2017b)

This passage corresponds to the logic of subaltern realism: the Third World needs strong states for its representation in world politics. Since Al Qaeda did not have a recognized state, its rhetoric often treated areas they occupied as states, as is the case with the so-called Islamic State:

> Today, Jihad in Pakistan has become a necessity for the defense of the Islamic Emirate in Afghanistan, a necessity for defending the Jihad center in Waziristan. It is the only possible solution to counter the enemy military and political traps in Pakistan itself. (Anonymous Jihadists of Pakistan, 2016)

The credibility among people in protected countries of the counter-cosmopolitan discourse that emphasizes the sanctity of state security depends on whether states are a better instrument for the well-being of citizens than a rule that is instituted by 'foreign powers'. Milošević outlines a narrative in which states, even when imperfect, are better for the well-being of citizens than external forces, terrorism or chaos. The fact that Serbia organized regular elections and the power of regimes was limited to just one term offered some credibility for Milošević's argument, despite the limitations of the democratic procedures and freedoms. It also enabled him to argue for the superiority of indigenous rule by referring to the ability of the citizens to participate in politics:

> Committed to the democratic functioning of the State and democratic society, the Socialist Party of Serbia not only expresses its deep concern for the fate of its beliefs, but expresses its most profound concern for the respect of fundamental human and civil rights in conditions when such rights are not protected by the competent institutions, but unidentified force will do all it can to suspend those institutions. (Milošević, 2000c)

Assad used a similar strategy of argumentation but added (to a disbelieving audience) the argument that he himself was elected in 2014 also with the votes of refugees and expatriates. Even if one might suggest that the context of war (and autocracy) made it difficult for people to trust in the anonymousness of the vote, people voting abroad should have been free to vote against Assad had they wanted to do so (al-Assad, 2014a).

For Saddam Hussein and Muammar Gaddafi, whose democratic credentials were less obvious, the argument in favour of the indigenous state was more modest. Both interpret the feelings of their people without hard evidence. According to Gaddafi 'the large majority of the Libyan population is opposed to the Benghazi-based Transitional Council' (Gaddafi, 2011d). 'On 1 July 2011, hundreds of thousands of Libyans supporters gathered in Green Square and surroundings. Some 1 700 000 people demonstrated to defend their country and to repudiate NATO's aggression' (Gaddafi, 2011d). Instead of claiming something about the preferences of his people, Saddam Hussein simply claimed that life was better for Iraqi citizens during the control of his state apparatus (Hussein, 2003a).

For Osama bin Laden, who had no claim for democracy,[9] the argument was turned around. He did not claim that the existing states were useful for citizens; he simply claimed that Western rule was even worse:

> For anyone who wants to know how the Peninsula will look, all you have to do is look at our people in Gaza and the West Bank. Under the same alliance, they kill the men, women, and children; destroy homes; and scrape [sic] farms and

> steal the fortunes of the farm land. They divided the West Bank with hundreds of barricades to humiliate and oppress the people, and put one-and-a-half million of our brothers in big Gaza prisons to die with their siege of disease and poverty due to malnourishment. And when the Jews want, they cut off the electricity and water; and when they like, they close the crossings and other catastrophes. The world headed by the Arab and Muslim rulers turns a blind eye to that great humanitarian catastrophe. (bin Laden, 2016b)

Protection to him implied tyranny, and its resistance was legitimate in the name of liberty: 'Our legitimate and blessed jihad has glorious goals and noble objectives. . .supporting and protecting His religion, enforcing righteousness, fending off tyranny and aggression, seeking to liberate people and nations, being merciful to all creatures, and benefiting all' (bin Laden, 2016a).

Yet, the democracy argument in support of the indigenous states, against protective interventions, is limited in the way it interacts with the Western discourse of protection. In many cases there has been confusion in the anti-cosmopolitan argument that makes democratic representation impossible and some of this confusion has been the motive for Western protection. For Milošević, the confusion was related to the word Serb, which confused Serb state and Serb ethnicity. He often emphasized his commitment to multi-ethnic statehood, but when he mobilized patriotic spirit he was unclear about whether he talked about Serbs as citizens or as an ethnic group (Milošević, 2000c). Similarly, both Al Qaeda and ISIS gave instructions on the benign treatment of non-Muslims and criticized 'foreign' rule as something hostile to local rule. Yet, when emphasizing the hostility of foreign rule they often used the word infidel or kafir to describe the foreign threat, which externalizes local non-Muslims (ISIS, 2015b; bin Laden, 2016b).[10] In Milošević's, Assad's and Gaddafi's rhetoric, opposition groups were often externalized and marginalized outside citizenship by their criminal, terrorist identity (al-Assad, 2014a; Gaddafi, 2011b; Milošević, 1999b). As a result, the state was not an instrument of *all* its citizens, and this was part of the humanitarian problem that protective operations aimed to fix in Kosovo, Syria, Iraq and Libya. Yet, foreign, non-UN troops were portrayed as occupiers and destroyers of the state as an instrument of its people, and this gave perceived legitimacy for the violent resistance of protection.

The other way of justifying violence against the humanitarian intervention and the US was related to the international norms of the UN role as the representative of humanity. As members of the UN, most dictators have ownership of the organization and cannot then credibly legitimize violence against operations that the United Nations conducts. Here, there is a difference between operations that are in line with UN rulings, operations that are mandated by the UN, and operations that the UN conducts itself. In the first type of operation it is possible to mobilize violence against the actors of the operations, unless the UN has mandated them, while in the second category it is possible to mobilize violence by referring to the ways in which the UN-mandated actors implement the mandate. Finally, for the mobilization of violence, the interpretation of what is in accordance with UN rulings, what constitutes a UN-mandated operation and what is a UN operation depends on those who need to be mobilized for violence, not those who are the targets of violence. So, mobilization works if those who are being mobilized (ISIS fighters, Serbian military, Syrian military, etc.) believe that the UN does not mandate the US.

Whenever there is confusion over the role of the UN, opponents of protective operations fail to see the UN role, while the implementors of these operations feel justified as implementors of a cause of the UN and humanity. This confusion causes mutual overconfidence of each of the conflict parties' moral positions – such overconfidence escalates conflict (Blainey, 1988).

Milošević was perhaps more explicit in his utilization of the UN argument in his mobilization of violence and resistance to the operations of the 'International Security Force' in Kosovo. For him, the force was a NATO force, and the involvement in Kosovo of the international actors was illegitimate and representative of 'the so-called international community'. He criticized the pressure on Serbia to accept:

> [. . .]outside mediation to go to the side which has provoked the conflicts, to treat the representatives for that side as well-meaning representatives of the international community, although we as all others in the world, knew perfectly well, that these are the representatives of an independent political will who usurped international rules of the game, harbouring ill-intentions towards stubborn and disobedient Serbs. (Milošević, 2000a)

And in a speech on an American TV show, Milošević claimed that the Western protection of Kosovo 'violate[s] the resolution of the UN Security Council on the basis of which arms deliveries are prohibited', that 'your country has practically banned the UN', and that 'you have abolished the UN. Your first bombs have destroyed the UN' (Milošević, 1999a).[11]

Gaddafi also presented the UN argument, and claimed that the Western intervention had overstretched its mandate (Gaddafi, 2011c), while the argument by Assad against US missile strikes in 2017 and 2018 referred to the UN Charter and its stipulations on sovereignty, and the requirements for UN Security Council authorization for international interventions for the protection of the international community from the threat to international security (al-Assad, 2017). While Assad can hardly claim any moral high ground, the inability of the UN Security Council to act as an agent of global humanitarian action weakens the legitimacy of protection and makes it more vulnerable to the rhetoric of legitimate resistance. Common agreement and ownership of humanitarian values and principles would make it easier to prevent resistance to the enforcement of humanitarian values.

The third line of argument among the dictators and terrorists against Western protective interventions relates to double standards. Protectors of humanitarian norms are not credible as agents of protection if they impose different standards on friends and enemies. Enforcement only in the latter countries exposes protective interventions to interpretations that operations are not really about enforcement of humanitarian norms, but rather about obedience to the Western domination. Saddam Hussein's argument justified his opposition to the US fight against terror on these grounds. According to the logic that Saddam Hussein emphasized, if the US fails to impose its norms on its own allies, it is not a legitimate agent for the imposition of norms on its enemies either. Terror can be condemned by the US only if it stops terror itself and if it stops its support of such terror by its allies.[12] The accusation against Israel often came to the fore:

> How many are those accused with killing and theft in other countries are now in the United States? If the United States presents such inventory to its peoples and to the World, and initiated implementing one standard and one norm on its agents and those I calls friends. And if it starts the same storm against the killers in the Zionist entity responsible of killing Palestinians in occupied Palestine and in Tunis and Lebanon. And if it charges its own secret services with what they committed of special actions and assassinations they brag to publish in the form of stories. Only then one can believe the new American slogans that America is trying to make them believe. Only then it becomes legitimate to ask the World to do what it believes is useful for its security and the security of the World. (Hussein, 2001; see also bin Laden, 2015b)

Milošević also used the argument of double standards in his defence against accusations of ethnic cleansing and genocide: 'We do not believe that the Serbs in Bosnia behaved any worse than Muslims and Croats', he repeated in his defence of the genocidal practices that the Serbian government under him practised against Bosnian Muslims and Kosovars (Milošević, 1998).

Enforcement of norms also requires that the actors that enforce such rules themselves follow those norms and that they subject themselves to similar enforcement of such norms. The fact that the US has fought against the imposition of the norms against war crimes, genocide, and ethnic cleansing (its refusal to be a state party to the Rome Statute of the International Criminal Court) and that it insists on bilateral treaties of immunity to accusations of such crimes, weakens the West's ability to enforce these norms on brutal dictators. The fact that the US is in violation of its commitments under the Chemical Weapons Convention and missed the extended deadline for destruction of its 3000 tons of chemical weapons (Griffin and Johnston, 2013) exposes the Western enforcement of the prohibition of chemical weapons to criticism.

In addition to these vulnerabilities, Milošević attacks the contradiction between NATO principles for itself and actions for others: 'NATO was formed to defend the western democratic nations from totalitarian aggression, not to commit aggression. We just want to be left alone and free' (Milošević, 1999b). However, instead of mobilizing just Serb violence against NATO, Milošević articulates an agency of nations vulnerable to external interference and tries to mobilize resistance to operations that violate the classical norm of sovereignty and non-interference. Milošević marginalizes the criticism of his government's genocidal policies in Kosovo and tries to explain them away by referring to ulterior motives: according to him, US operations in Kosovo are not about humanitarian norms, but about geopolitics:

> First is to prove U.S. leadership in Europe and the second to re-establish U.S. leadership in NATO in the post-Cold War era. Regretfully, we were targeted as a guinea pig to achieve those goals. Simply because of our weaknesses and of the internal problems we faced. But, as you know, you will find in at least 100 countries around the world different ethnic separatist movements. If you decide to support separatist movements it is very hard to believe any country can survive. There are 4,000 ethnic groups in the world and only 185 members of the United Nations. (Milošević, 1999b)

Gaddafi uses the same argumentative strategy, marginalizing criticism of his government as dual morality, and then explaining it away by referring to imperialist motives. He too warns other weak countries of geopolitical interests and articulates common anti-American identity for such Third World nations. Addressing all Third World nations, he said: 'The fight if it is not won in Libya will be coming to you. Prepare for it. Prepare traps for the invaders. You must defend your territory' (Gaddafi, 2011h). In addition to mobilizing developing countries against US selective acceptance of norms of sovereignty, he also lends support to bin Laden's assertion of US war on Islam, and tries to mobilize Arab and Muslim resistance to Western operations: 'Islamic nations, from Libya to Iraq and Pakistan, are being offensively attacked and bombed' (Gaddafi, 2011e).

While in the case of Sierra Leone the argument of illegitimate agency was raised, and the idea of foreignness as a source of illegitimacy was part of the rebel discourse, it was not the UK that was targeted in this critique.

First, it was mainly Nigeria that was accused of trying to gain geopolitical power, thus the agency of a neighbouring regional power was seen as more dangerous for the rebels and the power of Nigeria inside Sierra Leone was seen as a more provoking factor than the power of the UK, despite the latter's colonial history in Sierra Leone. Early reports of the Armed Forces Revolutionary Council of the role of the 'power hungry' Nigerian military force already show the resentment of the role of this regional power and so the role of Nigeria within the Military Observer Group (ECOMOG) of the Economic Community of West African States (ECOWAS) was viewed with greater sensitivity (Armed Forces Revolutionary Council, 1997) than the role of the UK.

Second, the UN's role was also criticized by the rebels side as being biased (Revolutionary United Front of Sierra Leone, 2000), yet the critique of the UN can never be as fundamental as the critique of unilateral actors. While the UK operation was not part of the United Nations Observer/Armed Mission in Sierra Leone (UNOMSIL/UNAMSIL), it continued from it after the collapse of the UN and ECOMOG seemed evident, and the entry of UK military in cooperation with the UN operation increased the legitimacy of the UK as an agent of protection (Nuamah and Zartman, 2001, p. 16).[13] This protection was based on the enforcement of an existing, indigenous peace agreement, rather than on a Western interpretation of global humanitarian norms.

Finally, the agency of the anti-cosmopolitan forces, the rebels and the former soldiers that started supporting the rebellion, was made so illegitimate by their obvious selfish interests and strategies that their resistance did not raise as many concerns for the legitimacy of the UK agency in the tamping down of the rebellion (Bendre, 2017; Johnstone, 2017). According to Nuamah and Zartman, the inability of the rebel side to stick to its own promises in the various peace agreements further delegitimized the rebel agency, and made enforcement of mutually agreed roles less controversial (Nuamah and Zartman, 2001, pp. 17–18).

The fact that UN military power simply turned out to be inefficient and insufficient after the departure of the ECOMOG troops late April 2000, and that the conflicting parties saw this within their own context (Bendre, 2017; Johnstone, 2017; Nuamah and Zartman, 2001) legitimized the UK as an agent of protection in a way that was not the case in other protective interventions. The fact that the rebel side was not the only illegal force in the country, but that there were also irregular militias (such as the Kamajors Forces) that fought the RUF, further consolidated the perception, even among the rebels (Armed Forces Revolutionary Council, 1998b; Revolutionary United Front of Sierra Leone, 2000), that the country needed order that the overwhelming power of the UK army could bring.

Nevertheless, while the case of Sierra Leone seems different from the other cases in the sense that the intervention could not be seen as 'foreign' and the agency of intervention not as illegitimate as in most cases of protective military operations, Sierra Leone is not entirely immune to provocations that relate to the foreignness of the agency of progress in the country. The development of state structures has not been impressive in the country and many of the reasons why there is less incentive in Sierra Leone for protest, are related to agency of external actors. The progress in the development of international market controls that reduce the ease with which conflicting parties can fund their war by using 'blood diamonds' have contributed to the decline of conflict incentives (Van Wauwe, 2018). At the same time, the governmental regulation of the small-scale mining industry has developed very slowly (Hilson, Hilson and Maconachie, 2017; Maconachie, 2018), creating a situation where the control of violence and development stays outside the country, in the hands of international forces that do not necessarily prioritize the interests of Sierra Leoneans. Without the development of indigenous capacity to control the violence and well-being of the country, without a state that could be an instrument of the citizens, the argument of foreignness of agency could eventually provoke resistance.

MILITARY MEANS OF PROTECTION AS A SOURCE OF LEGITIMACY OF ANTI-COSMOPOLITAN VIOLENCE

While suspicion of hidden agendas and the perceived illegitimacy of Western countries as enforcers of humanitarian norms and protectors of civilians provide perceived legitimacy for anti-cosmopolitan violence, it seems that the means of protection is an even more powerful source of perceived legitimacy of violence – violence of the protective operations constitutes legitimacy of the violence of the counter-violence (and vice versa). It seems that, at least on the level of discourse, violence in an interactive process is a mutually constitutive escalatory phenomenon. Similarly, Booth and Wheeler describe the structure of security dilemma and prescribe interactive understanding and security dilemma sensitivity (Booth and Wheeler, 2008), and it seems clear that there was a need on both sides to understand the symmetry and interaction that fuels processes of escalation. The way in which the Al Qaeda terrorist operation on September 11, 2001 boosted the US's international power position and its legitimacy as an actor of security and justified even the selfish motives in US overseas military operations (see Chapter 6) was diametrically opposed to the interests of Al Qaeda. Yet, nothing in the Al Qaeda discourse seems to suggest that the organization realized the disservice their violence did for their own position in world politics. As will be shown in Chapter 8, the same lack of understanding of the interactive nature of the mutual constitution of legitimate violence between conflicting parties also existed in the Western discourse on protection.

Even the lowest rationale of the enemies of Western protection justified their violence in interactive terms. Despite the rhetoric that distinguishes between believers and infidels, and despite the illogic of assuming legitimacy of civilian targeting if the enemy also targets its own civilians, even Al Qaeda defined its enemy as an aggressor and mobilized violence against agents it perceived as violent to its own constituency. Jihad was not targeted just against infidels, but also against aggressors: 'Jihad against the aggressors is a form of great worship in our religion, and killing us means a high status with our Lord' (bin Laden, 2015b). Staying on the offensive against terror was not, at least on the level of Al Qaeda rhetoric, an incentive not to continue terror, but a motive for violence: 'We, from our side, confirm that the Jihad will continue, God willing, against the occupying Infidels, and their bleeding will continue' (bin Laden, 2016d). Bin Laden frames wars as a battle of will where superior power will make the opponent yield – just what Kaldor accuses the US of in its war in Afghanistan and Iraq, assuming an outdated idea of current warfare (Kaldor, 2012, p. 152): 'The battle between the people and their rulers today is a battle of wills, and the revolution is based on pride and dignity' (bin Laden, 2016c). Furthermore, there is a failure of logic in Al Qaeda's discourse that escalates conflict regardless of the approach of the West. The organization identifies that attacks come from *some* Jews, Christians, and so on, and then sometimes concludes that *all* or a greater number of Jews, Christians, and so forth are legitimate targets. This obviously escalates conflict beyond those Jews, Christians and so on who wage war on terror against Al Qaeda: '[u]tilizing all their means, the enemies of Islam, to include Jews, Christians, and infidels combined, have waged an attack against Muslims and every aspect of their lives, in terms of doctrine, culture, economy, policy, and so forth' (Anonymous Jihadists of Pakistan, 2016).

Also, ISIS legitimizes its violence by referring to 'responses in kind' (obviously defined according to their, not Western or objective, criteria): 'And today it is necessary to have a studied plan that responds in kind and brings about like change in the profane abode of disbelief, expelling its people and killing its people until there is no base for them and the land is for God and his servants' (ISIS, 2015e). ISIS even believes that it is responding to rather than initiating terror (ISIS, 2013). Again, there is a clear blindness to the symmetry of violent interaction: while Western violence motivates ISIS violence, the assumption is that ISIS violence deters Western violence.

While Assad has not fought against the West he finds legitimacy against the West in his rejection of Western violence. His main target, the opposition of Syrian government, is defined as terroristic and thus their violent identity justifies the government's violence against them: 'Terrorism is a sick thinking, deformed belief as well as an odd practice and should be eliminated from its roots' (al-Assad, 2015). In the Syrian discourse then, the legitimacy of violence against the opposition is increased, not decreased, by the Western-supported military power of the opposition. Furthermore, the Western support externalizes the opposition in the Syrian government discourse: opposition is not part of the Syrian political system, it is not part of the minority that votes in the elections, it is part of a foreign hegemonic conspiracy (al-Assad, 2014b, 2016c). Assad sees the Syrian army fighting an 'aggressive terrorist attack against Syria. . .in the face of hegemony schemes and the new-old colonialism bids' (al-Assad, 2016a). There is no doubt that what is perceived as foreign aggression not just legitimizes, but also justifies and motivates violence against the opposition: 'Syrians are ever to defend their sovereignty, integrity and fight terrorism and are never to be taken by some foreign-agenda agents who are a floor cloth for their masters' (al-Assad, 2016b). Violence of the opponent takes away peaceful options in the Syrian rhetoric as '[t]he fight against terrorism is the sole alternative. . . Syria is never to surrender the homeland to the foreign-backed opposition nor to their masters' (al-Assad, 2015).

Milošević too justified violence by referring to the violence of the opposing side:

> NATO leaders' decisions were all criminal. They were simply killing our people and they have thrown more than 22,000 tons of bombs to [sic] hospitals, to apartments of civilians, to electricity facilities, water supply, bridges, railways, trains, refugees, and that was all one massive killing of innocent people and that was the real crime, so [the] right address for war crimes in Yugoslavia is NATO. (Milošević, 2001a)

Milošević also cites Western violence as a justification for a refusal to negotiate peacefully:

> I believe that it will be very easy to continue the political process after the aggression stops, after the bombing stops. . . The International Red Cross and the UNHCR may return immediately. I cannot say whether this applies to each and every humanitarian organization, as there have been certain so-called humanitarian organizations which have been organized to support terrorism or the separatist movement and which have functioned under the mask of the so-called humanitarian operations. . . They have spied in favour of NATO to explain to them the position of the sites that were to be bombed. (Milošević, 1999a)

Furthermore, violence of the opponent justifies militarization and increased military preparedness. When asked about the radical increase in the Serb military presence in Kosovo, Milošević asserts that this was 'because of the danger of aggression across our borders by NATO forces. . . But if the danger of NATO aggression is over, we can send our troops back to Serbia' (Milošević, 1999b).

Finally, Gaddafi's logic of aggression is also based on interaction: violence against Libya by the intervening forces justifies Libyan violence against others, while violence against the state apparatus by the opposition, which Gaddafi calls terrorists, justifies government violence against them. Furthermore, Gaddafi mobilizes broader Third World resistance against the US by referring to the US violence not just against Libya but also against other African and Third World countries (Gaddafi, 2011a).

Even if violence and force under protection may be part of the mutual constitution of legitimacy of violence on both sides, this is not to say that the use of force only has a negative impact on violence by dictators, terrorists and criminals – that would be an overly simplistic statement. The military defeat of Serbia in Kosovo and rebels in Sierra Leone, for example, is part of the reason for the end of anti-Western violence in these places. Organized guerrilla fighting and national military operations of Western enemies there required a unified capability, and once this capability was defeated by force the conflict was over. However, the situation was different in places where resistance was not unified. Terror is possible even if the centre of resistance has fallen. This could be the reason that the violence against civilians by terrorist groups (which may be defeated as an organization but which can always reorganize) tends to fail.

Yet, even terror groups are not entirely immune to forceful persuasion. Bin Laden instructed his militia leaders to seek escape routes before operations (bin Laden, 2017a) and thus revealed that an ability to prevent such exit could delay or prevent operations. Thus, force might be of benefit in protection. Gaddafi threatened Libyan opposition with revenge once the Western presence had left the country: 'NATO will not protect those agents forever' (Gaddafi, 2011g, 2011k). The Western presence thus prevented him from taking revenge before the exit of protective force.

It would also be simplistic to say that the logic of violent interaction only fuels violence. It does not, as violence implies normative costs. In some cases, the counter-cosmopolitan discourses also set limits on their violence and demonstrate some elementary sense of understanding the symmetry in violent escalation. Even the most brutal terrorists tend to realize some of the costs in legitimacy that excessive violence causes. Osama bin Laden sent many pieces of advice to jihadists, ordering discipline in the targeting of the enemy and in the use of violence. To win people over to one's side, one needs to target the regime without causing civilian fatalities: '*Every arrow should be aimed at bringing down the regime, and avoid the secondary fronts*' (bin Laden, 2016c; original emphasis). Avoiding Muslim and unjust fatalities was also important for the identity and image of the movement:

> I and other people have heard about the many accusations on the Internet directed against the jihadi movement by the enemy and the media. [The mujahidin have been accused] of killing Muslims and they have been portrayed as killers who are only interested in spilling blood, looting, and pilfering money, and of having no dignified goal, . . . The mujahidin leadership should advise the suicide bomber of this and warn them from being tricked or being sent to questionable suspicious targets of which they were not advised. (bin Laden, 2016a)
>
> We remind our brethren, the Mujahidin, . . .about the significance of forbidding the shedding of Muslim blood. God's Shari'a. . .forbids us from killing anyone, except for the requirements of justice. (ibid.)

Bin Laden spends surprising energy restraining his fighters from methods where it is not possible to control targeting and urging them to restrict it only to the justified persons. He advised against using 'explosions and using methods that kill generally and indiscriminately in Muslim mosques or similar, general gathering places, such as markets, streets, playgrounds, or whatever the target it may be, so as to control the situation, as a precaution, and to avoid mistakes and [collateral] damage' (ibid.).

Even ISIS felt it important for their 'legitimacy' to limit militarism: 'We inform our mujahideen brothers that it is absolutely forbidden for them to attack the homes and properties of the Kurds under any justification or pretext' (ISIS, 2015c, p. 9).

Also, Saddam Hussein's rhetoric aimed at creating legitimacy for his leadership with references to humanitarian, rather than militaristic principles: 'Our principles are not just national or pan-Arab, but they are humane principles. We believe in humanity. We believe that the world must seek to find opportunities for peace, not opportunities for war or opportunities for fighting or opportunities for venting or harming others' (Hussein, 2003a).

While the process of mutual constitution of legitimate violence also took place in Sierra Leone, the main conflicting parties based the legitimacy of their own violence on the violence of actors other than the UK. The Armed Forces Revolutionary Council brought violent 'law and order' to the country, referring to violence by their domestic (tribal armies and the illegitimate 'Sierra Leone People's Party government') and regional opponents (Nigerian warplanes): 'the AFRC/RUF. . .will defend this country against further Nigerian/Kamajor thuggery' (Armed Forces Revolutionary Council, 1998a; see also 1998b) and the fight by the

Revolutionary United Front statements tended to refer to the government as the culprit of violence, while occasionally referring to violence that the UN had allowed to take place (Revolutionary United Front of Sierra Leone, 2000; Sankoh, 2000).

In most places where protective operations were opposed by governments that had nationalist discourse and determination behind their arguments, or by religious militias that had God on their side, they were determined to die for their cause. Overwhelming force was not possible to persuade them of peace. Instead, violence just consolidated their image of the 'imperialist West', and escalated conflict. Kaldor's assumption about new wars is that overwhelming force can persuade the violent opponents of protection because they are opportunistic people with gainful motives. However, it seems that only in Sierra Leone did the counter-cosmopolitan forces as criminal and opportunistic people be persuaded, whilst elsewhere, opponents of the West were convinced of the rightfulness of their cause and thus violence could not overwhelm them without also consolidating their will to fight against what they saw as an illegitimate, militant enemy.

CONCLUSIONS

While the narratives of resistance of Western protection and global cosmopolitan enforcement of humanitarian norms are many, there are a few clusters of discursive strategies into which the most powerful strategies of mobilization and justification of counter-cosmopolitan violence can be classified. Based on the analysis of the texts of some of the key enemies in protective interventions – ISIS, Al Qaeda, Bashar al-Assad of Syria, Muammar Gaddafi of Libya, Saddam Hussein of Iraq and Slobodan Milošević of Serbia – it seems that legitimate violence is constituted in arguments against:

- perceived selfishness of the motives behind protective interventions;
- perceived power political unilateralism of interventions; and
- perceived militarism, or power bias in the ways in which protection is implemented.

On this analysis it is not possible to say if any of these arguments have any legitimacy based on any ethical theory. In any case, most of the actions that are mobilized with these counter-cosmopolitan discourses seem repulsive and violent. Yet, these discourses seem to manage to mobilize resistance and violence and this seems to be related to the findings of Chapter 4, according to which protective interventions are associated with the escalation of conflicts they respond to. This suggests that the grievances that violent opponents of protection refer to in their rhetoric seem to have some resonance and traction among the masses in fragile states of the Third World. Thus, it is important to use the analysis of the rhetoric of enemies of Western protective operations for the explanation of the failure of protection and for the analysis of better strategies for cosmopolitan policies. The analysis of what justifies terrorist and autocratic violence should also be used to address the grievances related to Western operations that are real among the ordinary people in fragile states. Thus, it makes sense to study how selfishness, unilateralism and power bias enter into protective interventions. All these features seem somehow contradictory to the cosmopolitan ethos of protection. Protection should be focused on the needs of the people that are being protected. Cosmopolitan protection should strengthen cosmopolitan rather than unilateral agency. And it should be caring rather than violent and power biased. Thus, the following three chapters will trace how cosmopolitan protection was manipulated towards these three deviations.

NOTES

1. The CIA declassified and released files recovered in the May 2011 raid on Osama bin Laden's compound in Abbottabad, Pakistan. These files were declassified in four batches between 2015 and 2017, and most of them are correspondence and drafts of correspondence between Osama bin Laden and his regional commanders and followers. The documents do not reveal the author of all the texts, but with a few exceptions only it seems clear that Osama bin Laden authors the texts. I have listed these documents as texts of bin Laden even though in some of the texts one cannot be sure if the author is him or one of his closest subordinates.
2. Given the origin of ISIS in Saddam Hussein's bureaucracy, this should perhaps not be so surprising. Even though ISIS has taken on a religious identity for its resistance of the US, Saddam Hussein utilized a nationalist identity for his articulation of difference from the US.
3. By 'revolution' Gaddafi probably refers to the Al-Fatah Revolution of 1969, a military coup led by Colonel Gaddafi, ten years after the discovery of significant oil reserves in Libya.
4. Personal interview on March 29, 2017 with Rajiv Bendre, former Director of the British Council in Sierra Leone, Jordan and Iraq [Skype].
5. Personal interviews on February 2, 2017 with Colonel Andrew Johnstone, a retired senior UK military officer. In 2003–2004 he was a senior military advisor in the International Military Assistance and Training Team (IMAITT), commanded by then Brigadier Adrien Freer in Sierra Leone, who was later seconded to the United Nations Mission in Kosovo, with responsibility for the Kosovo Protection Corps in the rank of Major General.
6. Interview in Bath, UK on 1 February, 2017 with Professor E. Thompson, Vice-Chancellor, University of Sierra Leone.
7. During the implementation of the Lomé Peace Agreement, the leader of the Revolutionary United Front, Foday Sankoh, wrote to the guarantors of the agreement. His first

complaint against the way in which the agreement was implemented was the following: 'Since the 3rd of October, 1999, when the Press Release issued by the Government of Sierra Leone confirmed my appointment as Chairman for the Commission for the Management of Strategic Resources, National Reconstruction and Development, I still do not know my salary. I have only received a little of Three Million Leones (Le 3,000,000), equivalent to One Thousand, Five Hundred United States Dollars (US$ 1,500). That was in November, 1999' (Sankoh, 2000).

8. See note 5, Chapter 3.
9. Bin Laden did suggest, in some of his instructions to his regional commanders, that followers should be allowed to choose their leaders, so that they would feel ownership of the rule that Al Qaeda enforced (bin Laden, 2016e), yet, he never allowed his own position to be questioned.
10. To some extent, Gaddafi also describes the foreigners as non-Muslim, and constitutes 'our side' in religious terms (Gaddafi, 2011e).
11. Yet, Milošević's critique was ambiguous with regard to the UN, as he felt that due to Western aggression, UN peacekeeping and other operations were legitimate only if they did not involve representatives of NATO countries: 'after all those crimes against our nation and its people, we cannot accept representatives of the countries that committed aggression against us' (Milošević, 1999b).
12. While this logic is used for the justification of actions that are not humane, it is clear that the delegitimation of an agent of protection and enforcement of humanitarian norms do not imply that the norms themselves would also lack legitimacy. While from the point of view of analytical ethics this seems clear, in the reality of mobilization of violence, incorrect logic often mobilizes almost as well as correct logic. One must realize though that this illogic also exists in the Western mobilization of protective operations (see, for example, Government of the United Kingdom, 2018). The fact that someone commits acts that are against humanitarian norms does not legitimize Western countries as actors that enforce these norms.
13. Nuamah and Zartman (2001) suggest that the UK operation could have received even more international legitimacy had it been part of the international observing mission under the UN that the rebel side had accepted in its peace agreement. While in some other protective operations disagreements between Russia (and China) and the Western permanent members of the UN Security Council have made operating within the UN difficult, in Sierra Leone this would not have been a problem. Instead of replacing the crumbling UN military force, the UK could have complemented it by resourcing it with sufficient military force.

6. Hidden agendas and the protection of civilians

INTRODUCTION

After revealing how protective interventions seem to be associated with increased conflict intensity and mounting fatalities, and after discovering the main sources of legitimacy for enemy violence, it is now possible to start investigating how these sources affect fatalities and interventions and how they emerge in the Western discourse strand on protection. As we discovered in the previous chapter, the first cluster of sources of enemy violence is related to various types of selfish, nationalistic hidden agendas behind the declaratory altruistic cosmopolitan motive of protection. This chapter will focus on the source of this resistance, how it affects protection and how it emerges in the cosmopolitan discourse of the West. I will first look at existing research on the possibilities of cosmopolitan altruism and research that suggests that such altruism is still contaminated and entangled by nationalistic and selfish discourses. I will look at the mechanisms by which selfish motives have been suggested to impact conflicts and protection, and how they have been assumed to affect the intensity of conflict. Then I will move on to the investigation of the US discourse strand on protection and see how much its referent object remains national and how such selfishness is related to the intensity of violence and incentives for protective interventions. Finally, I will then look at the discursive path through which selfishness has entered into and entangled with the discourse strand on protection in US presidential papers.

EXISTING LITERATURE ON SELFISHNESS AND PROTECTION

The theoretical roots of political cosmopolitanism show much optimism about the feasibility of selfless global thinking and political action that simply focus on the good of the human race rather than emphasize partisan national interests. Clearly, such theory is behind the declaratory level of the political reality of cosmopolitan protection. On the theoretical, scholarly plane of the discursive strand, we find texts by cosmopolitan scholars (Beck, 2006; Bray, 2009; Brown, 2000; Gilmore, 2014; Habermas, 2001; Hayden, 2005; Linklater, 2011) and theorists on new wars (Duffield, 2001; Gilbert, 2003; Kaldor, 1999; Malešević, 2008; Mello, 2010), many of whom call for humanitarian intervention and the enforcement of humanitarian order in conflicts where opportunist conflict entrepreneurs use chaos to achieve selfish gains by using violence against unarmed civilians. While global cosmopolitan protection helps civilians in failed and violent states it will eventually create a global order that is more humane and less violent (Elias, 1939, 1982; Pinker, 2011). National selfishness and self-help are no more natural a reality of governance than the security of the primitive order of families and tribes thousands of years ago, or the security of the feudal city-state governance hundreds of years ago. Kaldor argues that the transnational solidarity of non-governmental organizations during the European fight against communist totalitarianism was an example of the emergence of a global civil society, and that the same process has developed further in movements for global human rights (Kaldor, 2003, p. vii). For some, the European Union exemplifies a regional step towards cosmopolitan governance of security (Buzan, 1983). For Buzan, though, such supranational development of security governance is possible only among mature states, whose citizens have already passed the national stage of solidarity and who have started to develop a more global concept of solidarity and identity (or civil society as Kaldor imagines it). In this sense, Buzan can be seen as a bridge between cosmopolitan optimism and subaltern realist pessimism.

On another plane, we have the same discourse strand on protection in political texts by leaders in the United States, the United Kingdom and France. These texts oppose those conflict entrepreneurs who explicitly target civilians with their aggression, using authoritarian violence, weapons of mass destruction, or terror and crime (Blair, 2003; G.W. Bush, 2003d; Cameron, 2011; Obama, 2011a; Sarkozy, 2011).

At the same time, there are also theories that reject the possibility of cosmopolitan interest and loyalty and assume the naturality of national self-interest (Morgenthau, 2006). In addition to the naturality of national self-interest, many realists claim that the system of international relations is such that any efforts to promote supranational interests destabilize the system and result in greater numbers of conflict fatalities. This way, cosmopolitan altruism is not just impossible and unnatural, it is also dangerous (Kissinger, 2014).

Finally, according to another, subaltern, type of realist, it would be unrealistic to dream about supranational realities when even the national reality is still beyond the reach of most people in the world. If the existing functioning states develop supranational order and the people in the Third World, who live either in non-performing states or in autocracies, cannot participate in the development of such order, such an order would be a difficult sell for those who have failed to participate in its creation (Ayoob, 2001, 2016; Azar and Moon, 1988a, 1988c). Thus, while subaltern realists do not necessarily consider states as natural and sole possible units of governance, they feel that in this specific historical situation it will not yet be possible for the Western world to impose a supranational order. If the creation of such an order requires interaction between states, and only some people are represented by these states, then the creation of an order that is owned by all must wait until there are functioning democratic states to represent the people of the Third World.

As seen in the previous chapter, many of the sources of perceived legitimacy of terrorist, criminal or dictatorial violence draw from narratives of selfish imperialist exploitation by developed countries of the Third World. There are surprising similarities between theories of neocolonial and neoimperial intervention (Bukharin and Luxemburg, 1925 [1972]; De Alvarez, 2009; Forte, 2012; Lenin, 1999) and the rhetoric of some of the main opponents of Western humanitarian military operations. On the one hand, there is the narrative of economic ulterior motives that seems convincing especially in interventions in oil-rich countries, and then there is a narrative of power battle in which humanitarian norms and international law are but tools to be used selectively for the sake of selfish power interests (Chandler, 2000, 2002; Chomsky, 2016). While some of the Islamist enemies of Western protection saw these selfish power motives targeting Islam as a religion and culture, Milošević and Gaddafi saw it targeted at the type of social democracy their countries represented: more humane versions of economic systems that erode the legitimacy of the American type of capitalism, and limit the options of US multinational corporations for imperial exploitation (Gaddafi, 2011j, 2014; Milošević, 2000a). All these narratives were helpful for the legitimation of violence against the West and against the people the West intended to protect. Thus, these narratives contributed to the escalation of conflicts and to the increase in the number of fatalities humanitarian protection was associated with.

In addition to the impact of enemy narratives, Western selfishness has also been seen as directly resulting in fatalities. According to theories of imperialism, interventions may be initiated for economic reasons and if they are made politically possible by the cosmopolitan declaratory motive then the practice of 'protective' interventions costs lives (Snow, 2016). Cosmopolitan operations that lack sufficient resourcing and have to resort to strategies that minimize costs and compromise cosmopolitan priorities can also be costly in terms of human life (Falk, 2003). While Beck (2006) suggests that cosmopolitan commitment is deeply rooted in Western thinking, Mueller provides empirical evidence that suggests that Falk, rather than Beck is right: one American soldier is of more worth for an average US voter than tens of thousands of people the US aims at protecting (Mueller, 1996). As a result, cosmopolitan arguments justify operations that at least need to be conducted in a way that also serve national rather than cosmopolitan interests and therefore it is possible that more lives are lost than if the cosmopolitan arguments were unavailable.

Theorists of military myopia have examined the dynamics of this. According to this theory, warfare that is very averse to costs and fatalities on one's own side and that aims to avoid them even at the risk of not being very sensitive to even civilian fatalities and costs on the other side of the frontline might escalate conflict. When the US tries to avoid American fatalities, it tends to emphasize technological aspects of warfare and move the battle to the air. Decreased presence on the ground helps avoid US fatalities but it also tends to make it more difficult to assess the damage and differentiate between friends, civilians and foes. According to General Bontrager (Central Command's Deputy Director for Operations), 'It's a rare thing with strikes. . .that we can get on the ground in person, or that we can talk to anybody on the ground' (Knuckey et al., 2017). As a result, according to Lyall and Wilson, the mechanized, clinical mode of battle (with the extensive use of air power) may be efficient in interstate battles, yet in counter-insurgency this type of battle leads to the alienation of the effort from the worlds of the rebels – counter-insurgency effort remains insensitive to the grievances that fuel rebellion and might even strengthen the resolve of the people to fight (Lyall and Wilson, 2009), leading to interventions that kill a lot of people they are supposed to defend or protect (Mack, 1975; Merom, 2003).

NATIONAL AND COSMOPOLITAN JUSTIFICATIONS FOR HUMANITARIAN MILITARY INTERVENTIONS

Countries cannot launch military operations simply by justifying them in the UN with references to the natural resources that the targets of intervention possess. Interventions are not politically feasible as robberies; there is a need for an internationally acceptable justification. Yet, while international security operations or interventions might have an internationally acceptable justification, they tend to have a nationalistic justification as well. The interesting thing with regard to national selfishness is the balance between discourse on the internationally acceptable, here cosmopolitan, justification and the discourse with a nationally sellable argument for intervention. More specifically, the question is about the balance between national and non-national referent objects of protection. If the latter is overemphasized, there is a danger that operations do not get sufficient national funding or mandate, while if international operations are too much about the protection of the US and US interests, they may cause resentment and provoke escalation and justify violence among the enemies of such operations in the areas where they take place.

If we look at the dialogue where the word 'protection' (and its derivatives) is used as something that relates to foreign affairs (the threat against which one needs to protect someone or something is international), we can see that, since the end of the Cold War, the US and its security interests have been dominant. Almost half of such clauses in presidential papers on protection refer to Americans and their national interests (Figure 6.1).

All this seems to corroborate my previous findings on selfishness in diplomatic and military relationships from World War II to 2010, between the US and countries in the Middle East where most of the protective interventions take place. If one looks at the US policy of supporting democracy and human rights by comparing the level of US support (political, economic and military) and the level of democracy and autocracy in the Middle East as measured by Polity IV data (Marshall and Jaggers, 2000), one can see that, on average, US supports less democratic and more

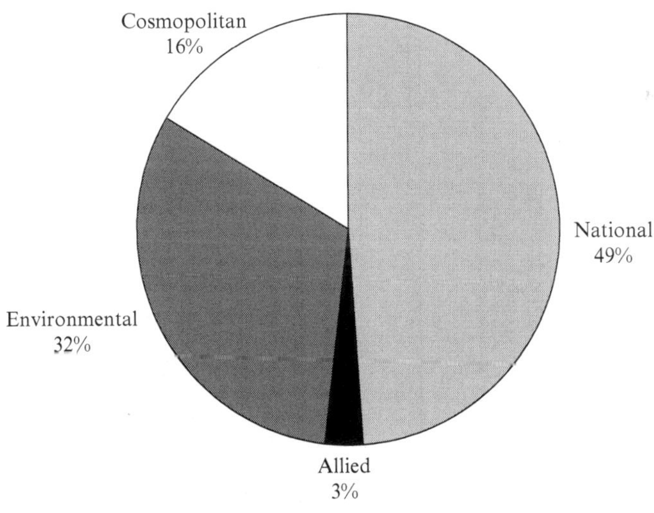

Figure 6.1 National and non-national interests in US protection (referent objects of US protection)

authoritarian countries than those it does not support (Kivimäki, 2012). Furthermore, countries that democratize tend to get less rather than more support, while countries where autocracy increases tend, on average, to get increased US support (Kivimäki, 2013) – all this despite the US rhetoric of promotion of democracy. While these studies did not reveal US preference for autocracy, they showed the primacy of US selfish strategic interest against Soviet Union and jihadist organizations, the US need to support Israel, and, in particular, the US need to consolidate friendly suppliers of energy resources. Thus, not only in protective military operations, but also in diplomatic, economic and military support, US policies were primarily driven by national rather than humanitarian interests.

However, as can be seen in Figure 6.2, nationalist discourse is very much dependent on the president in power. While Democrat presidents Clinton (1993–2001) and Obama (2009–17) were more hesitant to refer to national interests when using military power in areas outside US national borders, Republican presidents Bush (2001–09) and Trump (2017–) have been less restrained in this respect (even though quantitative data on Trump's texts are not yet available). Even if we can see that the party affiliation of the president affects the level of selfishness in protection, party affiliation should not be seen as an intervening variable to be controlled. Selfish discourses constitute selfish political cultures that voter agency follows

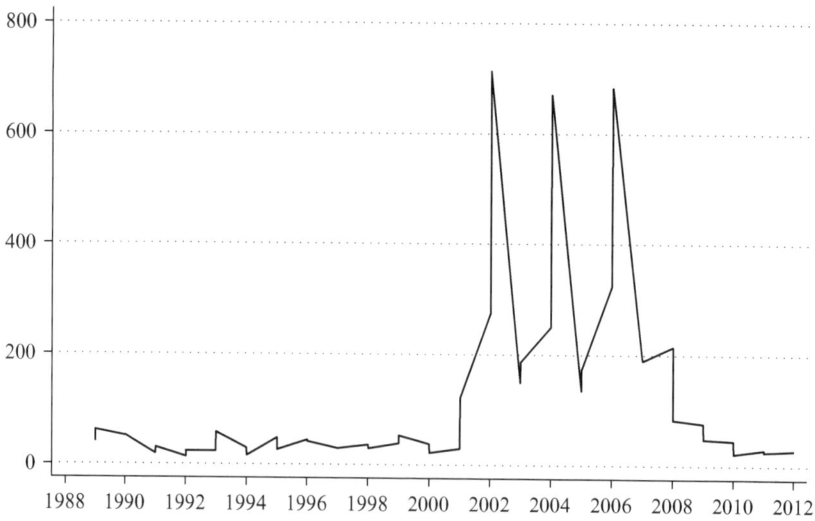

Figure 6.2 Development of national primacy in cosmopolitan protection – number of biannual presidential references (US security as referent option of protection)

and strengthens by selecting selfish presidents. This is part of the set of mechanisms in which discursive processes proceed.

The relationship between national selfishness, interventions and fatalities is complicated though. While, in general, an order in which the US simply focuses on its own security fails to justify cosmopolitan operations, US selfishness seems to be associated with reduced overall numbers of fatalities. UCDP fatality statistics are annual and we have data (Kivimäki, 2019b, forthcoming) on discourses for only 24 years, thus it is doubtful whether we can talk about statistical correlations with such a small number of observations. However, if we could, we would see that there is a highly significant relatively strong negative association[1] (–0.66) between the share of protection clauses that refer to the US nation and the overall number of conflict fatalities in the world. This could be interpreted that when cosmopolitan rationale is unavailable there are fewer fatalities in the world. This would probably not be a feasible interpretation though, given the fact that the number of protective operations are associated with the ability to use national/selfish rationales in support of protection and with the increase of conflict fatalities.. Perhaps a better interpretation of this association could be arrived at in a more path-dependent approach based on the development of the role of the national referent object of protection (Figure 6.2) and the development of fatalities (see Figure 4.6 in Chapter 4). The number of fatalities declined all through the 1990s, before the Western countries were ready for cosmopolitan military protection. Here the lack of legitimacy of military violations of sovereignty for the sake of protection of civilians inside a fragile state clearly influenced the declining tendency of conflict fatalities. The appetite for unilateral protective operations began to emerge only after the UN failures to protect in Bosnia and Rwanda. As will be shown in the next chapter, the floodgates of unilateral cosmopolitan protection were opened only in 1999, and soon after the nationalist rationalization of such operations emerged. However, that meant that when protective operations began, the overall number of fatalities was at its all-time low, and still when the nationalistic turn was triggered by the terrorist attack on September 11, 2001, the overall number of conflict fatalities was still very low and only started to increase slowly. This, rather than the immediate effect of nationalist reference object of protection, explains the correlation.

However, if we then look at the number of fatalities of protection wars (see the data, Kivimäki 2019b, forthcoming, as presented in Chapter 2) we can see that there is an almost equally strong statistically very significant positive association (0.56) with nationalist orientation. In a more path-dependent, historical analysis one can see that the first two operations, in Kosovo (1999) and Sierra Leone (2000), took place at the time when cosmopolitan protection could not be justified as selfish protection of one's own nation. These operations caused less resistance among the opponents of Western military operations than the operations that took place after the emergence of the nationalist justification for protection. Legitimacy for violations of sovereignty was thus gained during the time when nationalist justification was not yet acceptable, but once protective operations were already initiated and acceptable due to the cosmopolitan rationale of protecting strangers, the next step of protecting one's own citizens by means that violate the norm of non-interference was easier to take. Thus, it seems that when cosmopolitan rationale for interventions was already available, the focus on national interests became deadly.

This is still something that corresponds with our previous findings: first, that cosmopolitan protection wars have contributed to increased fatalities of conflict, and second, that nationalist selfishness of the protector provokes increased violence in protective operations. So far then the analysis of referent objects simply confirms our previous conclusions. However, what also can be found if one looks at the number of protective operations, is that nationalist rhetoric is needed to justify and launch operations more than rhetoric about the cosmopolitan need for protection. Thus, it seems that the main obstacles to operations are national rather than international: the international community's priorities and norms of protection take second place to domestic budgetary, legal and political concerns. Here we can resort to biannual statistics as we can identify the time of operations more precisely, and the number of clauses with reference to protection biannually.[2] Thus, with 47 biannual observations it is possible to come to somewhat more reliable statistical conclusions. The share of clauses with national references as objects of protection (rather than references to the environment, allies or global civilians) is strongly and statistically very significantly positively associated with the number of US protective operations (0.6317, $n = 47$, $p \sim 0.0000$).

If we look at presidential papers and individual protective operations, we can see that the highest peak in the number and share of nationalist reference objects of protection was when the US tried to sell its Iraq operation during the latter half of 2002. Then the main discussion was about Iraq and the terrorist strike on September 11, 2001. Furthermore, if one looks at developments month by month, one can see that the emphasis on the nationalist referent object continued until March 2003 when the Iraq intervention began. The first time in the post-Cold War period when the US presidential papers make no reference to the cosmopolitan referent to protection in two consecutive months, but consistently mention US and allied protection was at the end of 2002 and beginning of 2003, just before the most destructive protection war was about to begin. The second most nationalist debate on protection was just before the beginning of the Somalia operation at the end of 2006, while the largest share of the national referent objects of protection was at the end of 2004, when the protective operation in Pakistan had already started. The second and last two consecutive months without any references to cosmopolitan referent objects of protection were in January and February 2010, after the protective operation in Yemen had started in December 2009. Yemenese people have never been referred to in presidential papers as referents of protection. Thus, even though internationally protective operations are justified with cosmopolitan interests, they tend to reflect national rather than cosmopolitan concerns.

All this seems to corroborate the qualitative findings I present in Kivimäki (2019a, forthcoming) partly based on analysis of word frequencies:[3] humanitarian vocabulary seems to be negatively rather than positively correlated with protection vocabulary, and not consistently associated negatively or positively with the number of ongoing or new protective military operations. At the same time, the discourse strand on protection seems to be closely connected with military discursive strands. The correlations between the relative frequencies (per 1000) of the words 'protection' and 'threat' is 0.701 ($p \sim 0.0000$, $n = 47$)! The frequency of the word 'threat', again, is very strongly associated with the number of ongoing and new protective operations (Kivimäki, 2019a, forthcoming). Thus, it seems that Richard Falk (2002, 2003) was right: there is not enough cosmopolitan altruism in world politics to justify protective military operations. Thus, we should: (1) focus on the safety of the people we want to protect rather than on our own safety if we want to undertake protective military operations; and (2) if we cannot do that, then we should not be undertaking such military operations.

If we look at the clauses focused on the protection of Americans in sentences on international protective operations, we can see that most of them were related to presidential statements on the need to protect American soldiers in humanitarian operations first and foremost. Despite the fact that internationally these operations were justified as protection of global strangers, in the internal debate the idea of the protection wars was different: 'We're at war with an enemy that wants to hurt us again, and the American people expect the Commander in Chief to protect them, and that's exactly what I intend to do' (G.W. Bush, 2007d, p. 1). This suggests that one of the reasons why protective operations increased the intensity of conflict was related to military myopia (Lyall and Wilson, 2009; Mack, 1975; Merom, 2003): warfare was made clinical in the sense that American fatalities were to be limited to the extent that the ability to avoid collateral damage was compromised. Additionally, as Chapter 5 suggests, the self-interest in protective operations was recognized by the opponents of these operations and this provoked deadly counteraction both against the US, and, especially in the absence of US soldiers, against those whom protective operations were intended to protect.

The fact that selfish discourse is so clearly associated with deadlier protective operations and the fact that operations seemed to need national rather than international justifications, could also suggest that there is a problem with the agency of protective operations. If agency is with nations rather than representative international organizations such as the UN, it will be difficult to avoid selfishness, and thus to design military operations that will not escalate violence. This last finding will be studied in the next chapter, while in this chapter the focus will now move to the path in which the cosmopolitan discourse strand becomes entangled with discourse strands on nationalistic self-interest.

REALITIES, REAL AND IMAGINED, RELATED TO SELFISHNESS IN WORLD POLITICS

As has been shown above, selfish thinking has been part of existing protective operations, but this does not prove that this needs to be the case. Yet, a qualitative analysis of US presidential texts reveals that a belief in the necessity and naturality of national self-help is entangled in the discursive strand on protection even though internationally protective operations seek legitimacy and justification from cosmopolitan ideas that explicitly deny the naturality of and necessity for nationalist selfishness. Many of the arguments that justify selfish motives for protection in world politics relate to the realist misunderstanding of the relationship between potentiality and actuality and assume that the actual situation proves the 'realities' and the non-existence of alternative potentials. The fact that states behave selfishly is often seen as proof of the *reality* of selfishness in world politics. Thus, there is no potential for cosmopolitan thought in world politics unless it directly serves national interest. (This logic is quite evident from the very beginning of classical works of realism – see, for example, Morgenthau, 2006.) Partly, this misunderstanding is due to the import of natural science into social sciences. Natural science ideals have been imported into the analysis of world politics, and this has meant the decline of agency in the political understanding of the world (Heidegger, 1962). However, if we understand that world politics is partly about realities and partly about agency, we can also understand that existing national selfishness does not prove selfishness as a reality. In addition to realities and agency, the social reality of the natural science understanding of the world rules out the imagination of more cosmopolitan futures. States should therefore either accept cosmopolitan national altruism as a possibility, or they should stop legitimizing their military operations as cosmopolitan. Nationalist, selfish cosmopolitanism is an oxymoron.

Nevertheless, the contradiction between natural selfishness in cosmopolitan operations is very evident in presidential papers of each of the US presidents in the post-Cold War era. Obama still used the language of national necessity in his policies on Libya in 2012 (Obama, 2013b, p. 203) while the 'America First' ethos seems like a return to a natural state of affairs in President Trump's discourse (Trump, 2017b). Presidents Bush and Clinton both utilized the US constitutional framework as justification for the natural concept of selfishness: 'My job is to protect America, and that's exactly what I'm going to do' (G.W. Bush 2004e, p. 248). When Clinton rationalized the naturality of presidential national selfishness, he sometimes also offered some ideas of how the cosmopolitan and nationalist could be combined: 'My goals as President have been to preserve the American dream for all of our people, to bring the American people together, and to keep America the world's strongest force for peace and freedom and prosperity' (Clinton, 1996c, p. 1851). If America's power as a global nation of peace, freedom and prosperity is a national interest, then national interest could also serve other countries. Yet, just as the theory of military myopia suggests, national protection and a global role do not always go well together. Already long before the beginning of drone-based protection, which was guaranteed not to kill any Americans, protective operations were planned to limit costs for the US. Even the most humanitarian of overseas missions, such as the US mission to promote democracy and assist Haiti in a humanitarian emergency must be motivated by national interest. This is clear in Clinton's statement: 'My first concern, and the most important one, obviously, is for the safety and security of our troops. General Shalikashvili and Lieutenant General Hugh Shelton, our commander in Haiti, have made it clear to all involved that the protection of American lives is our first order of business' (Clinton, 1995, p. 1575).

Combining nationalist and globalist rationales in Clinton's previous quotation is very familiar from the realist literature and is strengthened by the American tradition of global leadership, which does naturalize selfishness, even in global governance. However, cosmopolitan protection also meets with obstacles in the institutions of decision-making. When leading the world, the US president must request funding from Congress, and, constitutionally, cannot declare war without the backing of Congress. Furthermore, when making decisions on security in Iraq, the US president has a mandate based not on Iraqi, but on US national and human concerns. This comes through in the US protection discourse. According to Clinton:

> Every office I have ever held of the public trust, from being attorney general of my state to being governor to being president, required me to swear an oath to protect the people I was elected to serve, to give people the security they need to live up to the most of their God given potential. (Clinton, 1996b, p. 1216)

Bush and Obama repeated the same thing, almost like a mantra. According to Bush, '[The] president's job is not to pass a "global test." The president's job is to protect the American people' (G.W. Bush, 2005e, p. 2383). Obama clarified the relationship between the institutional setting and the cosmopolitan mission most accurately when he said:

> As President, my greatest responsibility is to protect the American people. We are not in Afghanistan to control that country or to dictate its future. We are in Afghanistan to confront a common enemy that threatens the United States, our friends and our allies, and the people of Afghanistan and Pakistan who have suffered the most at the hands of violent extremists. (Obama, 2010a, p. 366)

The need to show that US power and US interests are also in the interests of those the West protects requires a lot of half-truths, outright lies and efforts to conceal parts of facts.[4] While the US's and the UK's own polls showed that Iraqi civilians did not much appreciate Western military role in their country (Hussain, 2016; Rayment, 2005), and while the main challenge in Afghanistan was to stop even the privileged Afghan elite killing American protectors, US presidents continued to articulate realities of support of the ordinary people:

> Most Iraqis, by far, reject violence and oppose dictatorship. In forums where Iraqis have met to discuss their political future and in all the proceedings of the Iraqi Governing Council, Iraqis have expressed clear commitments. They want strong protections for individual rights. They want their independence, and they want their freedom. (G.W. Bush, 2005j, p. 557)

President Obama used stories of individual global civilians to create a pattern of support of Western presence: 'I think of the Libyans who protected our airman when he ejected over their town because they knew America was there to protect them. . . I think of all the Libyans who were waving American flags' (Obama, 2013a, p. 661). The means of protection were also often beautified with denials of torture, and violations of the humanitarian norms that protective operations were supposed to enforce. Members of Al Qaeda were not killed, but 'brought to justice': 'We've brought 75 percent of Al Qaida to justice, and we're still working' (G.W. Bush, 2005k, p. 2131), while 'the prisoners are well-treated in Guantanamo. . .in total transparency' (G.W. Bush, 2006f, p. 1191). The reality of the failed states that protective operations often left (or failed to leave) were often described in a light that did not correspond to the judgement of history:

> Because we acted, torture chambers are closed. Because we acted, countries like Libya understood we meant business, and they voluntarily disarmed. Because we acted, there is a democracy beginning to grow in a part of the world that needs freedom and hope. Because we acted, this man's weapons programs will never be. (G.W. Bush, 2005a, p. 811)

Yet, the naturality of national selfishness was a domestic political power reality (albeit one that should have made cosmopolitan justification of military operations difficult). Presidents do need their funding from national rather than international parliaments, their legal control is mostly national, and their access to weaponry is through their national constitutional roles. Thus, protective military operations do require national justifications, and if the national mood is selfish rather than cosmopolitan, as Mueller's findings suggest (Mueller, 1996), presidents are in a difficult position when they try to protect global civilians. This institutional commitment to realist state thinking in American foreign policy limits the US commitment to global democracy and cosmopolitanism (Ralph, 2003, p. 209). It introduces selfish national interest to protection since the US constituencies were, in reality, not as cosmopolitan as Beck and others suggest (Beck, 2006). Thus, to reconcile the contradiction between global cosmopolitan roles and policies and national decision-making, one would need to strengthen genuinely globally representative institutions, rather than assume that individual nations can play global cosmopolitan roles. The question of cosmopolitan agency will be discussed in the next chapter, while in the next section I will show how national selfishness entered the cosmopolitan discourse in a way that was seen as legitimate (despite the apparent contradiction between altruist cosmopolitan morality and nationalist selfishness).

SEPTEMBER 11, 2001 AND THE CONTRIBUTION OF 'INNOCENCE', 'REVENGE' AND 'JUSTICE' TO SELFISHNESS IN PROTECTION

Even though the US presidential papers revealed the realist and hegemonic fallacies in the discourse strand on protection from the beginning of the post-Cold War era, it seems clear that military protection of civilians – war activities for the protection of citizens of fragile and dictatorial states – did not start immediately after the end of the Cold War. On the contrary, theorists on new wars complain that the very reason that new wars erupted was the abandonment by developed countries of fragile states:

> [T]he end of the Cold War has been accompanied by an apparently reduced willingness and ability to control internal violence. . . Governments and potential insurgents no longer have ideological patrons who provide them with the wherewithal to commit violence and then expect some influence over how that violence is carried out. (Snow, 1996, p. 46; see also Daalder, 1996, p. 462; Kaldor, 1999, p. 3)

According to Münkler, 'war has become endemic mainly in regions where a major empire held sway and then fell apart' (Münkler, 2002, p. 10). The willingness to see global civilians as important referent objects of protection, in conflicts where they could be protected, developed only slowly after the collapse of the ideological Cold War rationale for intervention had disappeared.

In my analysis of word frequencies (Kivimäki, 2019a, forthcoming) I show that the discourse on protection started to increase during the 1990s and interacted with the events in Bosnia and Rwanda. When the selfish or Cold War-oriented interpretations of the world failed to interpret the people's sentiment following the genocides, there was a need to use words and articulate interpretations that helped make sense not just of the world but also of the sentiments that distant tragedies evoked in the minds of Western voters. There was a need for a vocabulary that focused less on states and their security and more on human security. There was a need for interpretations that made sense of the need to focus on safety of distant strangers as the development of information technologies had brought them closer to ordinary people all over the world. It was possible to be sorry, sympathize and act upon global solidarity in the 1990s as global communication had made it possible for people to have as much interaction with Bosnians as they had with their fellow citizens just a decade ago. Yet, as Figure 6.1 shows, protection always seemed to define US citizens as the important referent objects, and the attack on American citizens on September 11, 2001 gave this nationalist orientation some new legitimacy.

As can be seen in Figure 6.3, before 2001, the US nation, its people and existential interests were the referent objects only in 20–30 per cent of clauses with the word 'protect'. This rose after the incident on September 11, 2001 from 23 per cent to 43 per cent in the latter half of 2001 (remember that almost half of the latter half of the year had already passed on September 11) and 60 per cent at the first half of 2002. While it seems clear that Republican presidencies are more nationalistic in their rhetoric of protection, Bush did not turn from cosmopolitan protection rhetoric to nationalist rhetoric before September 11, 2001. Thus, we must seek the reasons for the nationalist turn from this terrorist incident. At the same time, as Figure 6.3 shows, nationalist protection replaced not only more cosmopolitan discourse, but also, even more importantly, an environmental

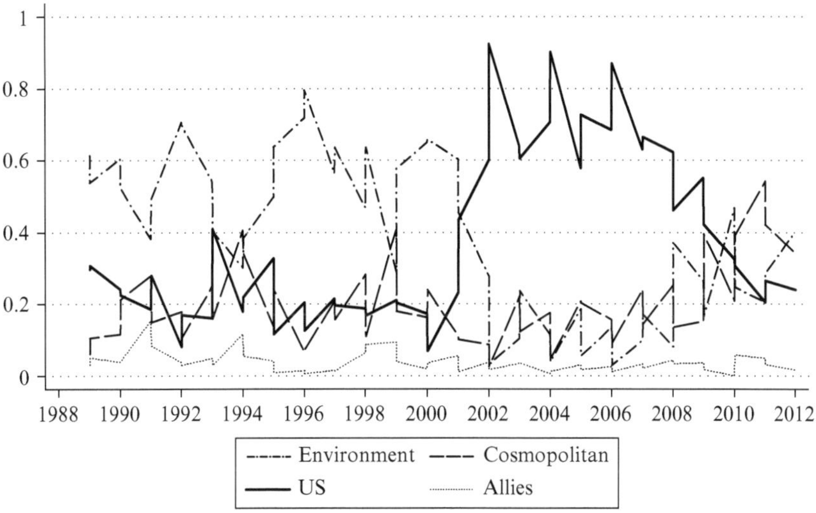

Figure 6.3 The rise of national selfishness: referent objects of protection (share of each object of all objects)

discourse of protection. The narrative of global threat moved from natural to agent-centric: the threat was no longer the common environment that made all countries face a common threat, but evil enemies, a framing in which the US was no longer *together* with others (other countries who were also threatened by global environmental threats), but primarily, *against* others (terrorists and dictators that supported terrorists).

The attack on the American heartland by Al Qaeda turned the concepts of protection and terror around. Previously, terrorism was resisted as part of the cosmopolitan ethos: terrorists were defined as people who targeted civilians and so were enemies of all civilians. Thus, the pursuit of human security required attention to the problem of terrorism. However, on September 11, 2001, terrorists became enemies of the United States. Protection discourse and protective operations were not associated with humanitarianism or civilians, but now protection and terror were framed where US power had been challenged and there was a very simple triangular relationship between the 'bad guys' (terrorists), 'good guys' (US), and the innocent civilians, who now were US citizens rather than global strangers: 'We have learned all too suddenly that there are evil people who have no regard for human life and will do whatever it takes to try to bring this mighty Nation to its knees' (G.W. Bush, 2002, p. 1326). The narrative of innocent objects of protection, innocent actors and guilty perpetrators can be seen in the association between the discourse stand on protection and on innocence. The word 'innocent' is strongly and statistically very significantly associated with 'protection' (0.624, $p \sim 0.0000$, $n = 47$) and the qualitative analysis of the relationship shows how the innocence of Americans killed on September 11, 2001 and the brutality of the terrorists justify US protective action that protects primarily Americans, disregarding global norms on how ('no matter how'). Innocence became a fixed identity that victimhood earned the US and this identity could not fade even if one's own operations were conducted in a way that disregarded humanitarian norms:

> We must never forget the day when the terrorists left their mark of murder on our Nation. We must never forget that day. We will remember the sorrow and the anger. We'll also remember the resolve we felt that day. All of us have a responsibility that goes on. We will protect this country, whatever it takes. (G.W. Bush, 2005h, p. 295)

While George W. Bush did not have a monopoly on the rhetoric[5] it was the context and frequency that testified to the importance of the terrorist attack on American soil in September 2001 to the US discourse strand on protection. The audience to whom he repeated the idea that the terrorist strike against the US justifies protection of the US 'whatever it takes' was almost always national, and thus the frequency of these few sentences with the reference to the attack, the justification and the idea of protecting 'whatever it takes' was repeated during Bush's re-election campaign in the latter half of 2004 123 times (as listed in the presidential papers).

The unfortunate confusion in which innocent victims are seen as immune to critique, as if one can only be either a perpetrator or a victim, but not both, is not brought to light in the academic literature on cosmopolitan protection (Kivimäki, 2019a, forthcoming). Yet, Joseph A. Amato, from outside the study of international relations, has derived this tendency to use victimhood as a claim with a political potency that purifies and justifies from the Christian narratives that have been used to make hardship more tolerable (Amato and Monge, 1990). While the crucified Christ has been the ultimate cultural reference, in international relations the narrative of the Holocaust has been the representative case of victimhood (Bouris, 2007) that has justified Israeli policies to secure the Jewish people. The moral problems that this 'purifying' victimhood pose have been dealt with in the academic literature (Levi, 2017; Spelman, 1998), but not in the cosmopolitan study of conflicts and new wars. In the Kaldorian conception of new wars, there is a conflicting party that benefits from violence and wants to continue the state of warfare as a social condition (rather than using violence instrumentally and conditional on compliance of the enemy), while the victim is simply on the receiving end of suffering (Chinkin and Kaldor, 2017; Kaldor, 2012, p. 126).

The fact that innocent victimhood in political literature focuses on actors (innocent people vs perpetrators) rather than on violent deeds has meant that the terrorist attack on the US has not sparked a reaction against terror and violence but rather against terrorists. As a result, instead of preventing violence, the discourse strand on innocence has legitimized violence. Bush's statements after the terror attack were explicit on the association between innocence and the right to act aggressively in self-interest. President Bush also portrays the September 11 attack as a personal tragedy for himself, making himself a victim. Throughout the last four months of 2004, he repeats this 40 times in the presidential papers with minimal variations, always saying that after the incident of September 11, he had woken up every morning thinking of the best strategy to protect the country or its people, always emphasizing that he would be prepared to do 'whatever it takes' to protect America. This, in a very concrete sense, shows the discursive path from victimhood to rough, selfish means of protection (Kivimäki, 2019a, forthcoming).

Furthermore, the fact that the enemy was not bound to a territory meant that self-defensive protection was legitimate throughout the globe. George W. Bush repeated how important it was to stay on the offensive:[6] 'We're hunting the Al Qaida terrorists wherever they hide, from Pakistan to the Philippines to the Horn of Africa to Iraq' (G.W. Bush, 2004a, p. 1277). Thus, while post-9/11 nationalist protection considered mostly US security, it was not bound to the state-centric norms related to sovereignty and non-interference. The argument has its academic version in Kaldor's cosmopolitanism regarding the nature of new wars: '[I]t is no longer possible to contain war geographically. Zones of peace and zones of war exist side by side in the same territorial space' (Kaldor, 2012, p. 185).

While the globality of the threat made the US national protection effort legitimately global, this again then confused the dividing line between crime prevention and defence and introduced many security elements into the crime discourse, while simultaneously introducing the idea of law enforcement to the global politics of protection. The disappearance of the dividing line between domestic law enforcement and global protection was characterized by President Bush: 'In our country it used to be that oceans could protect us. . . September the 11th, that changed. America is now a battleground in the war on terror' (G.W. Bush, 2004c, p. 152). The presidential papers emphasize this logic in the presidential introduction to the second volume of the 2001 collection and by repeating the above citation in slightly different variations in 2002 exactly 100 times. Analysis of the way in which the word 'crime' was used in Clinton's rhetoric and how the word 'terror' was used in George W. Bush's rhetoric reveals how the discourse of crime and terror were merged after September 11, 2001 (Kivimäki, 2019a, forthcoming). Consequently, many of the rules of crime prevention were exported to the world of global protection against terror. Intelligence by surveillance shifted focus from potential enemies (unfriendly countries) to potential criminals (terrorists AND ordinary citizens), and militarized means of law enforcement spread from military operations in enemy territories to domestic crowd control. Legally, the Patriot Act of 2001 merged the worlds of the intelligence community and law enforcement and allowed intelligence sharing, moving the use of CIA/National Security Agency intelligence into courtrooms to prevent terrorism (US Department of Justice, 2001). Institutionally, the creation of the Department of Homeland Security on November 25, 2002 merged the bureaucracies of crime prevention and prevention of international terrorism. All this had implications on the resourcing of crime and terrorism prevention too. The resources for terror prevention were tripled during the first two years after September 11, 2001 (G.W. Bush, 2005i, p. 116).

For the legitimacy of selfishness in global protection, all this meant another boost to national ruling on global issues. The merging of the prevention of terror with the police bureaucracy, and better resourcing and wider mandate of the activity, together with the change in the framing of protection from an environmental focus to a focus on the US need to fight concrete intentional enemies, all pushed protection in a more unilateralist, nationalist direction. There was no longer any need for UN acceptance to employ measures to prevent national crime (G.W. Bush, 2005f, p. 2392), even though – after September 11 – the criminal resided outside the US. While the unilateralism will be dealt with in the next chapter, the merger of crime and terror frames also had implications on the level of selfishness of priorities of protection.

Drone warfare seems the clearest consequence of the discursive entanglement of the terror and protection discourse strand and the strand on crime. Nationalistically motivated and authorized global law enforcement was added to the toolbox of US 'cosmopolitan protection', despite the fact that, in the international setting, legitimate legal norms were far less clear. Again, the right of the US to enforce its law and its interpretation of international law were not shared by the people in the areas where this law enforcement was conducted. As a result, conflicts escalated, and the people that cosmopolitan protection was supposed to shield died as a result.

Thus, the terrorist violence in the US changed the framing of protection in the following ways:

- Protection was no longer something in which all people in the world were on the same side against environmental degradation, but instead it was something in which one could distinguish the side of the good people from the side of the bad.
- Protection required military means over a broader territorial space.
- Protection referred to the United States rather than global strangers yet sought international justifications from the narrative in which US interest is a global interest.
- Protection by the US was justified mostly among Americans, while the audience of protection speeches used to be much more international.
- The issue had become so central (and securitized) that 'whatever it takes' could be done to protect Americans.
- Due to the entanglements between discourse strands on terror and crime, 'cosmopolitan' protection moved closer to the priorities of US national crime prevention. Together with the facilitating drone technology, individuals that were seen as a threat to the American understanding of legality began to be targeted as if the US criminal jurisdiction had become global.

CONCLUSIONS

National self-help and selfishness as such have no relationship to the increasing number of conflict fatalities in the world. On the contrary, there is a negative association between the frequency of the national referent object of protection and the number of overall fatalities in the world. Rather, the problem has been the contradiction between cosmopolitan international legitimation of intervention and the selfish nationalist ways of motivating and justifying it. Almost half the sentences on international protection and operations outside a country's own borders have referred to national rather than international security. Yet, they have been seen as cosmopolitanly and internationally acceptable. This, together with the expansion of the national institutionalization of global operations of protection, has contributed to the situation where the violence of the United States and other protecting Western powers provokes the enemies of protective operations, and the consequent violence by these powers further fuels Western interventions and military protection.

The fact that more countries were following the US lead in protection due to the victimization of the Western leader, together with these discursive changes, could help to draw the conclusion that the power-biased strategy of Al Qaeda of attacking the US had greatly damaged the organization and all the people Al Qaeda considered its constituency. Al Qaeda's violence had legitimized its opponent's violence and the consequent escalation of conflict served nobody's interest.

Yet, the same could be said about the Western reaction to terrorism. Staying on the offensive that was assumed to keep terrorists fighting in their own countries, rather than in the US, did not seem to yield the desired effects. Just as the West was provoked by the Al Qaeda intrusion in the US, ISIS has been justifying its operations in the West by referring to the Western intrusion in the 'Muslim lands'. If we look at the correlations between the share of nationalist definitions of the referent object of protection and the number of fatalities of protective operations, or the graphs on the development of fatalities of protective operations, we can see that these changes were very detrimental to the cosmopolitan objectives of protection. Operations in Kosovo and Sierra Leone, before the terrorist attack, were much more successful in terms of reducing fatalities and improving state strength, whereas the operations after the changes were, without exception, failures in both respects.

To reverse this process of escalation in which both sides find legitimacy for their violence in the violence of the other, there is a need to look at the crucial source of national selfishness in protection – national agency. Cosmopolitanism and the political practice of protection needs to turn from its focus on civil society and take representative institutions seriously. It is undoubtedly true that cosmopolitan ethics and motives for cosmopolitan politics arise from the emerging global solidarity among global citizens. It is undoubtedly a product of the emergence of a global civil society, rather than state-centric development. Yet, just as functionalist integration could not ignore the need for authoritative decisions made by representative institutions, the enforcement of cosmopolitan peace will require authoritative decisions that can only be made by representative institutions. Successful enforcement of a set of principles will necessarily require authoritative decisions on those principles, on the way they are enforced, and by whom. Thus, we cannot simply rely on the type of improvised governance that the popular revolt against communist dictatorships in Eastern Europe represented. A change from functionalist integration studies to neofunctional integration studies was needed there. We will need a change from cosmopolitan to neocosmopolitan theory. This would take the question of agency seriously, recognizing that building a global order requires representation and new types of representative institutions. The lack of representative agency is the root of selfishness that escalates protective operations. However, it is also a problem in itself, as legitimacy of protection is not only a problem of whose values are being protected, but also of who is doing the protection. The question of who protects is the topic of the next chapter.

NOTES

1. Most of the variables used for the analysis of this book are not normally distributed, thus the use of non-parametric correlations throughout this book.
2. The data (Kivimäki, 2019b, forthcoming) do allow monthly and clause-specific calculations on agents of protection, but such calculations tend to be less useful as they say more about some specific debates than about the overall mood and discursive setting. This is why, despite the fact that more detailed data are available in the data depository of this book, biannual data are used when not dealing with analysis that focuses on fatalities, that is, annual data.
3. When looking at word frequencies, I look at each word and at words that stem from them (protect, protected, protection etc.). Frequencies are adjusted to the total number of words in each book.
4. Here, text is my data on how social realities are constituted in speeches of US presidents, and it could be said that the text is not intended to reveal a truthful description of the realities in the world. When a text reveals a promise, a securitizing act, or articulates an interpretation of the social reality, it creates social reality, but when it claims that Iraqi people want US military operation to continue when the UK Ministry of Defence has in its polls revealed that this is not the case, the text does create realities that may persuade some to believe that Iraqi people are willing to host US troops, and it may consolidate the institution of lying in foreign relations, but it does not change the reality of Iraqi resentment of the US troops.
5. Clinton used the very same language already in 1993: '[Y]ou may be sure that we will do whatever is necessary to protect our own forces in Somalia and to complete our mission there' (Clinton, 1994c, p. 1668) and Obama continued along the same lines after Bush: 'When I took office, I pledged to do whatever was required to protect the American people and restore American leadership in the world' (Obama, 2011b, p. 1543).
6. It would be inaccurate to claim that this language of law enforcement outside US territory was introduced by the terrorist attack in the US, and that such argumentation did not take place before that. Clinton, too, spoke of law enforcement challenges outside US borders (see, for example, Clinton, 1998, p. 1690), but the idea of 'being on the offensive' was not a major element of the doctrine before September 11, 2001.

7. How did unilateralism sneak into cosmopolitan protection?

INTRODUCTION

The purpose of this chapter is to show how and why unilateralism crept into cosmopolitan protection of global civilians. It will reveal how legitimacy was constructed for unilateralism in the US presidential speech. The question of unilateralism is probably more specific to the US debate than selfishness or power bias. The UK and France may, at times, assume the naturality of their agency in protection in their former colonies, but not globally as is sometimes the case in US discourse. Yet, due to the hegemonic role of the US, French and British discourse on protection may assume the naturality of the agency of the US-led coalitions in the global protection of civilians and the enforcement of humanitarian norms in the world. Nevertheless, even though we can assume certain generality of some of the conclusions on the legitimation of unilateralism in this chapter, the focus is merely on the US discourse, not on any more general Western discourses.

EXISTING LITERATURE ON UNILATERALISM

Within the mainstream realist discourse, we cannot study whether the protection of global civilians should consider the question of agency. For the realist argument, unilateralism and the objective of increased power and control over global security issues is a 'natural', self-evident goal. Furthermore, the idea of interventions and military operations outside the calculus of national interest do not represent the 'intellectual toughmindedness' that Kissinger called for in world politics (Kissinger, 2014). For Kissinger, moralism, like the version of cosmopolitanism that legitimizes humanitarian intervention, is dangerous. Kissinger's realism represents thinking too honest to capture the logic of a realism that promotes national interest and makes it politically feasible by referring to cosmopolitan humanitarian norms. Moralism used to justify military intervention may disrupt the world order based on the sovereignty of states (ibid.) and delay state-building in developing countries (Ayoob, 1997; Azar and Moon, 1988a, 1988c). However, since the focus of this chapter is on cosmopolitan protection and the intention is to see how to avoid global fatalities through violence, the analysis must be integrated with literature that takes the interest of cosmopolitan protection seriously.

The discourse strand on cosmopolitan protection operates on at least two planes, academic and political, which interact with each other. On the one hand, we find this discursive strand in theoretical texts by cosmopolitan scholars of international relations,[1] emphasizing the need to focus on the well-being of individual human beings regardless of state borders, rather than on the sovereignty of states. Cosmopolitan theory denies the rigidity of territorial governance and downplays a clear agency in protection (except, most notably, Pattison, 2010). Instead, the polis that rules cosmos is not territorial in the way states have been: 'it is no longer possible to contain war geographically. Zones of peace and zones of war exist side by side in the same territorial space' (Kaldor, 2012, p. 185). In the place of a global state, cosmopolitan theorists imagine transnational governance, and a global civil society. This political and scholarly imagination is no doubt affected by the experience of the transnational civil society coalitions that helped liberate Eastern Europe and the Soviet Union from communist autocracy (Kaldor, 2003). The cosmopolitan literature is also closely related to the critical security studies that intended to broaden the concept of security outside the referent object of states (Wyn Jones, 1999).

Even though cosmopolitan theory emphasizes the need to protect individuals globally, in the form in which it often appears in the debate on international relations, it rejects the idea of a global state as the agent of global protection and the enforcement of humanitarian norms. Global policy is transnational and represents global solidarity, but it is not transnationally or globally representative in its agency:

> This global polity is not to be confused with a world state or government, but it does suggest the emergence of a realm of organized social and political life in which governance is becoming a transnational phenomenon effectively spreading across borders and being transmitted through various actors at levels from the local to the global. (Hayden, 2005, p. 4)

Kaldor talks about multilateral states or globalized states that are post-national and cosmopolitan, but not representative of the people of the cosmos. Their primary interest is in a multifaceted framework of rules, a system of 'glocal' governance (Kaldor, 2003, p. 137). Kaldor also talks about cosmopolitan powers (Norway, Canada, etc.), referring to states that focus on global good in their foreign policies (Kaldor, 2012, p. 139). In the same vein, Beck suggests that 'the politics of human rights. . .has become the civil religion, the faith of the United States itself' (Beck, 2006, p. 137). Thus, according to Beck, US foreign policy also reflects global rather than national priorities. However, these states, much like the enlightened autocrats, operate based on their own concept of cosmopolitan concerns, without subjecting their interpretations of the common global good to the test of global community.[2] Kaldor emphasizes the role of multinational organizations, revealing her pro-Western bias openly by endorsing 'multinational peacekeeping, arms control agreements involving mutual inspection teams, joint exercises, new or renewed organizations like the WEU [Western European Union], Partnership for Peace, NATO Coordination Council (NACC) – which constitute an intensification of trans-nationalization in the military sphere' (Kaldor, 2012, p. 139). The problem with Kaldor's treatment of multinational organizations is her failure to see the qualitative difference between their security role among their own members and the area outside. In the former context, this role follows the path of representative governance, but when operating in fragile states outside the area of the member organization, it does not represent the people whose security it governs.

Kaldor assumes, as do the supporters of enlightened autocracy, that the legitimacy of protection by these Western institutions comes from the quality of their operations rather than from their agency or local ownership:[3]

> [T]he new cosmopolitan troops will have to be professionalized. Since they are likely to comprise multilateral forces, integrated command systems, joint exercises and standard rates of pay and conditions would need to be introduced. The new cosmopolitan troops have to become the legitimate bearers of arms. They have to know and respect the laws of war and follow a strict code of conduct. Reports of corruption, of violations of human rights have to be properly investigated. Above all, the motivations of these new forces have to be incorporated into a wider concept of cosmopolitan right. (Kaldor, 2012, p. 131)

Kaldor even explicitly rejects the idea of consent of the ruled – thus going diametrically against the social contract vision of the original cosmopolitan theory that Immanuel Kant developed (Kant, 1996, pp. 90–91). In her cosmopolitanism: 'unqualified consent is impossible; otherwise there would be no need for peacekeeping forces. If, for example, protection of humanitarian convoys is based on consensus, then this can be negotiated as easily and perhaps more effectively by unarmed UN agencies or NGOs' (Kaldor, 2012, p. 126).

Texts by theorists of 'new wars' (Duffield, 2001; Gilbert, 2003; Kaldor, 1999; Malešević, 2008; Mello, 2010) can also be classified into the academic plane of the discourse strand on protection. Here, conflicting parties are mainly opportunistic actors rather than plaintiffs whose grievances should be addressed to end conflicts (Chinkin and Kaldor, 2017; Duffield, 2001;

Mello, 2010; Van Creveld, 1991). Consequently, the prevention of violence and protection of civilians is largely a question of peace enforcement and enforcement of humanitarian values. 'The analysis of new wars suggests that what is needed is not peacekeeping but enforcement of cosmopolitan norms, i.e. enforcement of international humanitarian and human rights law' (Kaldor, 1999, pp. 124–5).

The idea of enforcement of cosmopolitan norms by unilateral coalitions comes very close to the rhetoric of Western powers and the justification of protection wars. Yet, I do acknowledge that many theorists and politicians that could be considered contributors to this discourse strand have objected to the ways in which protective military operations have been conducted. Most scholars, including some of the main theorists of cosmopolitan protection, have criticized some of these operations (Bellamy, 2006), showing that they were not an appropriate reaction to the violence of new wars (Kaldor, 2012, pp. 159–61) or indeed, denying that they were humanitarian interventions at all (Kaldor, 2003, p. 134).

Furthermore, I will acknowledge the differences between the cosmopolitan and new war approaches to protection and between the approach of these two theoretical positions and the political approach of the main interventionist powers using the cosmopolitan argument. Still, there are important commonalities and interactions in these debates, thus it is possible to view them as part of the same discourse strand on protection.

Many of the core writings on new wars and cosmopolitanism resonate with the political debate in their unproblematic approach to the agency of protection. Legitimacy in protection is understood as a function of the merits of the operation and the cosmopolitan objectives of its actors. It is not related to the representativeness of the actors involved with global protection of people. In this way, the scholarship has implicitly repeated the arguments of enlightened authoritarianism and governance for the people, but not by the people.

THE COMMITMENT TO PROTECT AND THE NATURALNESS OF WESTERN LEADERSHIP IN PROTECTION

One can read in the speeches of US presidents that 'protection wars' were justified in part by the necessity of protecting the suffering people of the fragile states of the Third World. The cosmopolitan interest of protecting civilians, people that did not belong to 'our group' in any other sense than as fellow human beings, was part of the justification: in President Bush's words 'we're not only in a mission to protect our own security, we're on a humanitarian mission that will free young girls to be able to realize their dreams' (G.W. Bush, 2009a, p. 350).

US presidents after the mid-1990s consider it natural that the United States, its allies, a coalition the US has managed to gather for the mission of protection, or at least Americans together with a government they are supporting, will be included as the leading actors involved in protection. As can be seen in Figure 7.1, this was less the case during the George H.W. Bush presidency (1989–93), the first Clinton presidential term (1993–97), or the first two years of his second term (1997–1999). In the first Gulf War, in Somalia, and especially in Bosnia and Rwanda, for example, Bush Sr and Clinton had emphasized the role of the UN and its coordination of the rules so that the US would not be 'killing. . .the very people we're there trying to protect' (Clinton, 1994d, p. 734). However, something happened after that. The centrality of the UN and other representative agencies declined drastically in presidential papers (see Figure 7.1) and the wordings of US presidents started reflecting the idea of the naturalness of US, rather than UN, leadership.

In general, the issue of agency was not much addressed in protection speech. However, in the re-election campaign of George W. Bush, the fact that John Kerry, the Democratic candidate, suggested that the US should consult representative international organizations before launching military operations outside its borders forced President Bush to take up the question of agency in his speeches. While not presenting elaborate arguments for unilateralism, he rejected Kerry's idea of a 'global test' for US operations 47 times altogether in the speeches collected in the *Public Papers of the President* during his campaign. He considered it somehow ridiculous and impractical:

> Under this test, America would not be able to act quickly against threats because we'd be sitting around waiting for our grade from other nations. I have a different view. America will always work with our allies for security and peace, but the President's job is not to pass a 'global test'. (G.W. Bush, 2005e, p. 2383)

The reason for the naturalness of the US right to act unilaterally was partly related to the question of efficiency, but also to the identity of the United States, after September 11, 2001, as a victim. Both justifications will be discussed below.

Bush explicated the naturalness of Western agency in protection by referring to the agency of 'responsible governments', an expression that almost certainly not only refers to 'sane' leaders or democratic and human rights-protecting polities, but also political units that have historical and cultural affinities with Americans. This is suggested by the fact that when he spoke in London, after talking about responsible governments he immediately referred to the West and NATO:

> Our first choice and our constant practice is to work with other responsible governments. We understand as well that the success of multilateralism is not measured by adherence to forms alone, the tidiness of the process, but by the results we achieve to keep our nations secure. The second pillar of peace and security in our world is the willingness of free nations, when the last resort arrives, to restrain aggression and evil by force. . . The people have given us the duty to defend them, and that duty sometimes requires the violent restraint of violent men. In some cases, the measured use of force is all that protects us from a chaotic world ruled by force. Most in the peaceful West have no living memory of that kind of world. Yet in some countries, the memories are recent. The victims of ethnic cleansing in the Balkans, those who survived the rapists and the death squads, have few qualms when NATO applied force to help end those crimes. (G.W. Bush, 2004b, p. 1575)

Furthermore, Bush confused the national social contract between the state and the society with a global social contract. Even if Americans have democratically given the US president a 'duty to defend them', over 80 per cent of Iraqi citizens wanted US and Western forces out of their country (Hussain, 2016; Rayment, 2005).

In general, the pattern of US protection of global civilians was that new protective military operations relied on the agency of ad hoc coalitions that the US president felt were American-led. In most cases, the ad hoc agencies referred to UN Security Council (UNSC) resolutions for their international justification, always disregarding the question of agency in their legitimation. If the world organization agreed about the need to protect civilians somewhere, this still did not mean that they agreed about the Western implementation and US leadership in the protection. Often, the way in which protection was implemented was also something in which US presidents tended to assume great flexibility. The case of Iraq has been discussed elsewhere, while the protective operation in Libya is often seen as fully mandated by the UNSC. Yet, the conclusion that protection will necessarily mean regime change was something that was not subjected to Security Council decisions. On the contrary, President Obama concluded after a discussion with President Sarkozy of France: 'We agreed that we have made progress on our Libya campaign, but that meeting the U.N. mandate of civilian protection cannot be accomplished when Qadhafi remains in Libya directing his forces in acts of aggression against the Libyan people' (Obama, 2012c, p. 611). US presidents did recognize the problems that followed unilateralist operations, but instead of accepting that global decisions need global agency, the UN should simply give its mandate to US agency. President G.W. Bush claimed that the UN would not be relevant unless it mandated US action in Iraq, while President Obama tried to get a special arrangement (in relation to Kirgizia) to make its operations 'international' rather than national:

> One of the things that we discussed is creating a mechanism so that the international community can ensure that we have a peaceful resolution of the situation there, and that any actions that are taken to protect civilians are done so not under the flag of any particular country, but that the international community is stepping in. (Obama, 2011d, p. 864)

After the initial operation and regime change, the emphasis was on bilateral agency between the new leadership of the protected country and the United States. If we compare non-representative agency (US, allied, US ad hoc coalitions and US bilateral agency) with representative agency (UN and other international actors and agreements, such as the Organisation for the Prohibition of Chemical Weapons, International Criminal Court, Treaty on the Non-Proliferation of Nuclear Weapons, etc., where protection is collectively dealt with by the nations that are being protected), we can see that non-representative protection increased (Figure 7.1) at the same time that the US started to see protection of civilians as a key issue in world politics (Figure 7.2). This, again, coincides with the increase in fatalities during protection wars (see Chapter 4).

This is unexpected, on the one hand, given that US development cooperation in those countries where the US conducts its military protection emphasizes local ownership of operations. The discourse strand on

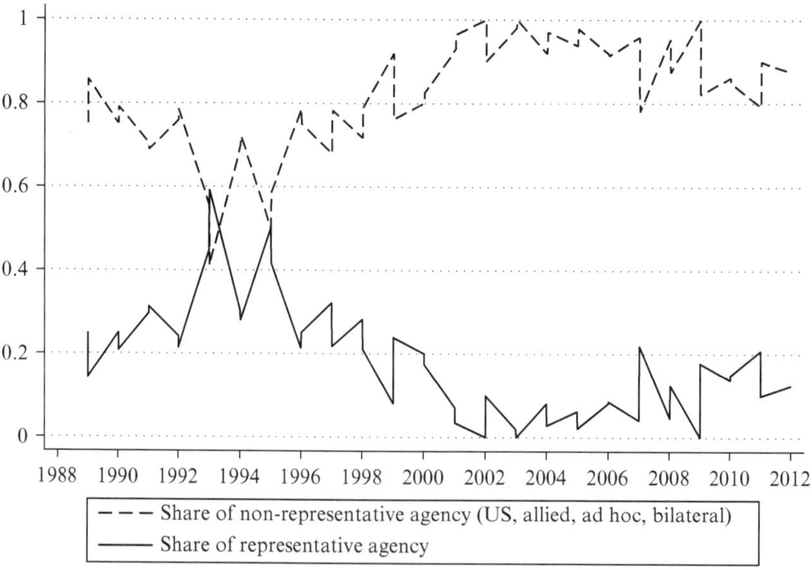

Figure 7.1 Agents of cosmopolitan protection: representative and non-representative protection

local ownership has not seriously penetrated the high-level US military debate, aside from speeches about the transitional nature of US military presence. According to President Bush, 'The government of Iraq and the future of your country will soon belong to you' (G.W. Bush, 2006c, p. 588). But the transition apparently did not belong to Iraqi people. Instead of seeking legitimacy for global protection through global participation and representation, protection has been legitimized by the nature of the activity, not the agency. According to President Barack Obama, 'our power grows through its prudent use. Our security emanates from the justness of our cause, the force of our example, the tempering qualities of humility and restraint' (Obama, 2010b, p. 2). The more US presidents have talked about cosmopolitan protection, the less they have talked about the United Nations; the more they have talked about crimes against humanity, the less they have talked about the International Criminal Court (of which they have refused to be a member).

All this seems contradictory. Apparently, central discourse strands of democracy and protection do not meet and interact in a presidential speech. Once this contradiction has been revealed, the next step is to trace the discursive processes that made this unilateralist development of protection justified for Americans.

THE PATH TO JUSTIFIED UNILATERALISM IN THE PROTECTION OF GLOBAL CIVILIANS

There is no conspiracy that explains the discursive path from post-Cold War conditions to the unilateral practice of protection as a conscious plan. Rather, it seems the path is only partly planned and mostly a result of interaction between international planning (agency) and material realities and social structures.

The discursive path to protection wars starts with conceptual conventions regarding the word 'protection'. These conventions smuggle the idea of a distinction between objects and subjects as a natural reality into the protection discourse strand. This idea was not challenged in the political discourse plane partly due to the entanglement of the discourse strand with apolitical discourse strands on crime, victimhood and global consensus, which were introduced quite consciously to serve the purpose of justifying protection. Interaction between the discourse and both national and international audiences pushed the discourse on the one hand, towards lesser respect for national sovereignty in violent anarchic countries and on the other, towards an exceptionally heroic unilateralist role played by the United States. Finally, international norms and nationalist and cosmopolitan pressures were reconciled by use of an ambiguous agency. The agents of protection were named 'international protection forces' – or something comparable that could be presented to national audiences as something controlled by the United States, while still giving an impression of allegiance to UN control when talking to international audiences. It seems that the referent objects of protection were involved only when the original military operations had been completed and the military presence had become more permanent. I will now reconstruct the path to justified unilateralism in cosmopolitan protection, step by step.

THE UNILATERALIST GRAMMAR OF 'PROTECTION'

The concept of protection, which is part of the internal logic of the discourse strand on cosmopolitan protection, is grammatically bound to an interpretation where someone is protected by someone. The identity of the subject and object are grammatically separate, which, in some discourse analyses, has been seen as a source of the naturalization of the binary framework of objects and subjects of protection (Muehlenhoff, 2017; Parashar, 2009). While according to feminist scholars this framework is gendered (weak women need to be protected by strong men), it is also race-specific and/or neocolonial in the international practice of protection (Connell, 2007; Tickner, 2001, p. 49). Because of underdevelopment in the developing world and because of the weakness of Third World states, there is a 'white man's burden' to protect the Third World. This logic focuses on the benefits to the object of protection, but hides the fact that it takes away the agency of the citizens of Iraq, Yemen, Afghanistan or Syria, since they are just objects of protection. The opinions of Iraqi people were occasionally measured in polls carried out by the defence ministries of the US and the UK (Hussain, 2016; Rayment, 2005) but the results (almost unanimous condemnation of the protective operation) were paid no attention.

Because of the unilateralist, undemocratic framings of the protection discourse strand, it is interesting to see how the general framing of foreign policy as protection developed in the post-Cold War period (Figure 7.2).

Genocide in Rwanda and Bosnia and the attack on September 11, 2001 interacted with the discourse strand on protection, making protection more central to politics. The discourse strand on protection also framed the reality of these events, making Rwandans, Bosnians and all victims of terror objects of protection.

It is interesting to note that the discourse strand on protection was also greatly utilized in the effort to legitimize legal changes – the 'Terrorist

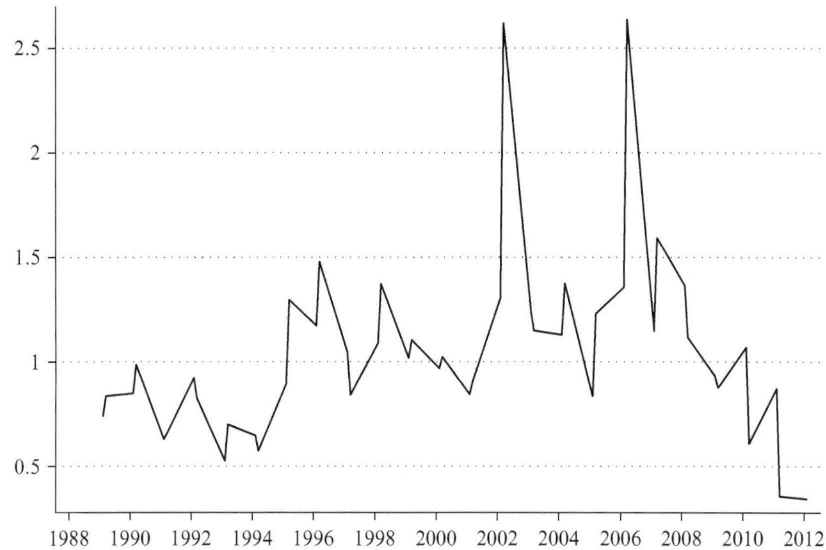

Figure 7.2 Centrality of protection – frequency of the word 'protect' (per 1000)

Surveillance Program', the continuation of the 'Patriot Act' and the CIA interrogation programme – that enabled 'professionals of security' to do their job and protect US citizens in 2006. In 2006, President Bush continued to depoliticize these 'tools of professionals' and appeal to the need to 'protect you'. Bush used expressions referring to the need to 'protect you' and the 'tools' needed for it by 'professionals' more than 200 times in 2006, almost four times more often than during the previous year. During the latter half of the year, Bush mentioned protection, referring either to protection of the nation, allies or global civilians (mostly Iraqis and Afghans) altogether 762 times. This demonstrates the centrality of 'protection' for reaction to threats and for Bush's argument for the legal 'tools' needed for security.

MAKING AGENCY IRRELEVANT: INNOCENCE, CRIMINALIZATION OF THE ENEMY, AND THE END OF HISTORY

If the grammar of protection creates an implicit distinction between objects and subjects of protection, this gendered and racialized implicit distinction was never explicitly challenged. This was partly due to the fact that the question of agency was made irrelevant by three discursive entanglements. These entanglements took place between discourse strands on protection on the one hand, and on crime, innocence and consensus on the other. With these entanglements, protection became self-evidently just – it was guided by universally accepted, uncontroversial principles. As such, the agent did not exercise political power in protection – it simply followed undisputable rules and enforced 'humanitarian norms'.

The first entanglement emerged in the new analysis of the perpetrators of violence. There was an assumption that the 'rogue quality' of enemy groups, dictators or states was indisputable. Enemies are criminals – as if there always had been a law and only one universal way to interpret, apply and enforce it – and thus they will have to be brought to justice. According to the oft-repeated phrase, enemies of the US in the Middle East:

> [. . .]are people that you just cannot reason with. You can't negotiate with them. Therapy is not going to work with them. [Laughter] They're coldblooded people. That's the way they are. And we have a solemn responsibility to the American people to bring them to justice. (G.W. Bush, 2005c, p. 1317)

But the idea of a criminal enemy was not just a metaphor, it was often taken very literally. Kaldor refers (approvingly) to Major General Raymond T. Odiero, Commander of the US Army's 4th Infantry Division, in her conclusion that the enemies of US protection wars were not people who were politically opposed to the US military occupation of their land but that they were petty criminals and contract killers: 'When we first got here, we believed it was about $100 to conduct an attack and $500 if you are successful. We now believe that it's somewhere between $1000 and $2000 if you conduct an attack and between $3000 and $5000 if you are successful'. According to Odiero, 70–80 per cent of captured insurgents were ordinary criminals (Kaldor, 2012, p. 165; see also p. 2). The identity of the police official who catches criminals is irrelevant, and if the law was already created in a fair political process, then the role of protectors of people against criminals is not a role that needed justification.

The concept of 'rogue state' (Raymond Tanter, then a member of the US Security Council, might have been the first to use this concept in relation to US foreign policy; see Tanter, 1998) expands this idea of a criminal enemy to the level of states. The practice of calling insurgents that fight US troops in the context of warfare 'terrorists' suggests the same; although the Department of State defines terrorists as people who target civilians, not US soldiers,[4] in other contexts, US officials sometimes also define terrorism as something that takes place outside the context of warfare.

The criminal and terroristic nature of those opponents of the US makes the agency of protection irrelevant and non-political. There is no need to negotiate with criminals, no need to give them any ownership of the norms and order one is enforcing.

Another way of making protection apolitical and the agent of protection irrelevant and uncontroversial, both in the theory of new wars and in the US political debate, is to focus on the innocence of the victims of those that protection has tried to oppose (tyrants and terrorists). When someone is being raped or murdered, there is no time to consider who would be the proper actor to offer help. Yet, the protector defines the political terms of safety, and chooses the values and people to be protected.

President George H.W. Bush uses this rhetorical method of apoliticization by focusing on the 'innocent' in his treatment of Iraq after the Iraqi invasion of Kuwait. He says:

> We must send a signal to any would-be Saddam Husseins that the world will not tolerate tyrants who violate every standard of civilized behaviour – invading, bullying, and swallowing whole a peaceful neighbour. We will not tolerate the raping and the brutalizing and the kidnaping and the killing of innocent civilians. (G.H.W. Bush, 1991, pp. 1668–9)

Here the focus of attention is on whether or not to tolerate the raping and brutalizing of the innocent, not on whether it is the United States that would need to tolerate or not tolerate something in the Iraqi reality. The frequency per 1000 of the word 'innocent' and words stemming from it have a strong statistically significant and very significant non-parametric correlation[5] with the frequency per 1000 of the word 'protection' (and words stemming from it) and a more modest association with the number of US military operations (per 1000 frequency of 'protection': 0.6240, $p \sim 0.0000$, $n = 47$; number of existing military operations: 0.4474, $p = 0.0016$, $n = 47$). Thus, the ontology articulated by innocence speech, where the agency of protection is irrelevant since terrorists and tyrants are killing innocent people, is clearly associated with military operations and the discourse strand on protection.

Third, the trivialization of the agency of protection and the justification for unilateral cosmopolitan protection was created with a frame referring to a global political consensus. It is born out of the history of the collapse of communism and the rise of liberal democracy and free market economy as the final, victorious ideology. If there is only one universally agreed-upon ideology to promote, its promotion becomes apolitical. Consequently, the agency of that protection becomes a non-issue. In the academic debate, this idea is often associated with the 'end of history' thesis (Fukuyama, 1992) and the history of the collapse of challenges to liberal capitalist democracy. President George H.W. Bush's new world order represented this optimism:

> The last decade of this century marks the beginning of a new era, the gateway to a new millennium of freedom, and yet the outcome is not predestined. It depends on our continued solidarity as an alliance and as an American people committed to providing leadership, protection, and encouragement for this process of peaceful transformation. (G.H.W. Bush, 1990, p. 1608)

The same idea that undisputable universal values make protection apolitical and make the question of who protects what kind of order a non-issue, still justifies unilateralist military operations. President Barack Obama was very clear about this in his justification of the role of the ad hoc international coalition and the way in which it decided to conduct its protection in Libya (even though it was objected to by two UNSC veto powers, Russia and China): 'freedom and self-determination are not unique to one culture – they are universal values. . .in Libya, where the fight for freedom was answered with the threat of a massacre, we joined an international coalition to protect the lives and aspirations of the Libyan people' (Obama, 2012a, p. v).

IMPACT OF NATIONAL AND INTERNATIONAL AUDIENCES ON THE DISCOURSE STRAND ON PROTECTION

There were two institutional contextual settings with which the discourse strand on protection interacted. One was the nationalist setting that enabled and constrained protection in US foreign policy. The other was the new power-political situation in the United Nations after the collapse of the Soviet Union.

When speaking about protection, US presidents had to convince their American constituencies to keep their mandate, they had to abide by US law, and they needed resources from the US Congress. The institutional context of the discourse strand on protection was fundamentally national. On the one hand, this made it important for the presidents to focus on the protection of the US rather than the protection of people in faraway places (cosmopolitan protection; see Chapter 6). However, already from the beginning of the post-Cold War era, presidents considered leadership in world affairs a US national interest and thus national institutions not only pushed the president towards national selfishness, but also to unilateralism. Obama demonstrated this clearly when he defined his institutional role: 'When I took office, I pledged to do whatever was required to protect the American people and restore American leadership in the world' (Obama, 2011b, p. 1543).[6] Due to the association between US power and US interest, it seems clear that the US presidents were pushed by their national constituencies towards greater unilateralism. If we look at the collections of US presidential papers from periods when there were elections and those from periods when there were no elections, it is clear that presidents emphasized US unilateral agency in cosmopolitan protection more during election campaign periods. Elections and the relative frequency of references to unilateral agency in cosmopolitan protection are significantly correlated (congressional elections: 0.3520, $p = 0.0152$, $n = 47$; presidential elections 0.2951, $p = 0.0440$, $n = 47$; presidential re-elections: 0.3049, $p = 0.0372$, $n = 47$).[7]

However, at the beginning of the 1990s, US presidents were unable to legitimize unilateral military operations outside the US. Presidents simply could not protect civilians abroad without the framework of the United Nations. Thus, the operations related to the first Gulf War, the Bosnian war and the Rwandan genocide were much more restrained by norms of sovereignty and controlled by the United Nations (see Figure 7.3).

However, the word 'sovereign' all but disappeared from political vocabulary towards the end of the 1990s and reappeared in the new millennium as something with a very different definition, now emphasizing the sovereignty of citizens rather than that of the state alone. The first signs of this decline came from a very anti-unilateralist direction, that of the United Nations. The new situation where Russia and the US were 'on the same side' and did not need to veto each other's UNSC resolution proposals gave rise to optimism. Perhaps it was possible in the post-Cold War era to prevent violence within dictatorial, fragile states using the mandate of the United Nations. The UN's *Agenda for Peace*, written by Secretary-General Boutros Boutros-Ghali, blamed conflicting parties for violence and encouraged third party intervention in conflicts: 'With greater unity has come leverage and persuasive power to lead hostile parties towards negotiations' (United Nations General Assembly, 1992, para. 35). The United Nations Development Programme's articulation of 'human security' some years later supported the idea of lowering state borders by focusing attention on security of global civilians rather than that of states (United Nations Development Programme, various years).

The tone of *Agenda for Peace* was also such that it affected the dominant idea of conflicts. While conflicts had previously been seen as reactions to grievances, this report saw conflicting parties as perpetrators. Prevention of violence was suddenly simple, but something conflicting parties often resisted:

> If conflicts have gone unresolved, it is not because techniques for peaceful settlement were unknown or inadequate. The fault lies first in the lack of political will of parties to seek a solution to their differences through such means as are suggested in Chapter VI of the Charter, and second, in the lack of leverage at the disposal of a third party if this is the procedure chosen. (United Nations General Assembly, 1992, para. 35)

The report also introduces the intrusive idea of peace enforcement. Finally, in paragraph 19 it prescribes democratic principles of governance, providing the first hints of the ideologies that could, in the post-Cold War era, justify intrusive operations of protection.

However, the report did not go any further towards dismantling the norm of sovereignty in international relations. Even though it accused conflicting parties and encouraged UNSC intervention, paragraph 30 did reaffirm the world organization's commitment to the norm of sovereignty. Furthermore, the report, especially paragraphs 44 and 45, systematically refers to the agency of the UN Security Council in decisions on peace enforcement and the use of force to restore peace, reaffirming ideas on the use of military force as stipulated by Article VII of the UN Charter. Thus, UN optimism and the UN's *Agenda for Peace* did not introduce unilateralism. The UN General Assembly reinforced the anti-unilateralist idea in its resolution soon after the publication of *Agenda for Peace* by emphasizing UN leadership in keeping order and enforcing peace in the world (United Nations General Assembly, 1992).

The texts of President Clinton in the mid-1990s, and again just before the protective operation against Serbia, show that UN optimism and the related active and more intrusive politics for peace and protection – as well as the idea that it is possible to insist on democratic principles from another state in its internal governance – survived failures of UN protection. However, due to the bloodshed in Rwanda in 1994 and in Bosnia in 1995, the idea of UN leadership weakened. As can be seen in Figure 7.1, the frequency of the mention of representative agents such as the UN as agents of protection had increased since 1989 and up until the two massive UN failures, but it declined for more than a decade after that. This can also be seen in Figure 7.3, in the near disappearance of the term 'United Nations' from US presidential papers until the end of 2002, when a UN resolution was attempted but not attained for the war against Saddam Hussein.[8] The combination of a disappearing reliance on the UN and an increasing eagerness to enforce peace and protect people in dictatorships led the discourse that created protection wars.

After the two UN failures, already during the aftermath of the conflict in Bosnia and the implementation of the Bosnian peace agreement, new methods began to emerge, pairing the need for efficiency that US

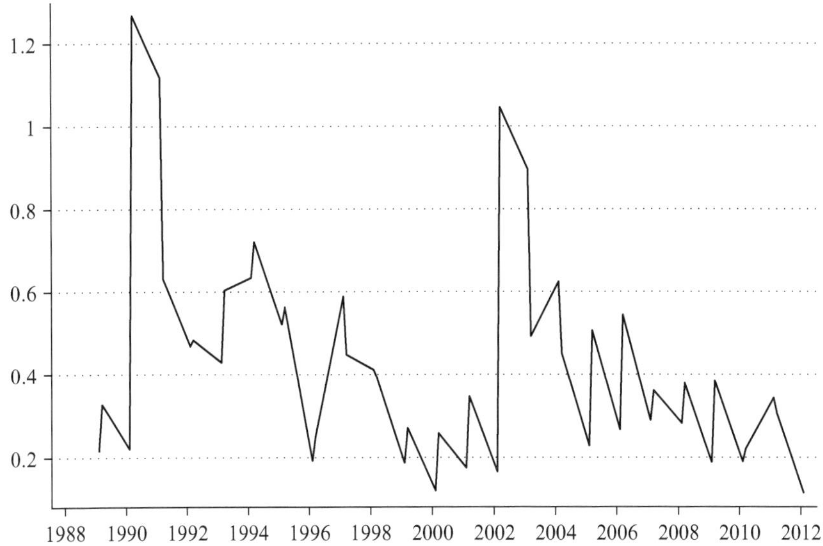

Figure 7.3 Centrality of the United Nations: frequency (per 1000) of the term 'United Nations'

leadership could offer and the legitimacy that only UN agency could provide. This formula was to be guided by the principles of the UN but would seek agency independent from the UN for more efficient exercise of power:

> Along with our allies we have taken a series of strong steps to strengthen the United Nations mission, to prevent further attacks on safe areas, and to protect innocent civilians: NATO has decided it will counter an assault on the remaining safe areas with sustained and decisive use of air power. Our response will be broad, swift, and severe, going far beyond the narrow attacks of the past. For the first time, military commanders on the ground in Bosnia have been given operational control over such actions, paving the way for fast and effective NATO response. (Clinton, 1996d, p. 1254)

This was the slippery slope to unilateral practices that were seen as illegitimate and imperialist by opponents of US protection. The fact that so many of the people the US wanted to protect sided with this view escalated the number of fatalities in conflicts that were meant to be controlled through external protection. The role and control of the UN was greater at first, but it gradually decreased, and already in the operation in Iraq in 2003 the UN role was very weak. In fact, most international lawyers would probably claim that the US-led coalition not only ignored the UN, but also explicitly went against the path the UNSC had prescribed.

AMBIGUOUS AGENCY AS A SOLUTION

The initiation of ambiguous international agency was a new strategy of the Clinton administration. In many places, but especially in Kosovo, Clinton created institutions that were collective, but not representative. The legitimacy of such institutions was based on inclusive policies, but not on inclusive agency. For example, Clinton created the International Security Force, which he (and not the UN, the Kosovars or Serbia, of which Kosovo was a province) could also invite countries to join, if they could work under NATO leadership. This non-representative, but neutral, even-handed security force was intended 'to return all the refugees to their rightful homes and their neighborhoods and their communities, under conditions of peace, and then have a secure environment that would also protect the Serb minority within Kosovo' (Clinton, 2000b, p. 568).

In Africa, Clinton developed a normative regime against threats to civilians by launching a summit meeting with the president of Uganda: the Entebbe Summit for Peace and Prosperity (Clinton, 1999a). In Latin America, Clinton's approach to cosmopolitan protection outside the UN was more bilateral (Clinton, 1999c, p. 578). The big change was that he replaced the UN as an agent of cosmopolitan protection with ad hoc coalitions that the US had the power to invite countries to join.

The principles of operation were created by the United Nations Security Council, but their implementation was then outsourced to or taken over by various US coalitions:

> The U.N. Security Council authorized member states to establish the international security presence in Kosovo in U.N. Security Council Resolution 1244 of June 10, 1999, for an initial period of 12 months. The mission of KFOR [Kosovo Force] is to provide a continued military presence in order to deter renewed hostilities; verify and, if necessary, enforce the terms of the Military Technical Agreement (MTA) between NATO and the Federal Republic of Yugoslavia (FRY); enforce the terms of the agreement of the Kosovo Liberation Army (KLA) to demilitarize and reintegrate itself into civil society; provide operational direction to the newly established Kosovo Protection Corps; and contribute to a secure environment to facilitate the work of the U.N. Interim Administration Mission in Kosovo (UNMIK) by providing, until UNMIK assumes these functions, for public security and appropriate control of the borders. . . The KFOR forces are under NATO command and control and rules of engagement. (Clinton, 2000a, p. 2304)

The implementation of arms control was also gradually shifted to become the responsibility of NATO and ad hoc US allied coalitions (see, for example, Clinton's confusion in the context of Iraq in Clinton, 2000g, p. 620). Concurrently, the interpretation and enforcement of UN Security Council resolutions suddenly became the responsibility of the United States. UNSC Resolution 1244 reconfirmed the full sovereignty of Yugoslavia in Kosovo, yet it could be interpreted in a way that allowed the US to oust Yugoslavia's own police force and army from Kosovo – and even gain 'day-to-day operative direction' of forces developed out of a separatist army. Regarding enforcement, President Clinton argued that:

> Mr. Milosevic refuses to abide by United Nations resolutions. So I'm trying to get the support not only of the leaders of both parties in our Congress but also of our Allies in NATO, to take aggressive action to protect those people's lives and restore peace there and stability, so that we won't have to do more there down the road and so that innocent lives can be saved. (Clinton, 1999b, p. 1760)

Also in Iraq, the US rhetoric used terms that sounded as if governance was using indigenous Iraqi or UN authorized structures (see, for example, G.W. Bush, 2004d, p. 1546). However, the Iraqi Governing Council (IGC), the provisional government of Iraq from July 13, 2003 to June 1, 2004, was established by and served under the US-led Coalition Provisional Authority (CPA). In Afghanistan, the Afghan Interim Authority was established after the US operation Enduring Freedom had toppled the Taliban government. It was established by the UN-sponsored Bonn Conference, with selected participants from all those anti-Taliban groups that the occupying US-led forces could identify.

A quantitative investigation reveals that the association between the number of US protective operations and the centrality of ad hoc coalitions as agents of cosmopolitan protection in presidential papers is relatively strong, and highly significant. If measured in absolute numbers, the non-parametric correlation between the frequency in which cosmopolitan protection was referred to as something that an ad hoc agent would do and the number of US operations was 0.6272 ($p \sim 0.0000$, $n = 47$) and between ad hoc agency and the number of new operations 0.4158 ($p = 0.037$, $n = 47$).[9] Even though random timetable-related issues obscure discursive trends in monthly analysis, the frequency of ad hoc agency references is very significantly associated with the number of ongoing US military operations (0.4009, $p \sim 0.0000$, $n = 282$).[10]

However, the association between ambiguous ad hoc operations that looked like UN operations but were US-led and the launching of new operations becomes more significant when we check the time during which this association was strongest (Figure 7.4). It seems that the ambiguous speech that hid Western unilateralism was crucial especially during the first operations that normalized the role of US-led coalitions of the willing. It all started with the extremely aggressive marketing of the idea of an ambiguous agency in Kosovo that was under NATO, but yet, still somehow international

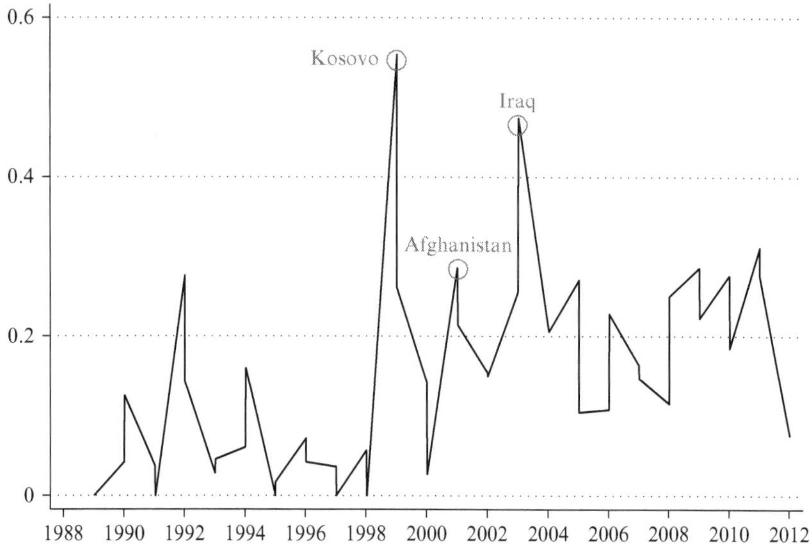

Figure 7.4 Development of US-led ad hoc agency of cosmopolitan protection

and UN-mandated. The fact that after the terrorist attack on September 11, 2001, the US was an innocent victim, made it easier to justify the protective operation in Afghanistan, and this may explain why the peak after 9/11 was not as high as the one in March 2003, when President Bush was able to launch a protective operation that he tried to sell as one with a UN mandate (and US leadership in implementation), but which did not have the support of all the UNSC veto powers, and which is usually considered by experts in international law to be illegal. After there was a practice of ambiguous, ad hoc agency, there was no longer as much need for words and justifying speech.

If we want to see whether ad hoc agency was a replacement for representative UN agency, we should not look at percentages but at absolute numbers because the share of ad hoc agency is conceptually negatively linked with the share of representative agency. Here, the association is still negative (even if statistically not significantly), even though one might think that the strategy of making ad hoc agency look like UN agency when legitimizing it to international audiences, and as a US/NATO operation when justifying it to voters and Congress, would make the association positive. Furthermore, when looking at absolute numbers one might assume that all agency of cosmopolitan protection would rise at times of humanitarian operations, yet this is not the case. Figure 7.5 shows how the peak of argumentation of

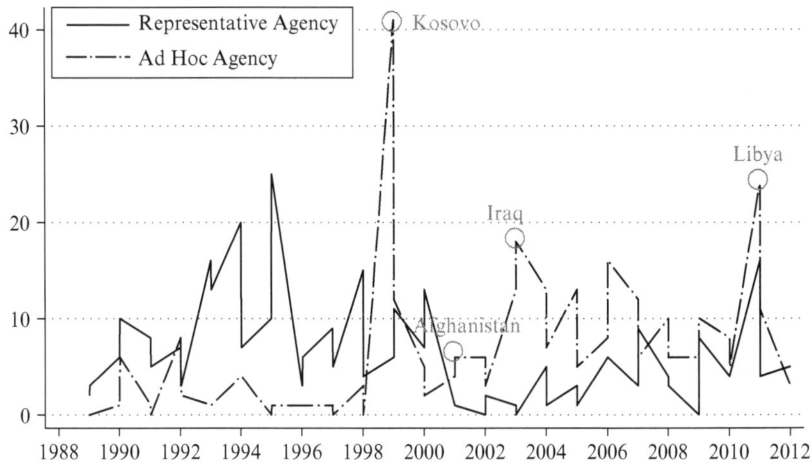

Figure 7.5 US-led ambiguous agency and UN-led representative agency: absolute frequencies

ad hoc agency reduced the primacy of UN agency in cosmopolitan protection. It seems quite clear that the introduction of ad hoc coalitions came at the expense of UN agency in cosmopolitan protection.

Only during the Libyan operation did the president of the United States talk about the United Nations Security Council as an agent and regard the NATO-led coalition as an implementer of a UNSC mandate. Yet, even there, two veto powers in the UNSC, Russia and China, felt that the mandate they had allowed to pass in the UNSC was not consistent with the operations that the NATO-led coalition conducted.

When there is ambiguity, different sides tend to interpret things differently. This feeds into both parties' overconfidence in their justification of their own position and thus escalation of conflict (Blainey, 1988; Johnson, 2004). If the US-led coalition is international (i.e., members other than the US participate) and relates its mission to UN resolutions or principles, there is a temptation on the US side to interpret this as global agency. Resistance to such an operation is then seen by the implementors of protection as resistance to the cosmopolitan, global will. At the same time, people on the receiving end of US-led military operations see US, UK and allied airplanes and do not interpret the operation as cosmopolitan or global. Obviously, Iraqis, Afghans and others are then convinced of the imperialist nature of the mission, rather than seeing it as an implementation of the will of humanity. The number of annual observations of conflict fatalities is too low (24) to make reliable observations on this basis, but if we look at the association between the number of protection war fatalities and the share of ad hoc agency in utterances on cosmopolitan protection we could find a relatively strong and statistically highly significant association (0.6634).

While initiation of new operations is dominated by speech emphasizing the agency of ambiguous US-led coalitions, continuing control of the 'protected' states is also associated with bilateral agency in the papers of US presidents. The absolute number of utterances of bilateral agency in cosmopolitan protection in presidential papers is not significantly correlated with the number of new operations (i.e., objects of cosmopolitan protection were neither asked nor involved when the operation started). However, bilateral agency of cosmopolitan protection in presidential papers is very significantly associated with the number of existing protective military operations. The non-parametric correlation between the two is 0.5593 ($p = 0.0000$, $n = 47$). If one looks at the relative share of bilateral agency, the correlation is weaker but still significant (0.4154, $p = 0.0037$, $n = 47$). The share of bilateral agency is also associated with the number of fatalities, but since the data on fatalities are annual, the number of observations is too low to make reliable conclusions.

CONCLUSIONS

Democracy has been an important factor in the cosmopolitan agenda, and the protection of civilians from ruthless dictators is a key focus. Yet, the theory has been ambiguous regarding the agency of protection – as if it was unimportant. The idea that policy is important and agency is not, is alien to democratic thinking. Thus, the blindness of cosmopolitan international relations and new wars theory is surprising. Despite cosmopolitan critique of protection wars (often coming long after it becomes clear that a conflict has escalated), and despite the obvious evidence of ulterior motives of Western military operations, the question of agency has not become an issue on the political or the scholarly platform of the discourse strand on protection. Theories of cosmopolitanism and new wars cannot be blamed as the foundation of politically disastrous incidences of global protection. Still, the ambiguity of these theories regarding agency must be part of the reason that cosmopolitan protection has not developed a global sharing of ownership for global protection of civilians. The agency of protection, the agency of defining who to protect and the question of which values to protect, constitute a dangerous blind spot in cosmopolitan theory. The idea of democracy and the Kantian version of cosmopolitanism that commits to the general contours of the social contract tradition advise us against ignoring agency in cosmopolitan governance. Only ownership of cosmopolitan norms – and an enforcement implemented by the objects of such enforcement – allows the norms their legitimacy amongst the people affected by them. If operations lack legitimacy, the enforcement of cosmopolitan values and the protection of civilians will have to focus on destroying dissent against something that we view as cosmopolitanism. However, such protection through destruction is viewed as imperialism not only by the enemies of protection, but often also by its objects. Thus, protection escalates rather than alleviates violence, as has happened in the protection wars of the new millennium.

Cosmopolitan theorists need to take the authoritative representative agency seriously. Even if cosmopolitanism draws from popular solidarity and global civil society, global representative institutions are needed to make it work. Cosmopolitan theory should therefore draw upon the cosmopolitanization of popular solidarity and loyalty, but it should include the question of a representative agency of global protection in its agenda and consider the enforcement of humanitarian norms as a necessary component of cosmopolitan progress.

NOTES

1. Beck (2006); Bray (2009); Brown (2000); Gilmore (2014); Habermas (2001); Hayden (2005); Kaldor (2013); Linklater (2011) When I talk about cosmopolitan theory in this book, I refer to these theorists of international relations, rather than to the original philosophers of cosmopolitanism.
2. For this critique, related to the partisan statutes of Western defence organization and the universalism of cosmopolitan missions, see Carati (2017) and Cunliffe (2010).
3. In this book, local ownership refers to a quality of projects that the local actor genuinely feels is its own. Unlike Ejdus, who defines local ownership as 'responsibilization for externally designed objectives', this book treats the concept as more genuine (Ejdus, 2017, p.28).
4. See Title 22 of the United States Code, Section 2656f(d) referred to in US Department of State (2004).
5. Most of the variables used for the analysis of this book are not normally distributed, thus the use of non-parametric correlations throughout this book.
6. Carati argues that the contradiction between NATO's partisan mandate and cosmopolitan universalism does not make allied protection any less problematic (Carati, 2017).
7. However, the association disappears when investigated with absolute numbers of sentences where the United States is the sole agent of cosmopolitan protection.
8. However, the frequency of the term 'United Nations' peaked in presidential papers, not during the genocides of the mid-1990s, but at the time of the first Gulf War.
9. If we look at relative frequencies, the association is slightly more modest (0.5529, p = 0.0001 and 0.3459, p = 0.0173). The investigation of absolute numbers focuses on how the amount of attention to the idea of ambiguous ad hoc agency is related to action, while the relational investigation focuses on how exactly such coalitions as agents of protection are seen as natural.
10. If we look at the share of references to ad hoc agency, the association is weaker: 0.3875, $p \sim 0.0000$, n = 260.

8. How did the preference for power-centric strategies emerge in cosmopolitan protection?

INTRODUCTION

While the problem of selfishness and unilateralism of 'cosmopolitan' operations deals with the question of why interventions are conducted, and who is conducting them, this chapter will deal with the question of how interventions are conducted. It deals with the preference for strategies to change someone else's behaviour to protect strangers over strategies to change one's own behaviour.

These preferred strategies emphasize power because power is required to change someone else's behaviour, and the obsession with changing someone else's behaviour is what anti-cosmopolitan discourse levels at cosmopolitan protection when talking about American or Western militarism and violence. There are two categorical alternatives to power-biased strategies. First, instead of changing enemy behaviour by using power, the US could change its own behaviour so that it could save more of the global strangers it intends to protect. This could be seen as a power-neutral category of strategies. Second, the US could protect by working with others to restrain its own and the enemy's power to injure (through arms control, peace negotiation, etc.). This would require constraints that reduce rather than increase power, and can thus be seen as a power-negative category of strategies.

The gun control debate, for example, deals with power-centric strategies and their alternatives. In President Trump's preferred power-biased strategy, people would maintain their power to shoot an offender for their own security. Obama's alternative strategy would be to constrain everyone's power to shoot by controlling arms sales. This would reduce the capacity of violent offenders and, of course, defenders too (*New York Times*, 2018). Connell treats the opposition to gun control in Australia and the movement that emphasized free gun ownership as a matter of human rights as an example of the defence of stereotypical masculinity. With guns seen, to use a cliché, as penis symbols, Connell likens the confiscation of guns in the stereotypical masculine debate to emasculation (Connell, 2005, pp. 212–16). This debate also suggests that we should be especially cautious of generalizations about 'Western discourse' on the basis of US presidential papers – the American debate on gun control demonstrates a more power-centric approach to security than can be found in other Western countries. Yet, my intention is not to assume that it is only US foreign policy that is power biased, because discourses that frame international relations constitute rationales for action for all foreign policy agents. Putin, for example, with his bear-wrestling, rodeo-riding and tough talk is certainly no exception.

As explained in Chapter 1, protection is coded as power biased (militarized) if something or someone needs to be protected against an intentional actor, either by deterring, destroying, incapacitating or weakening. Protection is coded as not power biased if protection does not affect the harming agent (offering asylum etc.); if action helps or facilitates protection directly, rather than affecting another agent's willingness and ability to threaten (offering aid for democratization is non-use of power, offering incentives to do so is use of power); if protection is targeting a non-intentional threat (poverty, disease, etc.); or if protection is by means of self-restraint (protecting democracy and improving relations by signing a mutual agreement, for example, the Helsinki Declaration, signed by 35 nations in 1975).

Power bias in protective interventions is sometimes analysed in the conceptual context of the distinction between old and new wars. Old wars are conflicts in which maximum power is exercised to destroy or subject the enemy to one's own will. Within this understanding of warfare, power is central. However, this Clausewitzian idea of warfare is, according to new war theorists, outdated. New wars are, as discussed in earlier chapters, those in which the context of violence is state weakness in a globalized world. There the main challenge is related to the building of structures of order that can control opportunistic violence (rather than simply destruction or subordination of the enemy) (Kaldor, 2012, p. 166).

Yet, a more explicit analysis of power-centricity exists in the feminist conceptualization of international politics. In feminist conceptualization, power bias is one of the features of stereotypical masculinity. Stereotypical masculinity in current security practice is not merely a materially reproduced feature – it is not caused by biological factors nor does power bias necessarily serve the material interests of states. Yet, the reality of continued masculine overrepresentation in security policies and the historical foundation of aggressive masculinity of men as defenders of families in primitive societies can be seen as the material foundations of power bias. According to Tickner, 'In today's world of about 190 states, less than 1 percent of presidents or prime ministers are women' (Tickner, 2004, p. 43).[1] '(I)f women's experiences were to be included, a radical redefinition of the field would have to take place' (Tickner, 1992, p. 5).

Today, however, all men are not doomed to stereotypically masculine behaviour, while women might also behave in a stereotypically masculine manner (Enloe, 2000, pp. 5–6; Tickner, 1992, p. 6). Stereotypical masculinity is not an essentialist masculine 'illness'. Masculinity for Enloe and Tickner (and for this chapter) is not what most men represent, but something that we have constructed as belonging to manliness. Furthermore, the hegemonic masculinity that feminists talk about is something that emerges as a naturalized default out of all the existing possible masculinities: 'Hegemonic masculinity is sustained through its opposition to various subordinated and devalued masculinities, such as homosexuality, and more important, through its relation to various devalued femininities' (Tickner, 1992, p. 6). Thus, stereotypical masculinity in feminist international relations theory is discursively reproduced, while both men and women perceive masculine conduct of security policies to be something that is biologically natural. While feminists (people critical of the naturality of masculine approaches) view world politics and the question of war and peace differently from the stereotypical masculine perspective, there is little difference between male and female perceptions on how questions of security should be handled (Tessler and Warriner, 1997). This is why some female leaders might be no different from their male counterparts in their assumptions that security issues should be handled the 'masculine' way.

EXISTING LITERATURE ON POWER-CENTRICITY IN COSMOPOLITAN PROTECTION

Power-centricity in security policies and in humanitarian intervention is often explained in the feminist literature as something that is inherited from the time when material conditions emphasized what feminist scholars call stereotypical masculinity. These historical material conditions were related to the biologically determined fact that only women can give birth and breastfeed children, and that before birth control women were either pregnant or caring for children during most of their adulthood (Gordon, 1997). This together with the separation of family from production during the period of industrialization meant that women were largely excluded from political life outside families (Jaggar, 1983, pp. 3–4). At the same time, the social reality of the production of security in primitive societies forced men to be prepared to incapacitate or destroy threats to family and clan. This created social practices that naturalized certain, power-centric identities for men and masculinity. These naturalized gender roles, however, have outlived the material and social contexts from which they emerged and created institutions, such as states, that reflect the societal power relationships of masculine dominance (Ball, 2014; Parpart and Zalewski, 2013; Tickner, 2001, p. 54). This is why fields of politics and foreign relations that have come to be seen as naturally masculine, tend to have these masculine, power-centric characteristics from which critical feminist security studies could emancipate us (Butler, 1990). 'Gender hierarchies that privilege men's knowledge and men's experiences. . .have formed the basis of most of our knowledge about international politics' (Tickner, 1992, p. xi). For Ann Tickner, one of the main characteristics of stereotypical masculinity in world politics is what I call in this book, power-centricity or power bias – the preference for strategies that change others' behaviour over strategies that change one's own behaviour (Tickner, 1992; Tickner has borrowed this idea of the relevance of a standpoint in the production of knowledge from the so-called 'standpoint feminists' – see, for example, Hartsock, 1998).

Cosmopolitan protection, which focuses on the security problems of weak state structures, has often been expected to represent a move from the stereotypical, state-centric, military type of masculinity in security policies to a more balanced approach (Hooper, 1998). The fact that cosmopolitan protection is focused on human security rather than state security is also a feature that Tickner considers as typical of feminist thinking on world affairs: 'whereas IR [international relations] has traditionally analysed security issues from a structural perspective or at the level of the state and its decision makers, feminists focus on how world politics can contribute to the insecurity of individuals, particularly marginalised and disempowered populations' (Tickner, 2001, p. 3). Primacy of human security over state security (which can, however, be an instrumental value) is also core in cosmopolitan and new war theories of world politics (Beck, 2006, p. 137; Habermas, 2000; Kaldor, 2003, p. 61). However, both Tickner and Kaldor suggest that the hardening of world politics after the terrorist attack on the US on September 11, 2001 has derailed this balancing tendency (Kaldor, 2012; Tickner, 2015).

According to Kaldor, the problem that caused the failure of protection in Iraq and Afghanistan was that the diagnosis the US prescription was based on was wrong: the US saw these wars as old Clausewitzian wars in which the intention was to impose one's will on the other by using superior military force. Also, the war on terror was aimed to be won simply by defeating the enemy (Kaldor, 2012, p. 166). Efforts at winning the hearts and minds in military operations worked to the opposite effect due to their power-biased approach (ibid., p. 165). 'Conventional military force cannot rebuild states. . .a serious civilian effort to reconstruct the state' was largely missing, especially in Iraq (ibid., p. 159). Instead of seeing power as a guarantee for security, feminist theory often assumes the opposite. According to Tickner, feminist international relations theory often focuses on security issues such as economic inequality and marginalized populations – that is, issues that do not even have an actor that needs to be destroyed or influenced (Tickner, 2001, p. 4). Security is often seen as threatened by violent structures rather than intentional agents, thus the focus is already that power to influence the threatening agent is not the solution. Furthermore, in feminist international relations theory, power is often a poor instrument of human security, and the lack of power may convince others of a lack of aggressive intentions, and this avoids provocation in the security environment (Tickner, 1992, pp. 62–3). Militarism and power-centricity are often seen as antithetical to individual security (Enloe, 2000; Tickner, 2001, p. 4): stereotypical masculinity that critical feminist theory (Zalewski, 2003) tries to denaturalize legitimizes war and militarization and this power-centric fact is seen as a problem rather than a solution to human security (Enloe, 2000; Tickner, 2001, p. 6).

Kaldor's analysis of what we call the military-minded, stereotypically masculine power bias also reveals the interactive logic of escalation, clearly seen in the empirical analysis of power bias in protective operations. If tension increases power-centricity, and the mutual willingness to deal with security issues by changing opponents' behaviour, even by force, it is clear that tension and the mutual power bias create a vicious cycle. In this vicious cycle, the knowledge of the preferability of power-centric approaches contributes to the mutual constitution in the interactive process between the 'protectors' and their enemies of legitimate violent strategies. This becomes clear if we compare the ways in which Chapters 4 and 5 reveal how both the United States and its enemies constitute their legitimate violence with the reference to each other's violence.

The futility of agent-centric 'security dilemma-insensitive' approaches to protection has already been revealed in the early stages of the development of security studies. And John Hertz (1950, 2003) has already revealed the collective irrationality of agent-centric strategies. When all agents of security bolster their security with power-centric approaches by increasing their individual military power, all actors end up worse off if the actors do not consider the structural impact of their individual strategies. Booth and Wheeler (2008) suggest, therefore, that security actors should be 'security dilemma sensitive' by considering the structural approaches of their individual strategies – by, for instance, trying to maximize their defensive power only or by negotiating power-restricting strategies with their enemies.

This kind of relational strategy would already come closer to the feminist approaches to security, but not far enough.[2] If the main focus could be placed on practices that were not power-centric at all – building relationships of mutual benefit, reducing structural violence, and building structures of just order – security dilemma could be avoided. If the rescue of Syrian civilians could be done through cooperative development efforts, common restraint or liberal immigration policies as a strategy, rather than the mutually violent effort of the US to change ISIS and Syrian government behaviour, of ISIS to change US and Syrian government behaviour and of the Syrian government to change ISIS and US behaviour, many lives could be saved.

MASCULINITY, AGGRESSION AND POWER BIAS IN COSMOPOLITAN PROTECTION

While unilateralism slowly crept into the discourse on protection after the failure of the UN to protect Bosnians and the Tutsis in Rwanda, and while selfishness was heightened by the experience of becoming a victim of global terror on 9/11, power bias has, nevertheless, been part of international relations and protection throughout history. Power-centricity increases when countries try to justify humanitarian operations, and undoubtedly events that require humanitarian action also focus attention on the need to use power and change the perpetrator's behaviour. While unilateralism and selfishness are not restricted to cosmopolitan protection or to the discourse that tries to legitimize intervention as cosmopolitan protection, power-centricity is a feature specific to the realm of security, as can be seen in Figure 8.1, which shows how often those clauses in US presidential papers that mention global civilians as referent objects of protection are power biased.

The way in which a crisis, in which humanitarian intervention is contemplated, fuels power bias and the way in which power-centricity fuels interventionist measures can be seen by comparing power-centric clauses that mention the name of one of the countries that were intervened in with all clauses (Table 8.1). While power-centricity is evident in 55 per cent of all cosmopolitan clauses (clauses that mention the word 'protect' and refer to global civilians) in US presidential papers, those clauses that refer to one of the intervened countries are power-centric in 74–100 per cent of the cases.[3]

Due to the consistent power-centricity and consistent association between it and the realm of security, it is possible to see highly significant and relatively strong statistical (non-parametric) associations between the discourse and military practices. In an annual investigation, the

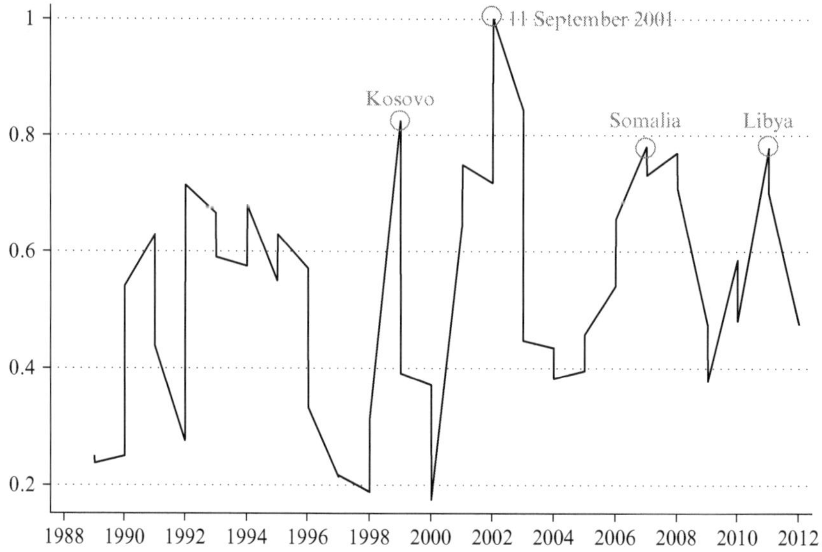

Figure 8.1 *Development of power bias: share of power-biased clauses of all clauses of cosmopolitan protection*

Table 8.1 *Representativeness of power-centricity*

	Power-centricity in Cosmopolitan Clauses (%)[a]
Kosovo	91
Afghanistan	76
(Pakistan)	83
Iraq	74
(Somalia)	100
Libya	92
Syria	92
Mali	82
All	55

Note: [a] Yemen is excluded from the comparison due to the complete lack of references to this intervention. The number of references to Somalia and Pakistan is also very low, hence they are in parentheses.

small number of years (24) of investigation does not warrant statistical analysis, but even if non-parametric correlations were calculated, the results between fatalities of protection wars and the number of power-centric clauses would be 0.487 and this would be statistically significant.

The share of power-biased clauses of all cosmopolitan protection clauses has a weaker relationship with fatalities of protection, but it too is clearly positively associated: the tougher we talk, the more fatalities we produce, but also the more violent the situation, the tougher we need to talk.[4] Since conflict fatalities are annual, this is the best one can offer in terms of the association between power bias and fatalities.

In a biannual investigation, it is possible to look at the relationship between power bias and new and ongoing US military operations to protect civilians from terror, dictators and criminals. There, the number of six-month periods is already 47, more suitable for elementary statistical analysis of associations. If we look at the number of power-biased cosmopolitan clauses in presidential papers we can see that it is somewhat associated with the number of new US military operations (Spearman correlation coefficient 0.3603, p = 0.0129, n = 47) and more strongly associated with the number of ongoing US protective military operations (Spearman correlation coefficient 0.5036, p = 0.0003, n = 47).[5] This shows that the more there is tough talk, the more there are protective operations, while protective operations also lead to tough talk. The fact that power-biased talk is more pronounced when there are already protective operations suggests that power-centricity plays a greater role in the legitimation than persuasion of militarism in protection.

In an annual investigation, it is possible to see the association between operation to protect and power bias by looking at the share of those clauses in US presidential papers where protection has abstract non-human referent objects. When, for example, one is protecting the environment, one is normally not focused on power, but on nurturing the flora and fauna of one's own country or globally. Clauses with environment as a referent object are strongly negatively associated with the number of new and ongoing military operations. The sum of clauses of environmental protection is strongly and statistically highly significantly negatively associated with protection fatalities (–0.635). The share of environmental focus in protection clauses is even more significantly and strongly negatively associated with protection fatalities (–0.641). Yet, in both cases, the number of observations is lower than is legitimate in statistical analysis.

However, if we then look at six-month periods we have 47 of them for our analysis. The number of new protective military operations and the number of ongoing protective military operations can be measured biannually and thus we can produce statistically more acceptable results for the association between environmental focus and the reluctance to use military forces for protection. The number of US military operations is very strongly negatively associated with the share of environmental speech of all relevant protection speech (–0.7245, $p \sim 0.0000$, n = 47). The number of clauses on environmental protection is also strongly, and statistically very significantly associated with ongoing protective US military operations (–0.6568, $p \sim 0.0000$, $n = 47$), but the negative association with new US operations fails to be statistically significant.

In sum then, it can be concluded that power bias is strongly associated with protective operations, especially ongoing operations: justifying ongoing operations requires power-biased ontologies, but power-centric ontologies are behind the motive to intervene. Perhaps more importantly though, power-centric ontologies increase escalation – the mutual need to use force and the mutual consolidation of power bias. The fact that such operations end up killing rather than protecting the people they were supposed to protect, and the fact that the enemies in such operations are mobilized by the power bias of Western operations, suggest that power-centric approaches to protection are problematic. Tension around an intervention gives rise to power-centric approaches, and according to the analysis of the enemy rhetoric in Chapter 5, power-centric strategies increase the perceived legitimacy of enemy violence. Thus, power-centricity in interactive tension creates a vicious cycle. If both sides need to change each other's behaviour and if they feel they have the right to use violence and threat thereof as means of power, it is clear that power-centricity leads to interactive escalation of conflict. This is why this aspect of the protection discourse is pertinent in the explanation of the failure to protect civilians in conflicts.

HOW DOES POWER BIAS ENTER PROTECTION WHEN TENSION INCREASES?

The 'Naturality' of Powerful Presidents

The power-centric idea that only tough action can work against terrorists and brutal tyrants, or that resisting evil opponents is the most cost-efficient way to save strangers, is not something that comes from objective necessity. Power bias is not materially needed as there are many other types of needs for protection that cannot be satisfied by means of power. Bush's focus on defeating terrorism and tyranny takes place at the time of an AIDS and malaria epidemy. The United States did work on these problems too, but such work did not receive, based on US presidential papers or budget shares, the full attention of the US presidents. Yet, even that little attention managed to help treat nearly 1.7 million people with AIDS and 25 million with malaria during Bush Jr's second term (Bush, 2009b, p. 1230) Even if we assumed completely unrealistic success for the US-led military operations, it would be impossible to even imagine similar cost-efficiency in terms of saved people/dollars. Why did power bias then already exist at the very beginning of the US protection discourse?

The development of power bias in cosmopolitan protection is partly outside our historical focus. The naturality of primacy of strategies in international politics has been articulated and sedimented in our diplomatic language and practices long before the emergence of cosmopolitan ideas in foreign policy practice. The overrepresentation of men in security policies combined with the historical social reality of men protecting their small children and their breastfeeding mothers is a context we have inherited from primitive societies and the birth of international relations. The key naturalization that brings power bias to cosmopolitan protection is the naturality of powerful men – a person is not a real man unless he is able to use power and get others to do what he wants them to do, and unless he can defend his family by destroying, incapacitating or powerfully persuading enemies. The literature on the relationship between violence and our construction of a man tells a story that is also outside our historical focus.[6] However, power bias also has its discursive path within the context of the history of cosmopolitan protection in the post-Cold War era.

One of the threads of power bias in cosmopolitan protection seems to be related to the naturality of power-centricity in positions of security administration. The role and identity of the US president is 'naturally' such in which the power to persuade is central. Speaker of the House of Representatives, Tip O'Neill (1977–87), revealed the meaning of President Reagan's intervention in Nicaragua in an interview with Larry King: 'It's being a man. [The president believes that] America has to show the firmness of manhood' (Booth and Wheeler, 2008, p. 64). If the president acts in a manly manner he gains the respect of a man when it comes to bargaining. A quotation from Bill Clinton after the Somali rebels had humiliated the US by killing one of the US soldiers suggests the same logic: 'I believe in killing people who try to hurt you, and I can't believe we're being pushed around by these two-bit pricks'. According to Henry Kissinger, a 'really strong overt act' by the president, such as bombing North Korea after its military provocation of the US, was 'essential to galvanize people into overcoming slothfulness and detachment arising from general moral decay' (Haldeman, 1995, p. 65; Young, 2000, p. 365).

Presidents 'must' weaken or destroy others to achieve the goals defined for the country. A head of state who does not focus on power will not be seen as credible or manly. The example of UK Prime Minister Neville Chamberlain is often mentioned as an example of a trusting leader who focused on mutual restraint rather than powerful influence on potential enemies. He negotiated peace with the devil in Munich in 1938 and believed an agreement was its foundation. As we know, war broke out soon after. Despite historical revelations (related to the plans of Lord Halifax) that could have changed the course of history (Offner, 1977), and despite an increasing body of evidence suggesting that negotiations can bring a lasting peace and that military power cannot, the example of Prime Minister Chamberlain has become a representative case in Western discourse on power as a natural primary instrument of security policies.[7]

The naturalization of masculine presidency in security policies can be pinned down to the discourse strand on protection. The reaction of the newly elected president Donald Trump after the devastating chemical attack in Khan Sheikhoun by the Syrian authoritarian government in April 2017 exemplifies the tendency towards stereotypical masculine power-centricity specifically in cosmopolitan protection. Trump was very concerned about changing President Assad's behaviour, while completely unwilling to accept refugees who were fleeing not just from Assad's cruelty, but also from the Western air operations and rebels that the United States sponsored:

> Using a deadly nerve agent, Assad choked out the lives of helpless men, women and children. It was a slow and brutal death for so many. Even beautiful babies were cruelly murdered in this very barbaric attack. No child of God should ever suffer such horror. . . Tonight I ordered a targeted military strike on the airfield in Syria from where the chemical attack was launched. (Trump, 2017c)

To broaden the focus from the individual incident to a more general consequence of Assad's authoritarian violence, Trump said: 'As a result, the refugee crisis continues, and the region continues to destabilise, threatening the US and its allies. Tonight I call on all civilised nations in seeking to end the slaughter and bloodshed in Syria and also to end terrorism of all kinds and all types' (Austin, 2017).

The 'children of God' escaping Assad, quickly become a destabilizing force, worth drowning for in the Mediterranean Sea, once they were described in a context that required power-neutral action. The children that, according to some sources, died in the US Tomahawk counter-strike, let alone US anti-ISIS airstrikes, do not even deserve a mention. Security policy is naturally power-centric and not for the faint-hearted. The association between power bias and the natural role of the president becomes clear in the representation of the airstrike in the media. When asked on CNN about what happened when the US hit the Syrian Air Force base from where the US assumed the chemical attack was launched, journalist Fareed Zakaria answered: 'I think Donald Trump became president of the United States. . . President Trump realized that the president of the United States does have to act to enforce international norms' (Zakaria, 2017). The naturality of such a powerful response for the president of the United States was emphasized in the reaction to the strike in *The Economist* (2017) that headlined the story as 'Donald Trump's foreign policy looks more normal than promised'. None of the biggest international newspapers paid attention to President Trump's unwillingness to accept new immigrants from Syria (except much later, after the second punitive strike against the Syrian government; see Amos, 2018). The interactive nature of power-centricity is revealed by the fact that Russian media reacted to the US airstrike by calling the chemical attack a false flag[8] incident and by repeating the Syrian (mis)reporting of deaths of children of the US counterstrike (RT, 2017). Fatalities caused by one's own side were ignored by both sides, while fatalities caused by violence of the opponent were portrayed as something that defines the identity of the opponent.

In addition to the naturalization of power-centricity of the role of the US president, power-centricity also enters the US discourse through the characterization of the enemy. Often, to legitimize violence to prevent anti-war protests US official discourse must make decisions on war more self-evident than they really are. There is a need for unity on the US side and thus opposition to US protective military operations needs to be marginalized. One method often used is by means of articulation of ontologies within which peaceful dialogue is not possible. Threats to global civilians need to be demonized in a way that makes all opposition to the weakening and destruction of them impossible. Despite the fact that many of these enemies of civilians (certainly Saddam Hussein, Osama bin Laden and Muammar Gaddafi) used to be US allies in anti-Iran, anti-Soviet and anti-terrorist operations, they all need to be demonized in a way that convinces allies and US citizens of the futility of peace dialogue with them. According to Bush Jr:

> We have a strategy to deal with Al Qaida in Iraq. But any time you say to a bunch of coldblooded killers, 'Success depends on no violence,' all that does is hand them the opportunity to be successful. And it's hard. I know it's hard for the American people to turn on their TV screens and see the horrific violence. It speaks volumes about the American desire to protect lives of innocent people, America's deep concern about human rights and human dignity. It also speaks volumes about Al Qaida, that they're willing to take innocent life to achieve political objectives. (G.W. Bush, 2008c, p. 522)
>
> We must see the terrorists for what they are: ruthless extremists who exploit the desperate, subvert the tenets of a great religion, and seek to impose their will on as many people as possible. (G.W. Bush, 2009b, p. 1227)

The idea of 'contest of will' that Kaldor sees as something that belongs to old wars is very much present in this argumentation. Wars are not won by cooperating with other states in the build-up of their nations, but instead, by destroying enemies and forcing them to our will. In doing that, signs of weakness embolden the enemy, while forceful unity and ruthlessness help in the Clausewitzian strategy of warfare. According to Bush Jr, for example:

> There can be no separate peace with the terrorist enemy. Any sign of weakness or retreat simply validates terrorist violence and invites more violence for all nations. The only certain way to protect our people is by united and decisive action. In this context of will and purpose, not every nation joins every mission or participates in the same way. Yet, every nation makes a vital contribution. (G.W. Bush, 2005g, p. 411)
>
> The Al Qaida terrorists who behead captives or order suicide bombings would not be satisfied to see America defeated and gone from Iraq. They would be emboldened by their victory, protected by their new sanctuary, eager to impose their hateful vision on surrounding countries, and eager to harm Americans. (G.W. Bush, 2008b, p. 541)

The 'Naturality' of Preference for Powerful Strategies

In addition to the identity of the 'president' and the 'enemy', power is also a natural preference in security strategy. Tickner talks about the naturalization of power bias in the mainstream realist tradition and cites examples where the lack of power is a great security political resource (Tickner, 1992, pp. 62–3). The statistical evidence on the greater number of terrorist fatalities in countries that participate in 'the protection against terror' compared to countries that do not, suggests that peace processes lead to more stable peace and security than military victories, and provides arguments for the idea that power is not a natural priority in security policies. In our analysis, the fact that Western enemies explicitly refer to the use of military power in their effort to constitute legitimate violent strategies for themselves suggests that strategies that focus on security from a relational perspective and try to reduce violent power in a relationship (by means of peace agreements, arms control, confidence-building measures etc.) could at least complement if not replace the power-biased strategies.

However, there are limits to how much relationality is possible in the current social structure in which foreign power-centricity is sedimented in foreign policy institutions and language. Symmetry in power-centric strategies is so difficult to understand within the logic of George W. Bush on the counter-terrorism strategy of 'staying on the offensive'. On the one hand, as discussed in Chapter 6, George W. Bush constructed legitimate violence against terrorists by using the reference to the violence the United States suffered on September 11, 2001 (the victimhood discourse strand). Due to the violence by terrorists against the US, America was justified to do 'whatever it takes' to destroy terrorists and to keep them out of the US (G.W. Bush, 2005h, p. 295).

When emphasizing the need to use violence, violate international norms, use taxpayer money, and make sacrifices, the violence the United States suffered on September 11, 2001 is referred to almost every time. While in his presidential campaign in 2004 President Bush repeated the same sentence 40 times about him waking up every morning after September 11, 2001 thinking about how to protect Americans, the following year, he kept on repeating another mantra:

> To accomplish this vital mission, we have a comprehensive strategy in place. We're working to protect the homeland. We're working to improve our intelligence, so we can uncover terrorist plots before they unfold, and we're staying on the offensive. We're fighting the enemy in Iraq and Afghanistan and across the world so we do not have to face them here at home. (G.W. Bush, 2006a, p. 1203)

In 2006, Bush combined the victimhood discourse of his presidential campaign with the new logic of 'staying on the offense':

> This Government is going to do whatever it takes to protect this homeland. We're not going to let their excuses stop us from staying on the offense. *The best way to protect America is defeat these killers overseas so we do not have to face them here at home.* We're not going to let lies and propaganda by the enemy dictate how we win this war. (G.W. Bush, 2007e, p. 1703; emphasis added)

This new mantra has an interesting, conflictual relationship with the previous one: while terrorist violence and entry into the homeland of Americans created legitimacy for US violence against terrorists 'wherever they may be', US violence in the homelands of the terrorists was supposed to deny legitimate violence from terrorists in the US and keep them fighting in the Middle East and Central and South Asia, instead of coming to America. What creates perceived legitimacy for one denies it for the other. This logic works only if one fails to see the symmetry between conflicting parties. The failure to see the symmetry, as the above example shows, leads to a security approach that is not sensitive to the logic of security dilemma: if one does not see symmetries one cannot see the game structures that explicitly prescribe less power-centric approaches to protection.

If one studies the strategic logic of protection in the US presidential discourse plane, one can see limits that prevent the understanding of the relational reality of symmetry between enemies in security policies. These limits can be analysed using a post-structuralist approach (Hansen, 2006; Howarth and Stavrakakis, 2000; Laclau and Mouffe, 2001; Mouffe, 1996) and the analysis of rhetoric approach (Enos, 1993; Kuusisto, 1998; Perelman and Olbrechts-Tyteca, 1968) to identify the grammatical connection between security and relationships. Due to the history of power-centricity in foreign affairs there is a language and normality where states have ministers for defence and security advisers. Security of the state is the core objective of the state machinery. This leads state behaviour to an agent-centric approach as security and defence in foreign policy parlance is always security and defence of an agent and it can only be threatened by another intentional enemy agent. Thus, security does not need a relationship: in fact, the statements by President Bush about the oceans protecting America before September 2001, shows that non-interaction with other actors is good for security. Another agent is needed only to define insecurity, and that agent is the one that needs to be destroyed or influenced.

Without the history of hegemonic masculinity, we might speak of peace, have ministries of peace and peace advisers to heads of state. The grammar of peace carries a bias towards relationship-focused rather than agent-centric politics. The only agent we need to define in peace speech is the one that we are at peace with. While it is possible to have security by destroying the enemy, peace is not possible through war and destruction (although it may be after such a phase). While security is associated with the demands states or groups make on each other (there is no security through surrender, security is safety of our values), peace is grammatically associated with compromise.

The two associations and dissociations that drive power-centricity then are: (1) the dissociation between human security on both sides in security grammar (there is an association between the two in peace speech as peace is between us and the other); (2) the association between political values and safety in security speech (there is a lack of such association in peace grammar, as peace requires willingness to compromise).

Without power-centric security thinking we could then assume that it would be easier to find solutions together with potential enemies and make compromises without seeing them as compromises to security. The fact that the US security apparatus is interested in President Trump's alleged good relations with some potential enemies and the fact that security specialists like Fareed Zakaria feel that Trump became a real president only once he launched a military strike on the 'baddies' is symptomatic of the situation. It speaks volumes about stereotypical masculinity, which has denied relational investigation of world politics and which has driven our focus on security rather than peace. The fact that the president's belligerent statements in relation to China, North Korea or Iran are not seen as security threats but as weak proof of his ability to handle security issues, may have something to do with the stereotypical masculinity in US security strategy – the concept of power-centric security, and the focus on security rather than peace.

The 'Naturality' of Demonizing Policy of Identities

In addition to identity of the enemy and the strategy of security, power bias enters protection discourse through the stereotypical strategy of identities. If the focus in protection is on potential enemies rather than on relationships that should be made more peaceful, then the focus, in the manipulation of one's own and the enemy's identity, is power-centric. In the power-centric security approach, the only other that needs to be defined is the enemy that threatens our security. Thus, the preferred power-centric approach is to weaken the other and emphasize the strength of oneself. In politics related to identities, such weakening implies isolation and demonization of actual and potential enemies. This strategy of identity politics is in use for cosmopolitan protection in the US presidential discourse: global civilians are, just as the free world was during the Cold War and the anti-fascist coalition during World War II, standing against crazy dictators and vicious criminals. An analysis of the US protection discourse also reveals the power-centric articulation of the United States in a way that exaggerates US strength:

> These terrorists and insurgents will use brutal tactics because they're trying to shake the will of the United States of America. That's what they are trying to do. They want us to retreat. They want us, in our compassion for the innocent. To say 'We're through.' That's what they want. They will fail. They do not understand the character and the strength of the United States of America. (G.W. Bush, 2006d, p. 1303)

Yet, to alter the behaviour of someone who one considers a threat to global civilians may be difficult if one does not offer more positive identities to one's enemies. A more relational and more sophisticated approach to the relationship between identities and policies would offer more successful ways of confronting groups that the US cosmopolitan protection considers enemies. It would be tempting to claim that this approach is missing because of stereotypical masculinity. It would be objectifying to claim that men are more violent and more demonizing than women by their objective nature despite the fact that of all the warriors, terrorists, murderers and violent offenders, a huge majority are men (Messerschmidt, 2000; Polk, 1994). Such a claim would go against our understanding of both male and female agency as something that is not determined by the objective characteristics of men and women. Yet, if our claim is that security policy has not benefited from female experience, due to the dominance of men in security roles, we could also say that, for example, domestic experiences, such as raising children, have not advised practices of security policies or cosmopolitan protection. Instead of portraying enemies as crazy dictators, securing them by weakening them with counter-force, a mother might try to influence motives rather than capabilities of conflicting parties, sometimes by tackling the interaction (rather than actors), referring to norms and by working with identities. Naughty children are not destroyed or weakened but taught with compassion. Even if we were to consider that the Taliban movement was detrimental to the human security of Afghan people, it has been shown that it was the militaristic interaction with the US military that created them as terrorists (Van Linschoten and Kuehn, 2012). A more interactive approach that could have accorded ethnic Pashtun leaders with identities more constructive for human security, could have worked better. When mediating in the conflicts of the former Yugoslavia, President Martti Ahtisaari of Finland took a more motherly, relational approach that appealed to the common norms and offered identities that could be useful for regional peace. The great power-nostalgic Russia was invited to a negotiation process that offered it a more positive identity in place of its former militaristic image. Ahtisaari's approach was like that of a mother who tries to induce more positive behaviour from a 'naughty child' by offering them the ability to see themselves as a more responsible and good child. Powerful Soviet Union was history, but Russia could be a meaningful force for peace in the world. Just like a mother might try to appeal to a child's willingness to be a 'good child', Ahtisaari tried to appeal to Russians and encourage them to constructively engage in the building of a more peaceful Europe by offering them a positive identity, not as a 'good child' but as a great power of peace.

Yet, in the end, this approach was destroyed in the first protective military operation in Kosovo by the stereotypical masculine need to humiliate Russia even in this peace process and deny its role in the design of the European security architecture. It was important (for the stereotypical masculine approach) to show who was the crazy dictator, and who had to be defeated. For the US, its strength had to be the backbone of security in Europe. Instead of focusing on relationships and approaches and deciding what would be a good approach and what kind of approaches should be avoided, the solution was to identify the guilty party (Milošević in Serbia, later the Taliban and Al Qaeda in Afghanistan, Saddam Hussein in Iraq, Muammar Gaddafi in Libya, etc.) and defeat it with military power or at least with sanctions. Security had to be guaranteed by partisan rather than common action. With a positive feminine alternative approach it might have been possible to identify hypothetical alternative ways of dealing with conflicts and to observe if any efforts in that vein had shown any success (Kivimäki, 2016, pp. 167–8).

CONCLUSIONS

The mutually constitutive relationship between tension, war, intervention and fatalities on the one hand and power bias on the other, can be clearly concluded on the basis of the study of the interaction between enemy discourses and on the study of US protective interventions and the discourse strand on protection in the US presidential papers.

The discourse on centricity of power in protection seems to fit very well with the descriptions of the feminist theory on power-centricity of hegemonic masculinity. There seems to be a naturalization of the relationship between the preference for powerful strategies and masculine identity and the identity of statesmen. To be a true man and to be a true statesman one needs to be prepared to use lethal power. Whoever does not fit the description will be considered unfit as a man and as a statesman. The UK's opposition leader, Jeremy Corbyn, is an interesting example of the extremities of this naturalization. After confessing that he would probably be unable to launch a second strike against the civilians of an enemy country he was judged to be a threat to security by the UK Prime Minister David Cameron and by the Secretary-General of NATO (Ridge, 2015; Stone, 2015). The development of President Trump's presidential identity suggests the same in the American security discourse. As an elected president he could be considered a real president only once he had shown his willingness to go to war and use lethal power in the way that statesmen are expected to.

In addition to naturalized identities, there are also naturalized strategies. Statesmanship is about the use of power. A president who argues for an intervention by referring to the victims of one's enemies can leave the same victims to die rather than accept them as refugees to one's own country, without being accused of inconsistency. People with tragic fates can be beautiful babies only if they are being mistreated by enemies whose behaviour can be changed by means of power. If these victims need protection by means of self-restraint or if they need to be accepted and nurtured as refugees, they are simply destabilizing forces.

Part of the power bias and stereotypical masculinity is sedimented in the language of security, and this way the grammar rules of that language reproduce the naturality of preferences for powerful strategies. The primacy of security speech in politics emphasizes agency, demands a definition of whose security, and only needs an enemy as a necessary other agent. The naturality of securitization (rather than 'peacification') of sources of existential threats sustains approaches that see communication with the enemy as treacherous, hides costs of wars and makes compromising dishonourable. This way, the language of security that smuggles power bias into security thinking rules out strategies that seek mutual benefit and offer positive, cooperative identities to potential enemies and aim at fixing relationships rather than weakening and destroying potential enemies.

Since all this contributes to the fatalities of protection wars, it seems clear that language and naturalized identities should be revealed, and feminine life experience should be introduced to cosmopolitan protection. One progressive step in this direction would require a greater representation of women in security administration. We have rejected essentialism – women do not have a peace gene that men lack, and some female leaders have had a hard time demonstrating their masculine credentials for their role as statesmen. Yet, it would be difficult to ignore the experience of Angela Merkel of Germany, as an example of the concrete benefits of feminine representation in security policies. Instead, of engaging in deadly interventions and exercise of power in the internal affairs of fragile countries, Germany has been the country that has absorbed the desperate refugees of wars that protective interventions have escalated. We should not forget that the main wave of refugees to Europe was from Syria and Iraq and that it emerged at the beginning of 2015 soon after the Western air operations had started in Autumn 2014. Given the percentage of the Iraqi population who have perished in the 15 years of battle that started with a protective intervention, and the fact that the conflict in Syria has not been any less intensive, it will be possible to calculate that of the million refugees that Germany has accepted from Iraq and Syria, up to tens of thousands would have perished without the feminine German protective operation of welcoming these refugees. Even if protective interventions could deliver the results that Western countries expected them to deliver, it would have been impossible to even imagine the kind of results Merkel's open-hearted immigration policies have achieved. Yet, Germany has not spent nearly as much money on the facilitation of such an immigration policy as the US has on its war efforts. After a while, Germany will have a productive, mostly educated, workforce from conflict areas, whereas the US will only have the economic burden of wounded American soldiers to take care of.

Finally, one can conclude, on the basis of the analysis in this chapter, that the democratization of cosmopolitan protection, which the two previous chapters have concluded as a prescription for cosmopolitan protection, will also require the inclusion of female agency in the global agency for protection. To create representative agency of protection will require the end of unilateralism, which then will deal with the problem of selfish ulterior motives. But to create representative agency will also require a cultural change in which the naturality of hegemonic masculine ways can be revealed as products of unfair, unequal conditions, and then changed into being more inclusive – cosmopolitan protection cannot remain a prerogative of the white Western men and the ways of protection cannot be Western, masculine ways only.

NOTES

1. While Tickner's argument of underrepresentation of women is correct, this statistical claim is obviously wrong. Less than 1 per cent would mean that there was at the most only one female president in the world at the time of writing of her article (2004), yet, Finland, Indonesia, the Philippines, Panama and Latvia were all led by female presidents at the time (Tarja Halonen, Megawati Sukarnoputri, Gloria Macapagal Arroyo, Mireya Moscoso and Vīķe-Freiberga, respectively).
2. Radical feminism, according to Tickner, endorsed values that were seen as feminine, and a worldview that was based on relationships and connections (Tickner, 2001, p. 14; see also, Jaggar, 1983). While treating these features as a product of the social construction of femininity, and while shying away from essentialism, and the objectivization of femininity, Tickner and Ruddick felt that feminine culture could enrich security policies that were guided by masculine experiences alone and approaches that represented stereotypical masculinity (Ruddick, 1995). This is the approach in this chapter, too. As a result, I will explore how relationality could serve as a substitute for agent-centric, harmful power bias in protection.
3. Reference to a country is coded if the passage where the referent object and agent of a clause is revealed also includes the name of the country. I have excluded Yemen from the comparison due to the complete lack of references to this intervention. The number of references to Somalia and Pakistan is also very low, hence they are in parentheses.
4. Since the assumption is that these simple non-parametric correlations reveal mutual constitution rather than one-directional causality, there is no need to deny the two-way effect, or for statistical operations to define which way causality goes.
5. This correlation survives even in the monthly investigation despite the fact that random events weaken any association when viewed against monthly developments. The correlation between the number of power-biased clauses and ongoing US protective operations is 0.3481 ($p \sim 0.0000$, $n = 282$).
6. Bowker (1997); Ellis (1989); Elshtain (1987); Heathcote (2017); Myrttinen and Swaine (2015); Polk (1994); Wood (2016); Young (2000).
7. Anti-Western discourses have their corresponding examples of the naturality of power in security policies. The increasingly assertive Russian foreign policy discourse uses the example of Party Leader Mikhail Gorbachev as a negotiator who was too trusting and was therefore left with a 'sucker's payoff'. His sin was the failure to demand guarantees for the non-expansion of NATO, which Russian diplomats feel was promised to the Soviet leader, even though this was not codified in the official agreements.
8. A deceptive operation that creates the appearance of a particular party being responsible for something, disguising the actual source of responsibility.

9. From cosmopolitanism to neocosmopolitanism: democratizing and degendering cosmopolitan protection

EMPIRICAL CONCLUSIONS: THE DIAGNOSIS OF FAILURE

The long history of violence suggests that when zones of order expand, and more people are included in the group that the unit of governance needs to protect, a lot of violence disappears. Tribal security orders have been better at limiting violence than family-based orders, larger societies better than tribal orders, nation-states better than city-states, and so on. Against this historical development, one would assume that the step from considering state security and restricting our solidarity to our compatriots to global ideas of human security, could be the next great step towards peace in the world. Furthermore, morally, it is difficult to justify restrictive ideas in which one's rights, well-being and even security and survival would need to be dependent on the colour of your passport. Cosmopolitan security thinking therefore, has its appeal.

While the attraction of cosmopolitan ideas varies in history, and some see pendulum movements with regard to the strength of cosmopolitan norms, one cannot deny the big normative trend towards greater cosmopolitan appeal. There is no doubt that people are now more interested in the well-being of individuals who live 5000 miles away than when people did not learn about or communicate with other people globally. Normative development has its material facilitators. While the use of money made it possible to establish units of security governance that were larger than city-states, because taxing people in faraway places was now possible, the cosmopolitan development also has its technological facilitators. The broadening access to the Internet, especially in developed countries, has enabled global solidarity and empathy is a material condition that will not disappear. Thus, there will be no pendulum movements in the development of cosmopolitan solidarity and interests in cosmopolitan human security even if one can see smaller variations of solidarity over shorter periods of time.

Yet, the cosmopolitan movement has not yet delivered peaceful progress. As shown in Chapters 3 and 4, the Western willingness to save strangers globally has not helped global civilians – quite the contrary. Protective operations have been associated with increased numbers of fatalities, globally, in countries where protection takes place, and specifically in conflicts where protective operations interfere in fighting. Furthermore, protective operations have been associated with further weakening of structures that could control violence. Protection has weakened states at a time when states are generally getting stronger and more able to control violence, even in areas that are marred with violence. Statistics of conflict, fatalities and state fragility make all this completely clear.

All this seems to correspond with the non-systematic observations that can be made of the perceptions of people escaping from conflict areas and returning to areas where control has been consolidated either under cosmopolitan powers or their enemies. These observations should be made much more systematically in the future scholarship of protection wars to ensure that what we find in the statistics of conflict fatalities and state fragility tells the whole story. While statistics of fatalities say nothing about the conditions of life – fear, repression, non-lethal violence – systematic studies of refugee and internally displaced person flows, with a more precise than annual temporal focus and more precise than national spatial focus, could be studied against the data on protective interventions. This way it would be possible to tap into the local knowledge without the need for extensive interviews: people indicate their observations on violence with their feet. To what extent they escape areas of protective operations measures the degree of devastation perhaps even better than annual statistics of national conflict fatalities. To what extent they escape areas in the control of groups and governments that Western protective operations protect people from says something about the need to protect these people. To what extent they escape from areas of protective operations tells about the costs of protection. To what extent they return to areas that have been put in order by the cosmopolitan powers, and to what extent they return to areas that enemies of Western protection control, says something of the need and the successfulness of the Western enforcement humanitarian order. The fact that this has not already been done in conflict studies, and the possible lack of data that could enable such study, clearly demonstrates the general disregard of the perceptions and feelings of the protected people. Perhaps it could be said that this demonstrates the idea of the protected global strangers as objects of protection rather than as political subjects.

To summarize the degeneration of the cosmopolitan agenda in the political discourse, it is possible to identify four steps to failure:

1. First, it was already laid down in the transition to cosmopolitan thinking. This was related to the easing of norms of sovereignty for the sake of human security. Optimism related to the ability of the international community to deal with issues of global human security was related to the diagnosis according to which the world already had common, universally owned principles that could regulate global security. In a unipolar world where veto powers of the UN could identify more commonness in their principles, there was a feeling that opportunistic violence could be dealt with by means of norm enforcement and peace enforcement. The UN report *Agenda for Peace* (United Nations General Assembly, 1992) outlined a view according to which norms of sovereignty could be eased and the UN could take on a stronger role for peace.
2. Second, after the failure to resource the UN security enforcement and the consequent failure to deal with the genocides of Rwanda and Bosnia, the norm on agency of protection was eased. This was done in the Kosovo operation by somewhat deceptive ways in which the US presidential discourse had two contradictory agencies for protective operations depending on the audience. In the international context, the operation in Kosovo was justified as a UN/global operation, whilst domestically it was justified as a NATO operation with US control and lead. This way the agency of global cosmopolitan protection was compromised.
3. Third, after the shock of the terrorist attack on the US on September 11, 2001, American audiences could no longer be persuaded to undertake international military operations merely by references to global human security. US presidential discourse started to define the protection of Americans as a necessary additional objective of global military operations. Here, even the cosmopolitan theory that is blind to the question of agency came to contradict cosmopolitan political practice. Operations cannot serve two fundamentally different objectives without compromising one or both. This way, the cosmopolitan justification of protection was also compromised.
4. Finally, while the Afghanistan operation was still very much focused on non-destructive aspects of operation, such as state-building, operations became more and more purely military at the end of President Bush Jr's term. The logical consequence of the protection of Americans was that American presence on the ground had to be limited. This moved protective operations to the air, where destruction rather than

Table 9.1 The phases of cosmopolitan protection

	1992 *Agenda for Peace*	1999 Kosovo Operation	2001 Afghanistan, War on Terror	Late Bush Years Onwards
Diagnosis	Conflicts gainful, not just grievance motivated	Conflicts gainful, not just grievance motivated	Conflicts gainful, not just grievance motivated	Conflicts gainful, not just grievance motivated
Objective	Global human security	Global human security	Global human security and protection of Americans	Global human security and protection of Americans
Agency	UN agency	Justification from UN principles, US agency	Justification from UN principles, US agency	Justification from UN principles, US/NATO agency
Method	Non-violent and violent (peace enforcement)	Violent	Violent	Violent. Air-based protection by the destruction of the enemy

state-building was the focus. This compromised the original, caring and nurturing nature of protection, and made it destruction rather than protection.

Table 9.1 summarizes this process of development.

Chapter 5 revealed the first layer of reason why protection fails. It has shown that the practice of cosmopolitanism has so far mainly provoked its opponents and helped justify and mobilize violent resistance to the Western enforcement of humanitarian norms and protection. Chapters 6 and 7 reveal that the cosmopolitan popular sentiment has not been strong enough to enable the strengthening of truly cosmopolitan agency and interests in world politics. These chapters show how national selfishness and unilateralism crept into the political discourse on protection after the rise of cosmopolitan thinking in world politics reduced hesitance to interfere in the internal security affairs of fragile states.

Statistical analysis of the relationship between operations and fatalities shows, interestingly, that selfish discourses are negatively associated with global numbers of fatalities. This is because before the beginning of protective military operations the number of fatalities was declining throughout the 1990s. Thus, the 1990s was a time with high, though declining numbers of fatalities of conflicts, and when the genocides in Bosnia and Rwanda then opened the floodgates for protective operations that did not comply with the traditional norms of sovereignty, the number of fatalities was declining. However, protective operations tended to escalate conflicts, and once the terrorist strike in the US in 2001 gave the West a perceived legitimacy to use such global protective operations also for national protection, the numbers of protective operations and the number of fatalities of such operations, and conflict fatalities in general, started their rise. The fact that cosmopolitan instruments of protection could be corrupted to serve national interests was at least partly related to the fact that cosmopolitan governance did not have representative global institutions, but instead, decision-making on cosmopolitan protection remained national.

Democratic countries that have conducted protective operations must know that legitimacy of governance is not just a matter of what values governance produces, but also who imposes these values and whether the subordinates of governance can participate in the selection of the values to be promoted and protected: enlightened autocracy does not avoid provoking resistance among the subordinates. Yet, this knowledge never entered the debate on protection. As a result, national agents have served selfish national as well as cosmopolitan purposes and this entanglement of cosmopolitan and selfish discourses has done exactly what Falk (2003) has suggested it will do: it has escalated conflict and helped legitimize violent practices and mobilize resistance, as opponents of protection have seen selfish imperialist, colonialist or anti-Islamic motives behind the apparently humanitarian protective operations.

In addition to the selfishness and national unilateralism, cosmopolitan normative power has not managed to prevent the diversion of strategies from efficient and violence-minimizing strategies to power-maximizing strategies. Chapter 8 reveals how the preference for overly militaristic, power-centric strategies of protection is linked with naturalized constructions of masculinity and statesmanship. Despite clear evidence against, the cosmopolitan statesmanship of protection and the terrorist or autocratic nationalist struggle against external enemies both believe that the other party could be forced and deterred from their violence. While the US president believes that staying in the offensive will keep the terrorists and dictators in the defence, the very reason for the US's own offensive is the offensive of the terrorists (9/11) and dictators (WMDs). Similarly, even though it was evident that the terrorist attack on the US invigorated American resolve to fight Al Qaeda, Osama bin Laden still felt that his 'constituencies' could be served and the US aggression in the Middle East could be ended by violent means. This mutual naturalization of power-centric strategies on both sides of the conflict created a vicious cycle of escalation that could be verified in Chapter 8 by statistical means: whenever the share of clauses on cosmopolitan protection referred by the act of protection to strategies that changed someone else's behaviour by means of power, fatalities of protection tended to increase, and military operations of protection tended to increase.

While the above summary has revealed reasons for the failure of most of the protective operations in terms of order-/state-building and prevention of fatalities, there is also a need to summarize why the intervention in Sierra Leone was so different. While the main textual material (US presidential papers) reveal very little on that, it seems clear that the analysis of the Western discourse and the analysis of the overall development of fatalities of conflict and protection wars provided some answers. It seemed that the case of Sierra Leone emphasizes the need to distinguish selfish and cosmopolitan interests from one another. The fact that the UK was not involved in the gainful side of the conflict, as the role of British actors in the country's diamond trade was negligible, made the UK resistant to accusations of hidden agendas. The fact that the intervention took place before the terrorist attack on the US in 2001 meant that the UK operation took place in a different discursive context than the operations after it. While the attack on the US opened the floodgates to selfish nationalist arguments for war on terror and protection of civilians from terror, the operation in Sierra Leone took place in a discursive context where cosmopolitan operation needed to be freer from selfish interests. This, together with the fact that the main opponents of the UK intervention were so clearly opportunistic themselves, might have been the reason why the argument of selfish Westerners did not offer legitimacy for violence against protection in Sierra Leone.

The case of Sierra Leone was different from most protective operations in the sense that the actor of intervention could not be accused of being an illegitimate actor and thus this illegitimacy did not fuel the conflict. Even though the UK was not a legitimate actor inside the border of Sierra Leone, in the sense that its intervention was not authorized by the United Nations Security Council (UNSC), the UK was operating in support of the conflicting party that most people in the country perceived as the legal and legitimate government. Thus, the intervention was not as unilateral as most of the protective interventions, and thus it did not justify violent reaction from its opponents. Furthermore, instead of defining its own objectives, the UK operation attempted to enforce an agreement that all conflicting parties had accepted. This way, the international intervention did not put aside local objectives and local agency, it merely enforced a local consensus. The claim that the opponent of the protective operation had a legitimate claim against the external dictation of the country's internal affairs is weaker in Sierra Leone than it was in any of the other protective operations. Finally, the UK came to the country in a situation where the under-resourced UN was about to fail. Thus, despite the lack of formal UNSC approval, the UK operation was very close to being an operation under a UN umbrella.

In addition to selfishness and unilateralism, the UK operation also avoids some of the accusations of power-centricity and militarism. The fact that the US did not conduct the operation helped in this as the overwhelming power of the US frames any intervention of the country in power-political terms. The UK also does not need to protect its power position in the way which the US does, and since the discourse on this operation was never entangled with the discourse on US protective operations, the power framing did not emerge as a militaristic operation. There was no need to react to the offences of the opponent in a way that protected the UK's power position because the UK did not need to defend such a hegemonic power position. In Sierra Leone, the situation was not one in which, 'America protects its own. Anyone, anyone, who takes on our troops will suffer the consequences. We will fight fire with fire' (Clinton, 1996a, p. 1787). The fact that the UK operation was integrated with the operations of many donors meant that the focus was not only on the military, but a fair share of attention was given also to state-building. There have been opinions that the UK and the international community should still have had a greater focus on economic development and social foundations of state-building, otherwise Sierra Leone might return to conflict one day. Yet, in Sierra Leone, state-building has received more attention than in most other countries of cosmopolitan protection.[1]

PROBLEMS OF THE COSMOPOLITAN THEORY OF PROTECTION

While the texts and numbers have helped build a diagnosis of the disease cosmopolitan protection is suffering from, the prescription will partly follow from the diagnosis, while partly it is always dependent on what we want and what we consider as morally acceptable. Making sense of the elements of the diagnosis has already required concepts and understandings that arise from interests and values (as the constructivist pragmatist philosophy of science guides the argument in this book), but the transformation of diagnoses to prescriptions bring normative and interest-driven thinking to the fore. Since the development of the prescription is partly theoretical and partly practical, I will discuss it first from a theoretical perspective and then move to more openly political prescriptions.

The theoretical ambition of this book was not to crush the prescriptions of the new war theory regarding the need for international enforcement of cosmopolitan law. The theory has been based on the assumption that the world in the 1990s was moving towards a more violent direction due to the lesser attention of great powers to the humanitarian problems in fragile states. Chapter 4 of this book has shown that this has been a fundamentally misguided assumption. Violence in the Third World was declining throughout the decade, most likely at least partly because of the great power abandonment of the Third World. As a result, the prescription that there should be greater big power attention and more robust military means to put fragile developing countries in order, seems to be in doubt.

Yet, even if it seems that operations that have been justified by protection discourse have failed to protect civilians, this does not mean that all protective military interventions should fail. Neither does it mean that it is the cosmopolitan prescriptions that have contributed to the failure of the operations, so far. Some of the international interventions in fragile states have been explicitly criticized by the cosmopolitan theorists and theorists of new wars, and thus we should not claim that the type of intervention that we can see in Afghanistan and in Iraq follows the prescriptions of the theory of new wars. Also, there is no doubt about the need to do something in the face of situations where brutal dictatorial regimes or criminal groups opportunistically exploit and violate civilians. The question is just what should be done and who should do it to produce positive outcomes rather than negative.

There should be systematic, evidence-based research on why different types of interventions perform differently. The case of international intervention in Sierra Leone should be used as one of the cases of clearly better results in terms of fatalities. While this book has touched upon this question, the case of Sierra Leone, and the political discourse on it in the UK, needs more serious attention.

However, one should also consider it possible that the new war theory is fundamentally wrong in some of its prescriptions. The rejection by new war theorists and some cosmopolitan scholars of the possibility of a 'world state' that could represent all and be owned also by the Third World, not only by the most developed Western capitalist coalitions of the willing, could be the source of fatal misunderstandings on protection. It may be that the asymmetry between willingness to protect and the unwillingness to share the agency of protection is the reason why protection is either seen as or why it actually is, nothing but a new justification for cynical power politics. It may be that this is the reason why military protection gives rise to so much resistance, and results in escalation rather than de-escalation of conflicts. New war theorists and others genuinely interested in the protection of global civilians should be open about this. Perhaps the reason why the US did not win the hearts and minds of Iraqi and Afghan people was not that it made mistakes in its global enforcement of norms, as Kaldor suggests (2012, p. 167), it may be that the whole idea of alien rule was what alienated the subjects of US norm enforcement, and gave nationalistic and religious legitimacy for the resistance that the US saw as terroristic. In any case, an effort to protect without sharing the agency of protection escalated conflicts, increased the number of fatalities and destroyed structures of control and prevention of violence.

FROM COSMOPOLITAN TO NEOCOSMOPOLITAN PRESCRIPTIONS

Moving from falsification to more positive engagement with existing literature, one can also identify several theoretical prescriptions that the investigation in this book has lent support to. It is possible to build on these theories and the empirical generalizations of this book and build a new theory with better prescriptions.

Falk and Gilmore (Falk, 2002, 2003; Gilmore 2014, 2015) have suggested that great powers are not yet ready for cosmopolitan protection. Genuine cosmopolitan action does not receive sufficient resourcing (Bosnia, Rwanda etc.), while non-genuine operations tend to be too much compromised by selfish rationales. Therefore, one should not call current protective operations humanitarian. In other words, there is a gap between practice and theory. This is related to the finding of Mueller (1996), according to which there is no global institutional agency, and unlike Beck (2006) suggests, citizens of the US vote for those that maximize US, not global interests.

This book has shown that the problem of selfishness is not just one that relates to poor humanitarian conduct of operations, but also to the interactive dynamics between protectors and their opponents: selfish hidden agendas of protection offer arguments and legitimacy for the violent opponents of protective operations, and the violence of these opponents then legitimizes even greater selfishness in protective operations. Given that each of the actors in protection wars view the situation from their own perspective, based on their own perceptions and with their own concepts, an interactive game emerges where the opponents play on entirely different playing fields. Rationalizations for their own selfishness that each side lives by do not affect the other, and as a result, the actors assumed to be perceived as civilized democratic actors whose democracy is envied by the enemy are seen as imperialists or infidels, while the just punishments or deterring signals against violence are seen as proofs of the aggressive nature of these imperialists or infidels. Imposition and enforcement of what is as a rule seen by the protectors as a humanitarian norm in a situation where the whole game-setting is seen fundamentally differently by the opponents of protective operations, is therefore not functional; they do not do what they intend to and thus they do not achieve the results they intended.

The fundamental problem of selfishness is related to the agency of global security governance. The analysis of the US presidential discourse on protection clearly revealed that the problem presidents faced with genuine cosmopolitan action was that they had to get acceptance – resources, manpower and mandate – from national bodies. If decisions are made by nations or partisan military alliances, protection will be a compromise between humanitarian and partisan interests. Enemies of such protection will often interpret even the humanitarian motives as selfish national and partisan perspectives and this enables them to legitimize violence in their constituencies. Thus, the development of *cosmopolitan agency* is what would be needed for the advancement of genuine global cosmopolitan security governance.

Etzioni (2004) suggests that an empire is more violent than a global community and that the difference between the two is that in the former order is not owned by all its subjects, while in the latter all members feel ownership of the rule. This book has supported this theoretical conclusion and added a few specifications to it. The importance of global rather than unilateral agency, from the point of view of success of protection of global civilians, is partly due to the problem of partisan and national selfishness, and partly due to the problems of imperial provocation. Protection in faraway places that is too much motivated by national priorities compromises the needs of the areas where protection is conducted. Furthermore, many individuals and groups in fragile states are provoked by the fact that the agency of protection is not legitimate, it does not enforce norms to its allies, and it does not comply with them itself. As a result, those that the West protects turn against the West and conflicts escalate. Legitimate cosmopolitan agency is emphasized in the original Kantian cosmopolitan theory, which has clear contractarian roots. However, this part of Kantian cosmopolitanism is neglected in the cosmopolitan ethics of the past two decades. To bring agency back to cosmopolitanism, first we need to remember that good governance is not sufficient for the legitimacy of governance. The governed need to be allowed to participate in governance; they need to be agents and subjects of protection, not just objects of protection. Enlightened autocracy is not stable, we need democracy for cosmopolitan politics. Second, we need to stop pretending that we can do politics without representative, authoritative actors. For cosmopolitan politics that actor will have to be global for it to be representative in a cosmopolitan sense.

It is possible to suggest, on the basis of the analysis of this book that the theory of cosmopolitanism should learn from the development of the closely related theory of integration. The functionalist integration theory (Mitrany, 1975) proposed that regional integration could only take place if people took control from the states and ignored state borders by interacting across borders as if they did not exist. Transnational loyalties, solidarity and eventually a regional civil society were the foundation of regional integration. The same could be postulated about the development of global, cosmopolitan solidarity and loyalty and this is very much what cosmopolitan scholarship claims to have happened to global security identities, security loyalties and solidarities and security priorities: Kaldor suggests that a global civil society is emerging, while the United Nations Development Programme outlines a global concept of human security. However, integration also requires authoritative, representative decision-making and institutions for it, as Ernst B. Haas (1964) has shown. Ad hoc civil society organization is not sufficient for authoritative democratic decision-making, and thus the step from functionalist integration theory to neofunctionalist theory required the recognition of another layer for successful integration. This discovery needs to be imported to the security theory of cosmopolitanism. While global security might require a global civil society, and while spontaneous popular movements might be the engine of change towards global human security, authoritative decision-making on and implementation of global security norms requires the strengthening of global representative institutions. Just like the theory of integration had to develop from the utopic version of functionalism, to a more realist neofunctionalism, also international political cosmopolitanism must develop from cosmopolitanism to neocosmopolitanism. We need to acknowledge that the implementation of the will of the global civil society requires authoritative, representative global institutions. The main addition to cosmopolitanism that neocosmopolitanism can offer is the realization that to make cosmopolitan dreams real and less violent we need a representative, democratic global state with a more inclusive representation than exists in the Western coalitions of the willing. The strengthening of the United Nations, rather than the United States, could be the first step in the creation of such an authoritative global agency.

The arguments against the gradual development of the United Nations into a more inclusive global actor, which have been presented in the

American political discourse, have often been related to the inability of the United Nations to function effectively. The explanation by President Bush of his effort to work through the United Nations in his intervention in Iraq testifies to the logic of this critique. The UN is relevant and efficient only when it acts on US orders. In this case, even the interests that UN action should serve were national:

> My job is to protect the American people. My job is to anticipate. And so I went to the United Nations. I went to the United Nations because I want the United Nations to be effective. I went to the United Nations and – to remind them that for 11 years, this man has defied 16 resolutions. Time and time and time again, he has ignored the United Nations. I basically said, 'You can be an effective body to help us keep the peace, or you can be the League of Nations'. (G.W. Bush, 2003b, p. 1733)

However, cosmopolitan agency is cosmopolitan exactly because it does not simply serve the US or any other nation in a partisan manner. Thus, whenever consensus cannot be achieved in the UN this is not inefficiency, it is the cosmopolitan will, not the US will.

Furthermore, instead of national cosmopolitan action the development of cosmopolitan governance requires cosmopolitan agency in the sense that nations, especially those who want to enforce cosmopolitan order, need to subject their own behaviour to the rules of the cosmopolitan agency. They should not use military force in a way that is in contradiction with the rulings of the cosmopolitan agent. The fact that in the US protection discourse such an idea is considered ridiculous, shows how far we are still from genuine cosmopolitan agency of protection. In his presidential re-election campaign, President Bush ridiculed his opponent for presenting an idea according to which the United States should subject its use of military force outside its own territory to international law and the international agency:

> When my opponent first ran for Congress, he argued that American troops should be deployed only at the directive of the United Nations. [Audience members: Boo-o-o!] You probably think I'm making that up. [Laughter] I thought it was wrong when I first read it. [Laughter] Now, to be fair, he's changed his mind, but it is a window into his thinking. [Laughter] Over the years, Senator Kerry has looked for every excuse to constrain America's action in the world. (G.W. Bush, 2005f, p. 2392)

Finally, the development of cosmopolitan agency requires the resourcing of the cosmopolitan agent. To say that the UN was unable to tackle the genocides in Bosnia and Rwanda and this is why the United States has to assume leadership of cosmopolitan protection is not a fair argument either, as the lack of capacity of the UN is not a primordial feature of this international actor. The lack of UN capacity is a function of the lack of cosmopolitan commitment to resource the UN. The main national actors of cosmopolitan protection tend to be among the least willing to resource the UN capacity to tackle peace and security problems. The US with 0 UN peacekeeping troops, and a total of 53 UN peacekeeping personnel is a prime example of this. With 0 troops, 41 staff officers, nine police officers and three United Nations Middle East Mission personnel (this is the US share) the UN cannot be expected to prevent genocides (United Nations Database, 2018). Given the centrality for success of the question of cosmopolitan agency, any country that does not contribute more to the UN peacekeeping and genuine UN (rather than national) security function, should not feel compulsion to conduct cosmopolitan operations on its own either.

Finally, some cosmopolitan scholars and scholars of new wars have suggested that protective operations should be conducted in a less militaristic, less power-centric manner. Glanville (2017) suggests that we should be looking at non-military means of protection rather than being obsessed about military means of protection. The analysis of discourse of protection in this book supports this track of thought: power-centric militaristic discourse is clearly associated with increased violence. We should be thinking of protection we could offer ourselves – such as accepting more refugees, or resourcing development funds – and we should be thinking of what we could do together with the protected people – such as development cooperation – making them agents rather than objects of protection. Finally, we should be thinking of things that build security by restraint rather than by power. Such a suggestion borrows from the feminist theory of international relations, most explicitly from Tickner and Enloe (Tickner, 1992, 2001, 2004; Enloe, 2000). Instead of focusing exclusively on forcing President Assad's compliance with chemical weapons prohibition and other humanitarian and arms control norms (there is no doubt Assad's violations of these norms is a challenge to global human security), the United States should finally stop stockpiling chemical weapons as per the stipulations of the Chemical Weapons Convention, it should join the International Criminal Court so that its own forces could be monitored for their compliance of norms against war crimes, and it should show signs of compliance with the Non-Proliferation Treaty by not accelerating the nuclear arms race, given that it has committed itself to nuclear disarmament rather than the nuclear arms race.

The naturalization of the preference for power (rather than mutual restraint) in security policies has also led protection agents into choosing strategies that are overly militarized and strategies that destroy rather than build state capacity, whose lack is often seen as the very problem in the opportunistic violence of fragile states. According to Tickner and Enloe, the understanding that the problems of world politics can only be resolved by using power and by changing other actors' behaviour is related to the historical overrepresentation of men in security policies and the consequent naturalization of behavioural patterns that can be characterized as stereotypical masculinity. While this book has not followed the discourse process from historical discourses that have not benefited from the advice of feminine experience, discourse analysis of US presidential texts could easily identify the elements that Tickner defines as stereotypical masculinity and the association between such a feature and the failure of protection could be easily verified by means of statistics of features of the US presidential discourse.

Thus, in addition to introducing representative global agency as the defining step from cosmopolitanism to neocosmopolitanism, there is a need to democratize our language and practices of cosmopolitan protection and in that way remove material, institutional and discursive obstacles to inclusive cosmopolitan agency. Masculine experience must be complemented by feminine experience in cosmopolitan protection. The stereotypically masculine ways of operating in global security policies need to be criticized and modified by exposing the masculine origin of power-biased ways of operating, by denaturalizing the preference for strategies that change the behaviour of others over strategies that aim at mutual restraint and reduction of violent power in international and intrastate interaction. This book has shown the futility of power bias in cosmopolitan protection, and this work needs to be complemented by efforts to reveal and test alternative, less power-centric strategies and prioritizations for their usefulness for protection (some of this has obviously already been done in Glanville, 2017).

Thus, it seems that in addition to the sharing of agency and ownership of protection with the protected citizens of fragile states, there is a need for a gender-based democratization of protection. While the agency of protection should be more inclusive towards the Third World and women, the transition from patriotic partisan ways of protection could not be successfully completed without democratic and international *matriotism*, and advice from such feminine experience that stereotypical masculinity of cosmopolitan protection has been left without.

NOTE

1. One might perhaps say, that the relative success of the operation in Afghanistan could also be attributed to the fact that also there, serious attention has been given to the economic recovery and social development of the country.

Bibliography

Adler, E. and Barnett, M. (eds) (1998). Security communities in theoretical perspective. In *Security Communities* (pp. 3–28). Cambridge, UK: Cambridge University Press.

Al-Assad, B. (2014a). 2014 inauguration speech, July 16, 2014. Accessed August 6, 2018 at http://www.presidentassad.net/index.php?option=com_content&view=article&id=1181:president-assad-2014-inauguration-speech-july-16-2014&catid=311&Itemid=496.

Al-Assad, B. (2014b). President Bashar al-Assad's Army Day speech, August 1, 2014. Accessed August 6, 2018 at http://www.presidentassad.net/index.php?option=com_content&view=category&id=311&Itemid=496.

Al-Assad, B. (2015). President al-Assad's speech on July 26, 2015. Accessed February 28, 2018 at http://www.presidentassad.net/index.php?option=com_content&view=article&id=1454:president-al-assad-s-july-26th-2015-speech&catid=319&Itemid=496.

Al-Assad, B. (2016a). Most able to encounter terrorism. Speech by Bashar al-Assad. Accessed August 9, 2018 at http://www.presidentassad.net/index.php?option=com_content&view=article&id=1541:most-able-to-encounter-terrorism&catid=323:2016&Itemid=496.

Al-Assad, B. (2016b). President Assad's Parliament speech, June 7, 2016. Accessed May 29, 2017 at http://www.presidentassad.net/index.php?option=com_content&view=article&id=1529:president-assad-s-parliament-speech-june-7-2016&catid=323&Itemid=496.

Al-Assad, B. (2016c). Bashar al-Assad – President Assad's Bar Associations speech, February 15, 2016. Accessed August 9, 2018 at http://www.presidentassad.net/index.php?option=com_content&view=article&id=1512:president-assad-s-bar-associations-speech-february-15-2016&catid=323:2016&Itemid=496.

Al-Assad, B. (2017). President Assad's Arab Forum speech, November 14, 2017. Accessed August 8, 2018 at http://www.presidentassad.net/index.php?option=com_content&view=article&id=1620:president-assad-s-arab-forum-speech-november-14-2017&catid=326:2017&Itemid=496.

Allansson, M., Melander, E. and Themnér, L. (2017). Organized violence, 1989–2016. *Journal of Peace Research*, **54**(4), 536–50.

Amato, J.A. and Monge, D. (1990). *Victims and Values: A History and a Theory of Suffering*. London: Greenwood Publishing Group.

Amnesty International and Human Rights Watch (2013). Will I be next? US drone strikes in Pakistan. Accessed August 6, 2018 at https://www.amnestyusa.org/reports/will-i-be-next-us-drone-strikes-in-pakistan/.

Amos, D. (2018). The US has accepted only 11 Syrian refugees this year. *NPR*, April 12, 2018. Accessed April 16, 2018 at https://www.npr.org/sections/parallels/2018/04/12/602022877/the-u-s-has-welcomed-only-11-syrian-refugees-this-year.

Annan, Kofi (1999). Secretary-General Presents His Annual Report to General Assembly. Press Release, SG/SM/7136, GA/9596. United Nations General Assembly, September 20, 1999. Accessed October 16, 2018. https://www.un.org/press/en/1999/19990920.sgsm7136.html.

Anonymous Jihadists of Pakistan (2016). Jihad in Pakistan (report to base). *CIA: Bin Laden's Bookshelf*, March 1, 2016. Accessed August 9, 2018 at https://www.dni.gov/index.php/features/bin-laden-s-Bookshelf?start=2.

Armed Forces Revolutionary Council (1997). Armed Forces Revolutionary Council press release, December 14, 1997.

Armed Forces Revolutionary Council (1998a). Civilians take up arms against the Nigerian forces. Armed Forces Revolutionary Council press release, February 9, 1998.

Armed Forces Revolutionary Council (1998b). Joe Dempsy sympathises with Freetonians. Armed Forces Revolutionary Council press release, September 10, 1998.

Aslam, M.W. (2015). Great power responsibility, side-effect harms and American drone strikes in Pakistan. *Journal of Military Ethics*, **15**(2), 143–62.

Associated Press (2013). US drone strikes in Afghanistan rose sharply last year, UN reports. *The Guardian*, February 19, 2013. Accessed August 6, 2018 at http://www.theguardian.com/world/2013/feb/19/us-drone-strikes-afghanistan-un-report.

Austin, H. (2017). Syria missile strike: Donald Trump calls on 'all civilised nations to end the slaughter and bloodshed'. *The Independent*, April 7, 2017. Accessed August 10, 2018 at http://www.independent.co.uk/news/world/americas/us-politics/donald-trump-latest-syria-missile-strike-tomahawk-cruise-missile-homs-a7671416.html.

Ayoob, M. (1991). The security problematic of the Third World. *World Politics*, **43**(2), 257–83.

Ayoob, M. (1995). The new-old disorder in the Third World. In T.G. Weiss (ed.), *The United Nations and Civil Wars* (pp. 13–30). Boulder, CO and London: Lynne Rienner Publishers.

Ayoob, M. (1997). Defining security: A subaltern realist perspective. In K. Krause and M.C. Williams (eds), *Critical Security Studies: Concepts and Cases*. London: UCL Press, pp. 121–48.

Ayoob, M. (2001). Humanitarian intervention and international society. *Global Governance: A Review of Multilateralism and International Organizations*, **7**(3), 225–30.

Ayoob, M. (2004). Third World perspectives on humanitarian intervention and international administration. *Global Governance: A Review of Multilateralism and International Organizations*, **10**(1), 99–118.

Ayoob, M. (2005). The future of political Islam: The importance of external variables. *International Affairs*, **81**(5), 951–61.

Ayoob, M. (2016). Why Arab states have failed: It's not about scripture, or Sunnis and Shia. It's about the West. *The National Interest*, September 19, 2016. Accessed July 10, 2017 at http://nationalinterest.org/blog/the-skeptics/why-arab-states-have-failed-17734.

Azar, E.H. and Moon, C. (1988a). Legitimacy, integration and policy capacity: The software side of Third World national security. In E.E. Azar and C.-I. Moon (eds), *National Security in the Third World: The Management of Internal and External Threats* (pp. 77–101). College Park, MD: Center for International Development and Conflict Management, University of Maryland.

Azar, E.H. and Moon, C. (eds) (1988b). *National Security in the Third World: The Management of Internal and External Threats*. College Park, MD: Center for International Development and Conflict Management, University of Maryland.

Azar, E.H. and Moon, C. (1988c). Rethinking Third World national security. In E.H. Azar and C.-I. Moon (eds), *National Security in the Third World: The Management of Internal and External Threats* (pp. 1–13). College Park, MD: Center for International Development and Conflict Management, University of Maryland.

Ball, N. (2014). *Security and Economy in the Third World*. Princeton, NJ: Princeton University Press.

Beck, U. (2006). *The Cosmopolitan Vision*. Cambridge, UK: Polity Press.

Bellamy, A.J. (2002). Pragmatic solidarism and the dilemmas of humanitarian intervention. *Millennium – Journal of International Studies*, **31**(3), 473–97.

Bellamy, A.J. (2006). No pain, no gain? Torture and ethics in the war on terror. *International Affairs*, **82**(1), 121–8.

Bellamy, A.J. (2016). Syria is a failure of commitment, not principle. *The Washington Post*, February 16, 2016. Accessed August 5, 2018 at https://www.washingtonpost.com/news/in-theory/wp/2016/02/16/syria-is-a-failure-of-commitment-not-principle/.

Bienen, H.S. and Van de Walle, N. (1991). *Of Time and Power: Leadership Duration in the Modern World.* (Data updated by Monty G. Marshall.) Stanford, CA: Stanford University Press.

Bin Laden, O. (2004). Full transcript of bin Ladin's [sic] speech – *Al Jazeera*, November 1, 2004. Accessed May 29, 2017 at http://www.aljazeera.com/archive/2004/11/200849163336457223.html.

Bin Laden, O. (2015a). Despotism of big money. *CIA: Bin Laden's Bookshelf*, May 20, 2015. Accessed August 8, 2018 at https://www.dni.gov/index.php/features/bin-laden-s-Bookshelf?start=3.

Bin Laden, O. (2015b). Letter to the American people. *CIA: Bin Laden's Bookshelf*, May 20, 2015. Accessed August 9, 2018 at https://www.dni.gov/index.php/features/bin-laden-s-Bookshelf?start=3.

Bin Laden, O. (2015c). To the American people. *CIA: Bin Laden's Bookshelf*, May 20, 2015. Accessed August 10, 2018 at https://www.dni.gov/index.php/features/bin-laden-s-Bookshelf?start=3.

Bin Laden, O. (2016a). Dear Muslim brothers and sisters. *CIA: Bin Laden's Bookshelf*, March 1, 2016. Accessed August 8, 2018 at https://www.dni.gov/index.php/features/bin-laden-s-Bookshelf?start=2.

Bin Laden, O. (2016b). Draft speech about Iran and America with Mahmud's comments. *CIA: Bin Laden's Bookshelf*, March 1, 2016. Accessed August 8, 2018 at https://www.dni.gov/index.php/features/bin-laden-s-Bookshelf?s tart=2.

Bin Laden, O. (2016c). Letter to the Muslim nation at large. *CIA: Bin Laden's Bookshelf*, March 1, 2016. Accessed August 9, 2018 at https://www.dni.gov/index.php/features/bin-laden-s-Bookshelf?start=2.

Bin Laden, O. (2016d). Letter to the Muslim nation on Eid al-Adha. *CIA: Bin Laden's Bookshelf*, March 1, 2016. Accessed August 8, 2018 at https://www.dni.gov/index.php/features/bin-laden-s-Bookshelf?start=2.

Bin Laden, O. (2016e). Tunis. *CIA: Bin Laden's Bookshelf*, March 1, 2016. Accessed August 9, 2018 at https://www.dni.gov/index.php/features/bin -laden-s-Bookshelf?start=2.

Bin Laden, O. (2017a). Letter about efforts in other regions. *CIA: Bin Laden's Bookshelf*, January 19, 2017. Accessed August 9, 2018 at https://www.dni.gov/index.php/features/bin-laden-s-Bookshelf?start=2.

Bin Laden, O. (2017b). Letter to the Muslim nation. *CIA: Bin Laden's Bookshelf*, January 19, 2017. Accessed August 9, 2018 at https://www.dni.gov/index.php/features/bin-laden-s-Bookshelf?start=2.

Blainey, G. (1988). *Causes of War* (3rd edition). New York: Free Press.

Blair, T. (1999). I have little doubt that we will win. Interview with Patrick Wintour, *The Guardian*, May 16, 1999. Accessed August 6, 2018 at https://www.theguardian.com/uk/1999/may/16/tonyblair.

Blair, T. (2003). Prime minister outlines vision for Iraq and the Iraqi people.

Comments made following a joint UK, US and Spain summit, The Azores, 16 March, 2003.

Böhnke, J.R., Koehler, J. and Zürcher, C.M. (2017). State formation as it happens: Insights from a repeated cross-sectional study in Afghanistan, 2007–2015. *Conflict, Security & Development*, **17**(2), 91–116.

Booth, K. and Wheeler, N.J. (2008). *The Security Dilemma*. New York: Palgrave Macmillan.

Bouris, E. (2007). *Complex Political Victims*. West Hartford, CT: Kumarian Press.

Bowker, L.H. (1997). *Masculinities and Violence*. London: SAGE Publications.

Bray, D. (2009). Pragmatic cosmopolitanism: A Deweyan approach to democracy beyond the nation-state. *Millennium – Journal of International Studies*, **37**(3), 683–719.

Brick, G. (2009). *Global Justice. A Cosmopolitan Account*. Oxford: Oxford University Press.

Briggs, T. (2014). Naw Bahar district 2010–11: A case study of counter-insurgency conducted by Naval Special Warfare in Afghanistan. *Small Wars & Insurgencies*, **25**(1), 122–36.

British Army (2009). *British Army Field Manual: Volume 1, Part 10: Countering Insurgency*. Army Code 71876. London: UK Ministry of Defence. Accessed August 10, 2018 at http://news.bbc.co.uk/1/shared/bsp/hi/pdfs/16_11_09_army_manual.pdf.

Brown, C. (2000). Cosmopolitanism, world citizenship and global civil society. *Critical Review of International Social and Political Philosophy*, **3**(1), 7–26.

Brown, E. (2014). In Gallup Poll, the biggest threat to world peace is. . .America? *International Business Times*, January 2, 2014. Accessed August 12, 2014 at http://www.ibtimes.com/gallup-poll-biggest-threat-world-peace-america-1525008.

Brown, M.E. (1996). *The International Dimensions of Internal Conflict*. Cambridge, MA: MIT Press.

Buchanan, A. (2004). *Justice, Legitimacy, and Self-Determination: Moral Foundations for International Law*. Oxford: Oxford University Press.

Buchanan, A. and Keohane, R.O. (2015). Toward a drone accountability regime. *Ethics & International Affairs*, **29**(01), 15–37.

Bukharin, N.I. and Luxemburg, R. (1925 [1972]). *Imperialism and the Accumulation of Capital*. London: A. Lane/The Penguin Press.

Bureau of Investigative Journalism (2015). Afghanistan: Reported US air and drone strikes 2015. February 12, 2015. Accessed May 24, 2016 at https://www.thebureauinvestigates.com/drone-war/data/get-the-data-a-list-of-us-air-and-drone-strikes-afghanistan-2015.

Bureau of Investigative Journalism (2016). Yemen: Reported US covert actions 2016. January 18, 2016. Accessed August 6, 2016 at https://www.thebureauinvestigates.com/drone-war/data/yemen-reported-us-covert-actions-2016.

Bureau of Investigative Journalism (2017a). CIA drone strikes in Pakistan, 2004 to present. Accessed November 28, 2017 at https://docs.google.com/spreadsheets/d/1NAfjFonM-Tn7fziqiv33HlGt09wgLZDSCP-BQaux51w/edit#gid=694046452.

Bureau of Investigative Journalism (2017b). Somalia: Reported US covert actions 2001–2016. Accessed May 24, 2016 at https://www.globalresearch.ca/somalia-us-covert-operations-2001-2016/5581718.

Burke, A. (2013). Security cosmopolitanism. *Critical Studies on Security*, **1**(1), 13–28.

Burke, P. (2004). A transcontinental movement of citizens: Strategic debates in the 1980s Western peace movement. In G.-R. Horn and P. Kenney (eds), *Transnational Moments of Change: Europe 1945, 1968, 1989* (pp. 189–206). Lanham, MD: Rowman & Littlefield.

Bush, G.H.W. (1990). Remarks and an exchange with reporters on the upcoming meeting with Soviet President Mikhail Gorbachev at Malta, November 30, 1989. In *Public Papers of the Presidents of the United States 1989, Book II* (pp. 1608–9). Washington, DC: US Government Printing Office.

Bush, G.H.W. (1991). Remarks to the military airlift command in Dhahran, Saudi Arabia, November 22, 1990. In *Public Papers of the Presidents of the United States 1990, Book II* (pp. 1666–9). Washington, DC: US Government Printing Office.

Bush, G.H.W. (2009). Remarks at the White House Summit on International Development, October 21, 2009. In *Public Papers of the Presidents of the United States 2008 Book II* (pp. 1327–34). Washington, DC: US Government Printing Office.

Bush, G.W. (2002). Remarks announcing the Lessons of Liberty initiative in Rockville, Maryland, October 30, 2001. In *Public Papers of the Presidents of the United States 2001, Book II* (pp. 1325–7). Washington, DC: US Government Printing Office.

Bush, G.W. (2003a). Address to the nation on Iraq from Cincinnati, Ohio, October 7, 2002. In *Public Papers of the Presidents of the United States 2002, Book II* (pp. 1751–7). Washington, DC: US Government Publishing Office.

Bush, G.W. (2003b). Remarks at a reception for gubernatorial candidate Mitt Romney in Boston, Massachusetts, October 4, 2002. In *Public Papers of the Presidents of the United States 2002, Book II* (pp. 1727–35). Washington, DC: US Government Publishing Office.

Bush, G.W. (2003c). President says Saddam Hussein must leave Iraq within 48 hours. Remarks by the President in an address to the nation, the Cross Hall, The White House, Office of the Press Secretary, March 17, 2003. Accessed August 6, 2018 at https://georgewbush-whitehouse.archives.gov/news/releases/2003/03/20030317-7.html.

Bush, G.W. (2003d). President Bush discusses freedom in Iraq and Middle East. Remarks by the President at the 20th anniversary of the National Endowment for Democracy. *Office of the White House*, November 6, 2003. Accessed August 9, 2018 at https://georgewbush-whitehouse.archives.gov/news/releases/2003/11/20031106-2.html.

Bush, G.W. (2004a). Remarks at Pease Air National Guard Base in Portsmouth, New Hampshire, October 9, 2003. In *Public Papers of the Presidents of the United States 2003, Book I* (pp. 1273–9). Washington, DC: US Government Publishing Office.

Bush, G.W. (2004b). Remarks at Whitehall Palace in London, United Kingdom, November 19, 2003. In *Public Papers of the Presidents of the United States 2003, Book II* (pp. 1573–9). Washington, DC: US Government Printing Office.

Bush, G.W. (2004c). Remarks following discussions with Prime Minister John Howard of Australia and an exchange with reporters, February 10, 2003. In *Public Papers of the Presidents of the United States, 2003, Book I* (pp. 151–3). Washington, DC: US Government Publishing Office.

Bush, G.W. (2004d). Statement on the announcement of a transition plan by the Iraqi Governing Council, November 15, 2003. In *Public Papers of the Presidents of the United States 2003, Book II* (p. 1546). Washington, DC: US Government Printing Office.

Bush, G.W. (2004e). The President's news conference, March 6, 2003. In *Public Papers of the Presidents of the United States 2003, Book I* (pp. 244–54). Washington, DC: US Government Publishing Office.

Bush, G.W. (2005a). Remarks and a question-and-answer session in Prairie du Chien, Wisconsin, May 7, 2004. In *Public Papers of the Presidents of the United States 2004, Book I* (pp. 808–23). Washington, DC: US Government Printing Office.

Bush, G.W. (2005b). Remarks at the swearing-in ceremony for John C. Danforth as US Representative to the UN, July 1, 2004. In *Public Papers of the Presidents of the United States 2004, Book II* (pp. 1221–2). Washington, DC: US Government Publishing Office.

Bush, G.W. (2005c). Remarks in a discussion at Mid-States Aluminum Corporation in Fond du Lac, Wisconsin, July 14, 2004. In *Public Papers of the Presidents of the United States 2004, Book II* (pp. 1316–38). Washington, DC: US Government Publishing Office.

Bush, G.W. (2005d). Remarks in a discussion in Portsmouth, Ohio, September 10, 2004. In *Public Papers of the Presidents of the United*

States 2004, Book II (pp. 1986–2006). Washington, DC: US Government Publishing Office.
Bush, G.W. (2005e). Remarks in Farmington Hills, Michigan, October 6, 2004. In *Public Papers of the Presidents of the United States 2004, Book III* (pp. 2383–6). Washington, DC: US Government Printing Office.
Bush, G.W. (2005f). Remarks in Wausau, Wisconsin, October 7, 2004. In *Public Papers of the Presidents of the United States 2004, Book III* (pp. 2387–95). Washington, DC: US Government Printing Office.
Bush, G.W. (2005g). Remarks on the anniversary of Operation Iraqi Freedom, March 19, 2004. In *Public Papers of the Presidents of the United States 2004, Book I* (pp. 410–14). Washington, DC: US Government Printing Office.
Bush, G.W. (2005h). Remarks on the anniversary of the United States Department of Homeland Security, March 2, 2004. In *Public Papers of the Presidents of the United States 2004, Book I* (pp. 291–5). Washington, DC: US Government Printing Office.
Bush, G.W. (2005i). Remarks to the United States Conference of Mayors, January 23, 2004. In *Public Papers of the Presidents of the United States 2004, Book I* (pp. 115–23). Washington, DC: US Government Printing Office.
Bush, G.W. (2005j). The President's news conference, April 13, 2004. In *Public Papers of the Presidents of the United States 2004, Book I* (pp. 557–71). Washington, DC: US Government Printing Office.
Bush, G.W. (2005k). Remarks and a Question-and-Answer Session in Derry, New Hampshire September 20, 2004. In *Public Papers of the Presidents of the United States 2004, Book II* (pp. 2115–33). Washington, DC: US Government Publishing Office.
Bush, G.W. (2006a). Remarks at the FBI National Academy in Quantico, Virginia, July 11, 2005. In *Public Papers of the Presidents of the United States 2005, Book II* (pp. 1202–7). Washington, DC: US Government Printing Office.
Bush, G.W. (2006b). Remarks on strengthening social security in Columbia, South Carolina, April 18, 2005. In *Public Papers of the Presidents of the United States 2005, Book I* (pp. 615–22). Washington, DC: US Government Printing Office.
Bush, G.W. (2006c). Remarks to military personnel at Fort Hood, Texas, April 12, 2005. In *Public Papers of the Presidents of the United States, 2005, Book I* (pp. 587–91). Washington, DC: US Government Printing Office.
Bush, G.W. (2006d). Remarks to the American Legislative Exchange Council in Grapevine, Texas, August 3, 2005. In *Public Papers of the Presidents of the United States 2005, Book II* (pp. 1295–304). Washington, DC: US Government Printing Office.

Bush, G.W. (2006e). Remarks to the Woodrow Wilson International Center for Scholars, December 14, 2005. In *Public Papers of the Presidents of the United States 2005, Book II* (pp. 1851–6). Washington, DC: US Government Printing Office.

Bush, G.W. (2006f). The President's news conference with Prime Minister Anders Fogh Rasmussen of Denmark in Kongens Lyngby, Denmark, July 6, 2005. *Public Papers of the Presidents of the United States 2005, Book II* (pp. 1189–96). Washington, DC: US Government Printing Office.

Bush, G.W. (2007a). Foreword. In *Public Papers of the Presidents of the United States 2006, Book I* (pp. v–vi). Washington, DC: US Government Printing Office.

Bush, G.W. (2007b). Remarks at a reception for Congressional candidate Dean Heller in Reno, Nevada, October 2, 2006. In *Public Papers of the Presidents of the United States 2006, Book II* (pp. 1743–9). Washington, DC: US Government Printing Office.

Bush, G.W. (2007c). Remarks at an Iowa victory 2006 rally in Le Mars, Iowa, November 3, 2006. In *Public Papers of the Presidents of the United States 2006, Book II* (pp. 2000–2008). Washington, DC: US Government Printing Office.

Bush, G.W. (2007d). Remarks to reporters following a visit with United States troops and an exchange with reporters in San Antonio, Texas, January 1, 2006. In *Public Papers of the Presidents of the United States 2006, Book II* (pp. 1–3). Washington, DC: US Government Printing Office.

Bush, G.W. (2007e). The President's news conference with President Hamid Karzai of Afghanistan, September 26, 2006. In *Public Papers of the Presidents of the United States 2006, Book II* (pp. 1700–703). Washington, DC: US Government Printing Office.

Bush, G.W. (2008a). Remarks to members of Armed Forces service organizations, April 16, 2007. In *Public Papers of the Presidents of the United States 2007, Book I* (pp. 416–18). Washington, DC: US Government Printing Office.

Bush, G.W. (2008b). The President's radio address, May 5, 2007. In *Public Papers of the Presidents of the United States 2007, Book I* (pp. 541–2). Washington, DC: US Government Printing Office.

Bush, G.W. (2008c). Remarks to the Associated General Contractors of America and a Question-and-Answer Session May 2, 2007. In *Public Papers of the Presidents of the United States, 2007, Book I* (pp. 517–31). Washington, DC: US Government Printing Office.

Bush, G.W. (2009a). Remarks to the National Religious Broadcasters Convention in Nashville, March 11, 2008. In *Public Papers of the Presidents of the United States 2008, Book I* (pp. 346–53). Washington, DC: US Government Printing Office.

Bush, G.W. (2009b). Remarks to the United Nations General Assembly in New York City, September 23, 2008. In *Public Papers of the Presidents of the United States 2008, Book II* (pp. 1227–31). Washington, DC: US Government Printing Office.
Butler, J. (1990). *Gender Trouble: Feminism and the Subversion of Identity.* London and New York: Routledge.
Buzan, B. (1983). *People, States, and Fear: The National Security Problem in International Relations*. London: Wheatsheaf Books.
Buzan, B. and Wæver, O. (2003). *Regions and Powers: The Structure of International Security*. Cambridge, UK: Cambridge University Press.
Cameron, D. (2011). PM's speech at London conference on Libya. Lancaster House, London, March 29, 2011. Accessed March 13, 2017 at https://www.gov.uk/government/speeches/pms-speech-at-london-conference-on-libya.
Caney, S. (2005). *Justice Beyond Borders. A Global Political Theory.* Oxford: Oxford University Press.
Carati, A. (2017). Responsibility to protect, NATO and the problem of who should intervene: Reassessing the intervention in Libya. *Global Change, Peace & Security*, **29**(3), 293–309.
Cardoso, F.H. and Faletto, E. (1971 [1979]). *Dependencia y Desarrollo en América Latina.* [Dependency and Development in Latin America]. Berkeley, CA: University of California Press.
Castells, M. (1996). *The Rise of the Network Society: The Information Age: Economy, Society and Culture, Volume 1.* Oxford: Blackwell.
Chabal, P. and Daloz, J.-P. (1999). *Africa Works: Disorder as Political Instrument.* Bloomington, IN: Indiana University Press.
Chandler, D. (2000). International justice. *New Left Review*, **2**(6), 55–66.
Chandler, D. (2002). *From Kosovo to Kabul.* London and Sterling, VA: Pluto Press.
Chinkin, C. and Kaldor, M. (2017). *International Law and New Wars*. Cambridge, UK: Cambridge University Press.
Chivvis, C.S. (2015). *The French War on Al Qa'ida in Africa*. Cambridge, UK: Cambridge University Press.
Chomsky, N. (2016). *Who Rules the World? Reframings*. New York: Penguin.
Clinton, W.J. (1994a). Exchange with reporters prior to a meeting with Congressional leaders, September 28, 1993. In *Public Papers of the Presidents of the United States 1993, Book II* (pp. 1624–25). Washington, DC: US Government Printing Office.
Clinton, W.J. (1994b). Letter to Congressional leaders on Somalia, July 1, 1993. In *Public Papers of the Presidents of the United States 1993, Book I* (pp. 969–71). Washington, DC: US Government Printing Office.
Clinton, W.J. (1994c). Remarks to the AFL–CIO Convention in San Francisco, California, October 4, 1993. In *Public Papers of the Presidents*

of the United States 1993, Book II (pp. 1667–76). Washington, DC: US Government Printing Office.

Clinton, W.J. (1994d). The President's news conference, April 20, 1993. In *Public Papers of the Presidents of the United States 1993, Book II* (pp. 732–6). Washington, DC: US Government Printing Office.

Clinton, W.J. (1994e). The President's radio address, June 12, 1993. In *Public Papers of the Presidents of the United States 1993, Book I* (pp. 839–40). Washington, DC: US Government Printing Office.

Clinton, W.J. (1994f). The President's news conference, October 14, 1993. In *Public Papers of the Presidents of the United States 1993, Book II* (pp. 1742–6). Washington, DC: US Government Printing Office.

Clinton, W.J. (1995). Remarks prior to a breakfast with President Jimmy Carter, General Colin Powell, and Senator Sam Nunn, September 19, 1994. In *Public Papers of the Presidents of the United States 1994, Book II* (pp. 1574–9). Washington, DC: US Government Printing Office.

Clinton, W.J. (1996a). Address to the nation on implementation of the peace agreement in Bosnia-Herzegovina, November 27, 1995. In *Public Papers of the Presidents of the United States 1995, Book II* (pp. 1784–7). Washington, DC: US Government Printing Office.

Clinton, W.J. (1996b). Remarks on environmental protection in Baltimore, Maryland, August 8, 1995. In *Public Papers of the Presidents of the United States 1995, Book II* (pp. 1215–18). Washington, DC: US Government Printing Office.

Clinton, W.J. (1996c). Remarks on vetoing budget reconciliation legislation, December 6, 1995. *Public Papers of the Presidents of the United States 1995, Book II* (pp. 1851–3). Washington, DC: US Government Printing Office.

Clinton, W.J. (1996d). Statement on vetoing legislation to lift the arms embargo against Bosnia, August 11, 1995. In *Public Papers of the Presidents of the United States 1995, Book II* (pp. 1253–4). Washington, DC: US Government Printing Office.

Clinton, W.J. (1997). Remarks on international security issues at George Washington University, August 5, 1996. In *Public Papers of the Presidents of the United States 1996, Book II* (pp. 1255–60). Washington, DC: US Government Printing Office.

Clinton, W.J. (1998). Remarks announcing the appointment of Togo D. West, Jr., as Acting Secretary of Veterans Affairs and an exchange with reporters, December 2, 1997. In *Public Papers of the Presidents of the United States 1997, Book II* (pp. 1688–90). Washington, DC: US Government Printing Office.

Clinton, W.J. (1999a). Communique: Entebbe Summit for Peace and Prosperity, March 25, 1998. In *Public Papers of the Presidents of*

the United States 1998, Book I (pp. 434–8). Washington, DC: US Government Printing Office.
Clinton, W.J. (1999b). Remarks at a Democratic National Committee dinner, 7 October 1998. In *Public Papers of the Presidents of the United States 1998, Book II* (pp. 1760–63). Washington, DC: US Government Printing Office.
Clinton, W.J. (1999c). Remarks to business and community leaders in Santiago, April 16, 1998. In *Public Papers of the Presidents of the United States 1998, Book I* (pp. 575–9). Washington, DC: US Government Printing Office.
Clinton, W.J. (2000a). Letter to Congressional leaders reporting on the deployment of United States military personnel to the Kosovo International Security Force, December 15, 1999. In *Public Papers of the Presidents of the United States 1999, Book I* (pp. 2303–5). Washington, DC: US Government Printing Office.
Clinton, W.J. (2000b). Remarks at a Majority 2000 luncheon in Dearborn, Michigan, April 16, 1999. In *Public Papers of the Presidents of the United States 1999, Book I* (pp. 563–9). Washington, DC: US Government Printing Office.
Clinton, W.J. (2000c). Remarks following discussions with NATO Secretary General Javier Solana and an exchange with reporters, April 22, 1999. In *Public Papers of the Presidents of the United States 1999, Book I* (pp. 601–3). Washington, DC: US Government Printing Office.
Clinton, W.J. (2000d). Remarks to American troops at Camp Bondsteel, Kosovo, November 23, 1999. In *Public Papers of the Presidents of the United States 1999, Book II* (pp. 2145–7). Washington, DC: US Government Printing Office.
Clinton, W.J. (2000e). Remarks to the veterans of foreign wars of the United States at Fort McNair, Maryland, May 13, 1999. In *Public Papers of the Presidents of the United States 1999, Book I* (pp. 656–762). Washington, DC: US Government Printing Office.
Clinton, W.J. (2000f). The President's news conference, March 19, 1999. In *Public Papers of the Presidents of the United States 1999, Book I* (pp. 409–21). Washington, DC: US Government Printing Office.
Clinton, W.J. (2000g). Washington Summit communique, April 24, 1999. In *Public Papers of the Presidents of the United States 1999, Book I* (pp. 613–22). Washington, DC: US Government Printing Office.
Clinton, W.J. (2000h). Interview With Yevgeniy Kiselev of Russia's NTV in Cologne June 20, 1999. In *Public Papers of the Presidents of the United States 1999, Book I* (pp. 973–76). Washington, DC: US Government Printing Office.
Coles, I. and Parker, N. (2015). How Saddam's fighters help Islamic State

rule. *Reuters*, December 11, 2015. Accessed January 4, 2016 at http://www.reuters.com/investigates/special-report/mideast-crisis-iraq-islamic state/.

Connell, R.W. (2005). *Masculinities*. Berkeley, CA: California University Press.

Connell, R.W. (2007). *Southern Theory: The Global Dynamics of Knowledge in Social Science.* Cambridge, UK: Polity Press.

Cunliffe, P. (2010). Dangerous duties: Power, paternalism and the 'Responsibility to Protect'. *Review of International Studies*, **36**(1), 79–96.

Daalder, I.H. (1996). The United States and military intervention in internal wars. In M. Brown (ed.), *The International Dimensions of Internal Conflicts.* Cambridge, MA: MIT Press, pp. 461–88.

De Alvarez, L.P.S. (2009). The theory of imperialism [recording from 1964]. *ISI Lecture Podcast, Volume 24*.

Deutsch, K. (1955). *Political Community and the North Atlantic Area.* Westport, CT: Greenwood Press.

Dodge, T. (2013). Intervention and dreams of exogenous statebuilding: The application of liberal peacebuilding in Afghanistan and Iraq. *Review of International Studies*, **39**(05), 1189–212.

Duffield, M. (2001). *Global Governance and the New Wars*. New York: Zed Press.

Duffield, M. (2002). Social reconstruction and the radicalization of development: Aid as a relation of global liberal governance. *Development and Change*, **33**(5), 1049–71.

Eck, K. and Hultman, L. (2007). One-sided violence against civilians in war. *Journal of Peace Research*, **44**(2), 233–46.

Economist, The (2017). Donald Trump's foreign policy looks more normal than promised. April 15, 2017. Accessed August 11, 2018 at https://www.economist.com/news/united-states/21720625-two-big-caveats-donald-trumps-foreign-policy-looks-more-normal-promised.

Ejdus, F. (2017). Local ownership as international governmentality: Evidence from the EU mission in the Horn of Africa. *Contemporary Security Policy*, **39**(1), 28–50.

Elias, N. (1939). *The Civilizing Process: Sociogenetic and Psychogenetic Investigations.* Cambridge, MA: Blackwell.

Elias, N. (1982). *Power and Civility, Volume 2: The Civilizing Process*. New York: Pantheon.

Ellis, L. (1989). *Theories of Rape.* New York: Hemisphere/Taylor & Francis.

Elshtain, J.B. (1987). *Women and War*. Chicago, IL: University of Chicago Press.

Elster, N. (2011). Danmark samarbeidet med Gaddafi [Denmark's cooperation with Gaddafi]. *NRK*, September 8, 2011. Accessed February 26, 2018 at https://www.nrk.no/urix/danmark-samarbeidet-med-gaddafi-1.7783633.

Enloe, C. (2000). *Bananas, Beaches and Bases: Making Feminist Sense of International Politics*, Berkeley, CA: University of California Press.

Enos, R.L. (1993). Viewing the dawns of our past days again. In T. Enos and S.C. Brown (eds), *Defining the New Rhetorics* (pp. 8–21). Newbury Park, CA: Sage.

Etzioni, A. (2004). *From Empire to Community.* New York: Palgrave Macmillan.

Falk, R. (2002). Testing patriotism and citizenship in the global terror war. In K. Booth and T. Dunne (eds), *Worlds in Collision: Terror and the Future of World Order.* London: Palgrave, pp. 325–35.

Falk, R. (2003). 'Humanitarian wars', realist geopolitics and genocidal practices: 'Saving the Kosovars'. In K. Booth (ed.), *The Kosovo Tragedy: The Human Rights Dimension* (2nd edition) (pp. 325–34). London: Frank Cass.

Farmer, B. (2013). Syria: Nearly half rebel fighters are jihadists or hard-line Islamists, says IHS Jane's report. *The Telegraph*, September 15, 2013. Accessed February 22, 2015 at http://www.telegraph.co.uk/news/worldnews/middleeast/syria/10311007/Syria-nearly-half-rebel-fighters-are-jihadists-or-hardline-Islamists-says-IHS-Janes-report.html.

Fearon, J.D. (1995). Rationalist explanations for war. *International Organization*, **49**(3), 379–414.

Fearon, J.D. and Laitin, D.D. (2004). Neotrusteeship and the problem of weak states. *International Security*, **28**(4), 5–43.

Fearon, J.D. and Laitin, D.D. (2014). Does contemporary armed conflict have 'deep historical roots'? Accessed August 5, 2018 at https://papers.ssrn.com/abstract=1922249.

Forte, M.C. (2012). *Slouching Towards Sirte: NATO's War on Libya and Africa*. Montreal: Baraka Books.

Foucault, M. (1974). *The Archaeology of Knowledge.* London: Tavistock Publications.

Fukuyama, F. (1992). *The End of History and the Last Man*. New York: Free Press.

Fukuyama, F. (2011). *The Origins of Political Order from Prehuman Times to the French Revolution*. New York: Farrar, Straus & Giroux.

Gaddafi, M. (2011a). Muammar Gaddafi's UNGA speech on behalf of the AU. *Libya 360° Archive*, March 1, 2011. Accessed March 8, 2018 at https://libyadiary.wordpress.com/2011/03/01/muammar-gaddafis-unga-speech-on-behalf-of-the-au/.

Gaddafi, M. (2011b). Muammar Gaddafi: 'The West is to be forgotten'. *Libya 360° Archive*, March 16, 2011. Accessed August 9, 2018 at https://

libyadiary.wordpress.com/2011/03/16/muammar-gaddafi-the-west-is-to-be-forgotten/.

Gaddafi, M. (2011c). Muammar Gaddafi, April 30, 2011. *Libya 360° Archive*, April 30, 2011. Accessed April 26, 2018 at https://libyadiary.wordpress.com/2011/04/30/muammar-gaddafi-april-30-2011/.

Gaddafi, M. (2011d). Muammar Gaddafi: Tripoli's Green Square, July 1, 2011. *Libya 360° Archive*, July 7, 2011. Accessed March 8, 2018 at https://libyadiary.wordpress.com/2011/07/07/tripolis-green-square-july-1-2011/.

Gaddafi, M. (2011e). Muammar Gaddafi: Zawiya, July 19, 2011. *Libya 360° Archive*, July 19, 2011. Accessed March 8, 2018 at https://libyadiary.wordpress.com/2011/07/19/muammar-gaddafi-zawiya-july-19-2011/.

Gaddafi, M. (2011f). Message from Muammar Gaddafi, August 23, 2011. *Libya 360° Archive*, August 23, 2011. Accessed March 8, 2018 at https://libyadiary.wordpress.com/2011/08/23/message-from-muammar-gaddafi-august-23-2001/.

Gaddafi, M. (2011g). Muammar Gaddafi, September 7, 2011. *Libya 360° Archive*, September 7, 2011. Accessed March 8, 2018 at https://libyadiary.wordpress.com/2011/09/07/muammar-gaddafi-september-7-2011/6.

Gaddafi, M. (2011h). Message from Muammar Gaddafi, October 6, 2011. *Libya 360° Archive*, October 6, 2011. Accessed February 28, 2018 at https://libyadiary.wordpress.com/2011/10/06/message-from-muammar-gaddafi-october-6th-2011/.

Gaddafi, M. (2011i). Last message from Muammar Gaddafi. *Libya 360° Archive*, October 23, 2011. Accessed February 28, 2018 at https://libyadiary.wordpress.com/2011/10/23/last-message-from-muammar-gaddafi/.

Gaddafi, M. (2011j). Letter from Muammar Gaddafi, September 12, 2011. *Libya 360° Archive*, November 16, 2011. Accessed March 8, 2018 at https://libyadiary.wordpress.com/2011/11/16/letter-from-muammar-gaddafi-september-12-2011/.

Gaddafi, M. (2011k). Message from Muammar Gaddafi, September 27, 2011. *Libya 360° Archive*, November 16, 2011. Accessed March 8, 2018 at https://libyadiary.wordpress.com/2011/11/16/message-from-muammar-gaddafi-september-27th-2011/.

Gaddafi, M (2014). Gaddafi's last formal speech to the people of Libya, April 17, 2011. *News Rescue*, August 10, 2014. Accessed February 27, 2018 at http://newsrescue.com/gaddaffis-last-formal-speech-people-libya/.

Gholiagha, S. (2015). 'To prevent future Kosovos and future Rwandas': A critical constructivist view of the Responsibility to Protect. *The International Journal of Human Rights*, **19**(8), 1074–97.

Giddens, A. (1985). *The Nation-State and Violence, Volume 2: A Contemporary Critique of Historical Materialism*. Cambridge, UK: Polity Press.

Gilbert, P. (2003). *New Terror, New Wars.* Edinburgh: Edinburgh University Press.

Gilmore, J. (2014). Protecting the other: Considering the process and practice of cosmopolitanism. *European Journal of International Relations*, **20**(3), 694–719.

Gilmore, J. (2015). *The Cosmopolitan Military: Armed Forces and Human Security in the 21st Century*. London: Palgrave.

Glanville, L. (2017). Responsibility to perfect: Vattel's conception of duties beyond borders. *International Studies Quarterly*, **61**(2), 385–95.

Glanville, L. (2018). The limits of rhetorical entrapment in a post-truth age. *Critical Studies on Security*. Accessed August 6, 2018 at https://doi.org/10.1080/21624887.2018.1441624.

Gleditsch, N.P., Wallensteen, P. and Eriksson, M. et al. (2002). Armed conflict 1946–2001: A new dataset. *Journal of Peace Research*, **39**(5), 615–37.

Goldberg, M.S. (2018). Casualty rates of US military personnel during the wars in Iraq and Afghanistan. *Defence and Peace Economics*, **29**(1), 44–61.

Gordon, L. (1997). The struggle for reproductive freedom. In A. Tone (ed.), *Controlling Reproduction: An American History* (pp. 147–56). Lanham, MD: Rowman & Littlefield.

Government of the United Kingdom (2018). Read the full legal case for the British government's strikes in Syria. *The Telegraph*, April 14, 2018. Accessed August 9, 2018 at https://www.telegraph.co.uk/news/2018/04/14/read-full-legal-case-british-governments-strikes-syria/.

Griffin, D. and Johnston, K. (2013). The United States is still getting rid of its chemical weapons. *CNN*, October 14, 2018. Accessed August 17, 2018 at https://edition.cnn.com/2013/10/11/us/u-s-chemical-weapons/index.html.

Gurr, T.R. (1970). *Why Men Rebel*. Princeton, NJ: Princeton University Press.

Gurr, T.R. (1993). *Minorities at Risk.* (Updated by M.G. Marshall and V. Asal.) Washington, DC: United States Institute of Peace Press.

Gurr, T.R. (2000). Ethnic warfare on the wane. *Foreign Affairs*, May/June, 53–4.

Haas, E.B. (1964). *Beyond the Nation State: Functionalism and International Organization*. Stanford, CA: Stanford University Press.

Habermas, J. (2000). Bestialität und Humanität: Ein Krieg an der Grenze zwischen Recht und Mora [Bestiality and humanity: A war on the border between legality and morality]. In R. Merkel (ed.), *Der Kosovo Krieg un das Völkerecht* (pp. 51–65). Frankfurt am Main: Suhrkamp.

Habermas, J. (2001). *The Postnational Constellation: Political Essays*. Cambridge, MA: MIT Press.

Haldeman, H.R. (1995). *The Haldeman Diaries: Inside the Nixon White House.* New York: HarperCollins.

Hansen, L. (2006). *Security as Practice: Discourse Analysis and the Bosnian War*. London: Routledge.

Harbom, L., Melander, E. and Wallensteen, P. (2008). Dyadic dimensions of armed conflict, 1946–2007. *Journal of Peace Research*, **45**(5), 697–710.

Hartsock, N.C.M. (1998). *The Feminist Standpoint Revisited and Other Essays*. Boulder, CO: Westview Press.

Hayden, P. (2005). *Cosmopolitan Global Politics*. London and New York: Routledge.

Heathcote, G. (2017). Women and children and elephants as justification for force. *Journal on the Use of Force and International Law*, **4**(1), 66–85.

Heidegger, M. (1962). *Being and Time.* Oxford: Blackwell.

Hertz, J.H. (1950). Idealist internationalism and the security dilemma. *World Politics*, **2**(1), 157–80.

Hertz, J.H. (2003). The security dilemma in international relations. Background and present problems. *International Relations*, **17**(4), 411–16.

Heupel, M. and Zangl, B. (2010). On the transformation of warfare: A plausibility probe of the new war thesis. *Journal of International Relations and Development*, **13**(1), 26–58.

Hilson, G., Hilson, A. and Maconachie, R. (2017). Artisanal and small-scale mining (ASM) in Sub-Saharan Africa: Re-conceptualizing formalization and 'illegal' activity. *Geoforum*, **83**, 80–90.

Hoffman, B. (2004). *Insurgency and Counterinsurgency in Iraq*. Santa Monica, CA: Rand Corporation.

Hollis, M. and Smith, S. (1990). *Explaining and Understanding International Relations.* Oxford: Clarendon Press.

Holsti, K.J. (2006). The decline of interstate war: Pondering systemic explanations. In R. Väyrynen (ed.), *The Waning of Major War: Theories and Debates* (pp. 135–60). London and New York: Routledge.

Hooper, C. (1998). Masculinist practices and gender politics: The operation of multiple masculinities in international relations. In M. Zalewski and J. Parpart (eds), *The Man Question in International Relations.* Boulder, CO: Westview Press, pp. 25–53.

House of Commons and Foreign Affairs Committee (2015). *The Extension of Offensive British Military Operations to Syria: Second Report of Session 2015–16*. London: The Stationery Office Limited.

Howarth, D. and Stavrakakis, Y. (2000). Introducing discourse theory and political analysis. In D. Howarth, A.J. Novral and Y. Stavrakakis (eds), *Discourse Theory and Political Analysis: Identities, Hegemonies and Social Change* (pp. 1–23). Manchester: Manchester University Press.

Hudson, L., Owens, C.S. and Callen, D.J. (2012). Drone warfare in Yemen:

Fostering emirates through counterterrorism? *Middle East Policy*, **19**(3), 142–56.

Hume, D. (2000). *An Enquiry Concerning Human Understanding.* (Edited by T.L. Beauchamp.) New York: Clarendon Press.

Hussain, M. (2016). Young Iraqis overwhelmingly consider US their enemy, poll says. *Global Research*, April 15, 2016. Accessed March 24, 2017 at http://www.globalresearch.ca/young-iraqis-overwhelmingly-consider-u-s-their-enemy-poll-says/5520310.

Hussein, S. (2001). Saddam Hussein: Second open letter to the American people. *American Rhetoric: Rhetoric of 9-11*, September 18, 2001. Accessed March 8, 2018 at http://www.americanrhetoric.com/speeches/sadaamhusseinopenlettertous.htm.

Hussein, S. (2003a). Transcript: Saddam Hussein interview, Pt. 1. *CBS News*, February 24, 2003. Accessed March 8, 2018 at https://www.cbsnews.com/news/transcript-saddam-hussein-interview-pt-1/.

Hussein, S. (2003b). Raw data: Text of Saddam's speech. *Fox News*, March 20, 2003. Accessed August 8, 2018 at http://www.foxnews.com/story/2003/03/20/raw-data-text-saddam-speech.html.

ISIS. (2013). Specimen 5V: Notification: 'Emirate of Azaz'. *Archive of Islamic State Administrative Documents*, September. Accessed August 9, 2018 at http://www.aymennjawad.org/2015/01/archive-of-islamic-state-administrative-documents.

ISIS (2015a). General/public call for the citizens of the Islamic State. *Archive of Islamic State Administrative Documents*. Accessed August 6, 2018 at http://www.aymennjawad.org/2015/01/archive-of-islamic-state-administrative-documents.

ISIS (2015b). Specimen 3Z: Notice to the soldiers of Kweiris airbase, Aleppo province. *Archive of Islamic State Administrative Documents*. Accessed March 1, 2018 at http://www.aymennjawad.org/2015/01/archive-of-islami c-state-administrative-documents.

ISIS (2015c). Specimen 9Z: Prohibition on attacking Kurdish property in Raqqa. *Archive of Islamic State Administrative Documents*. Accessed March 1, 2018 at http://www.aymennjawad.org/2015/01/archive-of-islamic-state-admiznistrative-documents.

ISIS (2015d). Specimen 12G: Ban on satellite reception apparatuses [i.e., satellite TV]. *Archive of Islamic State Administrative Documents*. Accessed March 1, 2018 at http://www.aymennjawad.org/2015/01/archive-of-islamic-state-administrative-documents.

ISIS (2015e). The Isis papers: A masterplan for consolidating power. *The Guardian*, December 7, 2015. Accessed February 28, 2018 at http://www.theguardian.com/world/2015/dec/07/islamic-state-document-masterplan-for-power.

ISIS (n.d.). Specimen 5M: Notification for Kurds to leave Raqqa city. *Archive of Islamic State Administrative Documents*. Accessed March 1, 2018 at http://www.aymennjawad.org/2015/01/archive-of-islamic-state-administrative-documents.

Jäger, S. (2001). Discourse and knowledge: Theoretical and methodological aspects of a critical discourse and dispositive analysis. In R. Wodak and M. Meyer (eds), *Methods of Critical Discourse Analysis* (pp. 32–62). London: Sage.

Jaggar, A.M. (1983). *Feminist Politics and Human Nature*. Totowa, NJ: Rowman & Littlefield.

Johnson, D.D.P. (2004). *Overconfidence and War: The Havoc and Glory of Positive Illusions.* Cambridge, MA: Harvard University Press.

Jones, C. (1999). *Global Justice: Defending Cosmopolitanism.* Oxford: Oxford University Press.

Kaldor, M. (1999). *New and Old Wars: Organized Violence in a Global Era.* Stanford, CA: Stanford University Press.

Kaldor, M. (2003). *Global Civil Society: An Answer to War.* Malden, MA: Polity Press.

Kaldor, M. (2012). *New and Old Wars: Organized Violence in a Global Era* (3rd edition). Stanford, CA: Stanford University Press.

Kaldor, M. (2013). Comment on security cosmopolitanism. *Critical Studies on Security*, **1**(1), 42–5.

Kalyvas, S.N. (2001). 'New' and 'old' civil wars: A valid distinction? *World Politics*, **54**(1), 99–118.

Kant, I. (1996). *Metaphysics of Morals.* (Edited by M. Gregor.) Cambridge, UK: Cambridge University Press.

Kant, I. (1999). *Toward perpetual peace*. In M.J. Gregor (trans.), Practical Philosophy: The Cambridge Edition of the Works of Immanuel Kant. Cambridge, UK: Cambridge University Press.

Keen, D. (2005). *Conflict & Collusion in Sierra Leone.* New York: Palgrave.

Kissinger, H. (2014). *World Order*. London: Penguin.

Kivimäki, T. (2012). Democracy, autocrats and US policies. *Middle East Policy*, **XIX**(1), 64–71.

Kivimäki, T. (2013). The United States and the Arab Spring. *Journal of Human Security*, **9**(1), 15–26.

Kivimäki, T. (2014). *The Long Peace of East Asia*. London: Routledge.

Kivimäki, T. (2016). *Paradigms of Peace*. London: Imperial College Press.

Kivimäki, T. (2019a, forthcoming). How does nationalist selfishness creep into cosmopolitan protection? *Global Responsibility to Protect*, **10**(1).

Kivimäki, T. (2019b, forthcoming). *Coding of US Presidential Discourse on Protection.* University of Bath Research Data Archive. doi:10.15125/BATH-00535

Knuckey, S., Solvang, O., Horowitz, J. and Almutawakel, R. (2017). Pentagon admits major investigation flaw: They rarely talk to air strike witnesses or victims. *Just Security*, June 29, 2017. Accessed August 22, 2017 at https://www.justsecurity.org/42675/pentagon-admits-rarely-talks-air-strike-witnesses-victims/.

Kratochwil, F.V. (1989). *Rules, Norms and Decisions.* Cambridge, UK: Cambridge University Press.

Krause, K. (1998). Theorizing security, state formation and the 'Third World' in the post-Cold War world. *Review of International Studies*, **24**(01), 125–36.

Kuperman, A. (2013). A model humanitarian intervention? Reassessing NATO's Libya campaign. *International Security*, **38**(1), 104–36.

Kuusisto, R. (1998). Framing the wars in the Gulf and in Bosnia: The rhetorical definitions of the Western power leaders in action. *Journal of Peace Research*, **35**(5), 603–20.

Lacina, B.A. (2009). *The PRIO Battle Deaths Dataset, 1946–2008, Version 3.0: Documentation of Coding Decisions*. Peace Research Institute Oslo. Accessed August 4, 2018 at http://www.prio.no/Global/upload/CSCW/Data/PRIObd3.0_documentation.pdf.

Lacina, B.A. and Gleditsch, N.P. (2005). Monitoring trends in global combat: A new dataset of battle deaths. *European Journal of Population*, **21**(2–3), 145–65.

Laclau, E. and Mouffe, C. (2001). *Hegemony and Socialist Strategy: Towards a Radical Democratic Politics*. London: Verso.

Lenin, V.I. (1999). *Imperialism: The Highest Stage of Capitalism*. London: Resistance Books.

Levi, P. (2017). *The Drowned and the Saved*. New York: Simon & Schuster.

Lichbach, M.I. and Gurr, T.R. (1981). Forecasting domestic political conflict. In J.D. Singer and M.D. Wallace (eds), *To Augur Well: Early Warning Indicators in World Politics*. Beverly Hills, CA: Sage, pp. 3–38.

Linklater, A. (2002). The problem of harm in world politics: Implications for the sociology of states-systems. *International Affairs*, **78**(2), 319–38.

Linklater, A. (2011). *The Problem of Harm in World Politics: Theoretical Investigations*. Cambridge, UK: Cambridge University Press.

Linklater, A. (2017). *Violence and Civilization in the Western States-Systems*. Cambridge, UK: Cambridge University Press.

Lyall, J. and Wilson III, I. (2009). Rage against the machines: Explaining outcomes in counterinsurgency wars. *International Organization*, **63**, 67–106.

Mack, A. (1975). Why big nations lose small wars: The politics of asymmetric conflict. *World Politics*, **27**(2), 175–200.

Maconachie, R. (2018). *Voices from the Mine: Artisanal Diamonds and*

Resource Governance in Sierra Leone [Documentary]. University of Bath, UK.

Mahmood, M. (2014). US air strikes in Syria driving anti-Assad groups to support Isis. *The Guardian*, November 23, 2014. Accessed August 6, 2018 at http://www.theguardian.com/world/2014/nov/23/us-air-strikes-syra-driving-anti-assad-groups-support-isis.

Malešević, S. (2008). The sociology of new wars? Assessing the causes and objectives of contemporary violent conflicts. *International Political Sociology*, **2**(2), 97–112.

Mamdani, M. (2010). Responsibility to protect or right to punish? *Journal of Intervention and Statebuilding*, **4**(1), 53–67.

Marshall, M.G. and Elzinga-Marshall, G. (2017). *Global Report 2017: Conflict, Governance, and State Fragility*. Vienna: Center for Systematic Peace.

Marshall, M.G. and Jaggers, K. (2000). *Polity IV Project: Political Regime Characteristics and Transitions, 1800–1999: Dataset User Manual.*

Marshall, M.G. and Ramsey Marshall, D. (2016). *Coup d'État Events 1946–2015*. Vienna: Center for Systemic Peace.

Marx, K. (1990). *Capital, Volume 1*. London: Penguin.

McGreal, C. (2000). Drinking gin and wearing flipflops, the bandits who ambushed the Royal Irish. *The Guardian*, August 28, 2000. Accessed March 6, 2018 at http://www.theguardian.com/world/2000/aug/28/sierraleone.

Melander, E., Öberg, M. and Hall, J. (2009). Are 'new wars' more atrocious? Battle intensity, genocide and forced migration before and after the end of the Cold War. *European Journal of International Relations*, **15**(3), 505–36.

Melander, E., Pettersson, T. and Themnér, L. (2016). Organized violence, 1989–2015. *Journal of Peace Research*, **53**(5), 727–42.

Mello, P.A. (2010). In search of new wars: The debate about a transformation of war. *European Journal of International Relations*, **16**(2), 297–309.

Merom, G. (2003). *How Democracies Lose Small Wars: State, Society, and the Failures of France in Algeria, Israel in Lebanon, and the United States in Vietnam.* Cambridge, UK: Cambridge University Press.

Messerschmidt, J.W. (2000). *Nine Lives: Adolescent Masculinities.* Boulder, CO: Westview Press.

Miller, G. (2013). CIA ramping up covert training program for moderate Syrian rebels. *The Washington Post*, October 2, 2013. Accessed August 6, 2018 at http://www.washingtonpost.com/world/national-security/cia-ramping-up-covert-training-program-for-moderate-syrian-rebels/2013/10/02/a0bba084-2af6-11e3-8ade-a1f23cda135e_story.html.

Milošević, S. (1998). Interview of Slobodan Milosevic to the *Washington Post*. Belgrade, December 16, 1998. Accessed August 6, 2018 at http://www.slobodan-milosevic.org/int-WP98.htm.

Milošević, S. (1999a). Interview of Slobodan Milosevic to KHOU TV. Belgrade, April 21, 1999. Accessed August 6, 2018 at http://www.slobodan-milosevic.org/int-KHOU99.htm.
Milošević, S. (1999b). Interview of Slobodan Milosevic to UPI. Belgrade, April 30, 1999. Accessed August 6, 2018 at http://www.slobodan-milosevic.org/int-upi99.htm.
Milošević, S. (1999c). President Slobodan Milosevic's address to the nation. Belgrade, June 10, 1999. Accessed February 23, 2018 at http://www.slobodan-milosevic.org/news/milosevic061099.htm.
Milošević, S. (1999d). Interview of Slobodan Milosevic to Politika. Belgrade, December 31, 1999. Accessed August 6, 2018 at http://www.slobodan-milosevic.org/int-pol99.htm.
Milošević, S. (2000a). Closing statement of Slobodan Milosevic at the Fourth SPS Congress, February 17, 2000. Socialist Party of Serbia. Accessed August 6, 2018 at http://www.slobodan-milosevic.org/sps4.htm.
Milošević, S. (2000b). President Slobodan Milosevic's address to the nation, October 2, 2000. Accessed August 6, 2018 at http://www.slobodan-milosevic.org/spch-oc2000.htm.
Milošević, S. (2000c). Closing statement at the Fifth SPS Congress, November 25, 2000. Accessed August 16, 2018 at http://www.slobodan-milosevic.org/sps5.htm.
Milošević, S. (2001a). Interview of Slobodan Milosevic to the Fox News Channel, August 24, 2001. Accessed August 6, 2018 at http://www.slobodan-milosevic.org/int-FNC01.htm.
Milošević, S. (2001b). Statement of President Slobodan Milosevic on the illegitimacy of the Hague 'Tribunal', August 30, 2001. Accessed August 6, 2018 at http://www.slobodan-milosevic.org/spch-icty.htm.
Mitrany, D. (1975). *The Functional Theory of Politics*. London: London School of Economics & Political Science.
Morgenthau, H.J. (2006). *Politics Among Nations: The Struggle for Power and Peace* (7th edition). (Revised by K.W. Thompson and W.D. Clinton.) New York: McGraw-Hill.
Mouffe, C. (1996). *Deconstruction and Pragmatism: Simon Critchley, Jacques Derrida, Ernesto Laclau and Richard Rorty.* London and New York: Routledge.
Muehlenhoff, H.L. (2017). Victims, soldiers, peacemakers and caretakers: The neoliberal constitution of women in the EU's security policy. *International Feminist Journal of Politics*, **19**(2), 153–67.
Mueller, J.E. (1996). Fifteen propositions about American foreign policy and public opinion in an era free of compelling threats. Paper prepared for presentation at the National Convention of the International Studies

Association San Diego, California, April 16–20, 1996. Accessed August 6, 2018 at http://politicalscience.osu.edu/faculty/jmueller//isa1996.pdf.

Münkler, H. (2002). *The New Wars.* Cambridge, UK: Polity Press.

Myrttinen, H. and Swaine, A. (2015). Monster myths, selfies and grand declarations. *International Feminist Journal of Politics*, **17**(3), 496–502.

Nafziger, W., Steward, F. and Väyrynen, R. (eds) (2000). *Weak States and Vulnerable Economies: Humanitarian Emergencies in the Third World.* Oxford: Oxford University Press.

New York Times (2016). How the US became more involved in the war in Yemen. October 15, 2016. Accessed August 6, 2018 at https://www.nytimes.com/interactive/2016/10/14/world/middleeast/yemen-saudi-arabia-us-airstrikes.html.

New York Times (2018). Trump suggests giving teachers guns [Video]. Accessed August 10, 2018 at https://www.nytimes.com/video/us/politics/100000005756976/trump-says-arming-teachers-could-solve-your-problem.html.

Nuamah, K. and Zartman, I.W. (2001). Case study: Intervention in Sierra Leone. Center for International & Security Studies at Maryland. Accessed August 11, 2018 at http://drum.lib.umd.du/handle/1903/7934.

Obama, B. (2010a). Remarks on United States military and diplomatic strategies for Afghanistan and Pakistan, March 7, 2009. In *Public Papers of the Presidents of the United States 2009, Book I* (pp. 365–70). Washington, DC: US Government Publishing Office.

Obama, B. (2010b). Inaugural Address, January 20, 2009. In *Public Papers of the Presidents of the United States 2009, Book I* (pp. 1–4). Washington, DC: US Government Publishing Office.

Obama, B. (2011a). Remarks by the President in address to the nation on Libya, National Defense University, Washington, DC, March 28, 2010. Accessed June 14, 2011 at http://www.whitehouse.gov/the-press- office/2011/03/28/remarks-president-address-nation-libya.

Obama, B. (2011b). Remarks on the resignation of James L. Jones, Jr., as National Security Adviser and the appointment of Thomas E. Donilon as National Security Adviser, October 8, 2010. In *Public Papers of the Presidents of the United States 2010, Book II* (pp. 1543–5). Washington, DC: US Government Publishing Office.

Obama, B. (2011c). The President's news conference in Lisbon, Portugal, November 20, 2010. In *Public Papers of the Presidents of the United States 2010, Book II* (pp. 1840–48). Washington, DC: US Government Publishing Office.

Obama, B. (2011d). The President's news conference with President Dmitry A. Medvedev of Russia, June 24, 2010. In *Public Papers of the*

Presidents of the United States 2010, Book I (pp. 855–64). Washington, DC: US Government Publishing Office.

Obama, B. (2011e). Statement on the 15th anniversary of the Srebrenica genocide, July 11, 2010. In *Public Papers of the Presidents of the United States 2010, Book II* (p. 1055). Washington, DC: US Government Publishing Office.

Obama, B. (2012a). Foreword. In *Public Papers of the Presidents of the United States 2011, Book I* (p. v). Washington, DC: US Government Publishing Office.

Obama, B. (2012b). Letter to Congressional leaders on deployment of United States Armed Forces to Central Africa, October 14, 2011. In *Public Papers of the Presidents of the United States 2011, Book II* (pp. 1278–9). Washington, DC: US Government Publishing Office.

Obama, B. (2012c). Remarks following a meeting with President Nicolas Sarkozy of France in Deauville, May 27, 2011. In *Public Papers of the Presidents of the United States 2011, Book I* (pp. 610–11). Washington, DC: US Government Publishing Office.

Obama, B. (2012d). Remarks on the situation in Libya, March 18, 2011. In *Public Papers of the Presidents of the United States 2011, Book I* (pp. 246–8). Washington, DC: US Government Publishing Office.

Obama, B. (2012e). Statement on sanctions against Libya, February 25, 2011. In *Public Papers of the Presidents of the United States 2011, Book I* (p. 155). Washington, DC: US Government Publishing Office.

Obama, B. (2012f). The President's news conference with President Carlos Mauricio Funes Cartagena of El Salvador in San Salvador, El Salvador, March 22, 2011. In *Public Papers of the Presidents of the United States 2011, Book I* (pp. 282–91). Washington, DC: US Government Publishing Office.

Obama, B. (2013a). Commencement address at the United States Air Force Academy in Colorado Springs, Colorado, May 23, 2012. In *Public Papers of the Presidents of the United States 2012, Book I* (pp. 659–63). Washington, DC: US Government Publishing Office.

Obama, B. (2013b). Letter to Congressional leaders on continuation of the national emergency with respect to Libya, February 23, 2012. In *Public Papers of the Presidents of the United States 2012, Book I* (p. 203). Washington, DC: US Government Publishing Office.

Obama, B. (2014). President Obama's message on Ebola, September 2, 2014. US Embassy in Mauritania. Accessed March 5, 2018 at https://mr.usembassy.gov/president-obamas-message-on-ebola/.

Obama, B. (2015). President Obama: 'We will stand with the people of Mali'. *Daily Mail Online*, November 25, 2015. Accessed March 5, 2018 at http://

www.dailymail.co.uk/video/news/video-1230810/President-Obama-stand-people-Mali.html.

Offner, A.A. (1977). Appeasement revisited: The United States, Great Britain, and Germany, 1933–1940. *The Journal of American History*, **64**(2), 373–93.

O'Neill, O. (2000). *Bounds of Justice*. Cambridge, UK: Cambridge University Press.

Parashar, S. (2009). Feminist international relations and women militants: Case studies from Sri Lanka and Kashmir. *Cambridge Review of International Affairs*, **22**(2), 235–56.

Paris, R. (2014). The 'Responsibility to Protect' and the structural problems of preventive humanitarian intervention. *International Peacekeeping*, **21**(5), 569–603.

Parpart, J.L. and Zalewski, D.M. (2013). *Rethinking the Man Question: Sex, Gender and Violence in International Relations*. New York: Zed Books Ltd.

Pattison, J. (2010). *Humanitarian Intervention and the Responsibility To Protect: Who Should Intervene?* Oxford: Oxford University Press.

Perelman, C. and Olbrechts-Tyteca, L. (1968). *The New Rhetoric: A Treatise on Argumentation*. Notre Dame, IN: University of Notre Dame.

Pinker, S. (2011). *The Better Angels of Our Nature: The Decline of Violence in History and its Causes.* London: Allen Lane/Penguin.

Polk, K. (1994). *When Men Kill: Scenarios of Masculine Violence.* Cambridge, UK: Cambridge University Press.

Posen, B.R. (1993). The security dilemma and ethnic conflict. *Survival*, **35**(1), 27–47.

Posen, B.R. (2014). *Restraint: A New Foundation for US Grand Strategy*. Ithaca, NY and London: Cornell University Press.

Poulton, R.E. and Youssouf, I. (1998). *A Peace of Timbuktu: Democratic Governance, Development and African Peacemaking.* Geneva: UNIDIR.

Ralph, J. (2003). Between cosmopolitan and American democracy: Understanding US opposition to the International Criminal Court. *International Relations*, **17**(2), 195–212.

Rayment, S. (2005). Secret MoD poll: Iraqis support attacks on British troops. *The Telegraph*, October 23, 2005. Accessed August 4, 2018 at https://www.globalpolicy.org/component/content/article/168/37188.html.

Revolutionary United Front of Sierra Leone (1995). Footpaths to democracy. *Fas.org*. Accessed August 8, 2018 at https://fas.org/irp/world/para/docs/footpaths.htm.

Revolutionary United Front of Sierra Leone (2000). Presentation by the Revolutionary United Front Party to the second meeting of the Joint Implementation Committee of the Lomé Peace Agreement, January 24,

2000. Accessed March 6, 2018 at http://www.sierra-leone.org/AFRC-RUF/RUF-012000.html.

Richards, P. (1996). *Fighting for the Rain Forest: War, Youth and Resources in Sierra Leone.* Oxford: The International African Institute.

Ridge, S. (2015). Corbyn: Nukes 'didn't do USA much good on 9/11'. *Sky News*, September 30, 2015. Accessed August 11, 2018 at https://news.sky.com/story/corbyn-nukes-didnt-do-usa-much-good-on-911-10344618.

Rosenberg, J. (1994). The international imagination: IR theory and 'classical social analysis'. *Millennium: Journal of International Studies*, **23**(1), 85–108.

Rosenberg, M. and Mazzetti, M. (2016). US ship off Yemen fires missiles at Houthi rebel sites. *The New York Times*, October 12, 2016. Accessed August 6, 2018 at http://www.nytimes.com/2016/10/13/world/middleeast/yemen-rebels-missile-warship.html.

RT (2017). Women & children among casualties of US missile strike – Homs governor. April 7, 2017. Accessed March 29, 2018 at https://www.rt.com/news/383968-civilians-killed-syria-airbase-attack/.

Rubin, A.J. and Barnard, A. (2015). France strikes ISIS targets in Syria in retaliation for attacks. *The New York Times*, November 15, 2015. Accessed August 6, 2018 at http://www.nytimes.com/2015/11/16/world/europe/paris-terror-attack.html.

Ruddick, S. (1995). *Maternal Thinking: Toward a Politics of Peace*. Boston, MA: Beacon Press.

Sankoh, F. (2000). RUF leader Foday Sankoh's letter to guarantors of the Lomé Peace Accord alleging violations of the agreement, February 24, 2000. *Sierra-leone.org*. Accessed March 6, 2018 at http://www.sierra-leone.org/AFRC-RUF/RUF-022400.html.

Sarkees, M.R. and Wayman, F.W. (2010). *Resort to War: A Data Guide to Inter-State, Extra-State, Intra-State, and Non-State Wars, 1816–2007.* Washington, DC: CQ Press.

Sarkozy, N. (2011). Statement by the President of the Republic at the Paris Summit for the support of the Libyan people, March 19, 2011. Accessed June 14, 2011 at http://fr.ambafrance-us.org/spip.php?article2241.

Scahill, J. (2015). *The Assassination Complex: Inside the Government's Secret Drone Warfare Program*. London and New York: Simon & Schuster.

Schweller, R.L. (1999). Forum: Fantasy theory. *Review of International Studies*, **25**(01), 147–50.

Seybolt, T.B. (2007). *Humanitarian Military Intervention: The Conditions for Success and Failure.* Stockholm: SIPRI and Oxford University Press.

Shaw, M. (2003). *War and Genocide: Organized Killing in Modern Society*. Cambridge, UK: Polity Press.

Singer, P. (1972). Famine, affluence and morality. *Philosophy and Public Affairs*, **1**(1), 229–44.

Snow, D.M. (1996). *Uncivil Wars: International Security and the New Internal Conflicts*. Boulder, CO: Lynne Rienner Publishers.

Snow, D.M. (2016). *The Case Against Military Intervention: Why We Do It and Why It Fails.* New York and London: Routledge.

Snyder, J. (1993). Nationalism and the crisis of the post-Soviet state. In M.E. Brown (ed.), *Ethnic Conflict and International Security.* Princeton, NJ: Princeton University Press, pp. 5–26.

Spelman, E.V. (1998). *Fruits of Sorrow: Framing Our Attention to Suffering*. Boston, MA: Beacon Press.

Stone, J. (2015). David Cameron claims Jeremy Corbyn is a 'threat to national security'. *The Independent*, September 13, 2015. Accessed December 5, 2016 at http://www.independent.co.uk/news/uk/politics/david-cameron-claims-jeremy-corbyn-is-a-threat-to-national-security-10498651.html.

Suganami, H. (1996). *On the Causes of War.* Oxford: Clarendon Press.

Sundberg, R., Eck, K. and Kreutz, J. (2012). Introducing the UCDP Non-State Conflict Dataset. *Journal of Peace Research*, **49**(2), 233–46.

Tanter, R. (1998). *Rogue Regimes: Terrorism and Proliferation*. London: Palgrave Macmillan.

Taylor, M. (1982). *Community, Anarchy, and Liberty.* New York: Cambridge University Press.

Teimouri, H. (2015). Protecting while not being responsible: The case of Syria and Responsibility to Protect. *The International Journal of Human Rights*, **19**(8), 1279–89.

Tessler, M. and Warriner, I. (1997). Gender, feminism, and attitudes toward international conflict: Exploring relationships with survey data from the Middle East. *World Politics*, **49**(2), 250–81.

Thakur, R. (2016). The Responsibility to Protect at 15. *International Affairs*, **92**(2), 415–34.

Thompson, M. (2009). The CIA's silent war in Pakistan. *Time*, June 1, 2009. Accessed August 6, 2018 at http://content.time.com/time/magazine/article/0,9171,1900248,00.html.

Tickner, J.A. (1992). *Gender in International Relations.* New York: Colombia University Press.

Tickner, J.A. (2001). *Gendering World Politics*. New York: Columbia University Press.

Tickner, J.A. (2004). Feminist responses to international security studies. *Peace Review*, **16**(1), 43–8.

Tickner, J.A. (2015). Revisiting IR in a time of crisis. *International Feminist Journal of Politics*, **17**(4), 536–53.

Tilly, C. (ed.) (1975). *The Formation of National States in Western Europe.* Princeton, NJ: Princeton University Press.

Tilly, C. (1990). *Coercion, Capital and European States, AD 990–1990.* Cambridge, MA: Basil Blackwell.

Trump, D. (2017a). Full text: Trump's 2017 U.N. speech transcript. *Politico*, September 19, 2017. Accessed September 27, 2017 at http://politi.co/2heOtM3.

Trump, D. (2017b). Read Donald Trump's full Inaugural Address. *Time*, January 24, 2017. Accessed August 5, 2018 at http://time.com/4640707/donald-trump-inauguration-speech-transcript/.

Trump, D. (2017c). Full transcript: Trump statement on Syria strikes. *Politico*, April 6, 2017. Accessed August 6, 2018 at http://politi.co/2nJqo1a.

UCDP (2012). *Battle-Related Deaths Dataset v.5-2012*. Uppsala Conflict Data Program, Uppsala University. Accessed August 6, 2018 at www.ucdp.uu.se.

United Nations Database (2018). Contributors to UN peacekeeping operations by country and post. United Nations, March 31, 2018. Accessed August 11, 2018 at https://peacekeeping.un.org/sites/default/files/1_summary_of_contributions_1.pdf.

United Nations Development Programme (various years). *Human Development Report.* New York: UNDP.

United Nations General Assembly (1992). *An Agenda for Peace: Preventive Diplomacy and Related Matters*. December 18, 1992. United Nations General Assembly, A/RES/47/120. Accessed August 10, 2018 at http://www.un.org/documents/ga/res/47/a47r120.htm.

United Nations General Assembly (2005). Resolution Adopted by the General Assembly on 16 September 2005. 60/1. 2005 World Summit Outcome. United Nations General Assembly, September 16, 2005. https://documents-dds-ny.un.org/doc/UNDOC/GEN/N05/487/60/pdf/N0548760.pdf?OpenElement.

United Nations Office on Genocide Prevention and the Responsibility to Protect (n.d.). About. Accessed August 15, 2018 at http://www.un.org/en/genocideprevention/about-responsibility-to-protect.html.

Uppsala University, Department of Peace and Conflict Research (n.d.). Definitions. Accessed May 31, 2016 at http://www.pcr.uu.se/research/ucdp/definitions/.

USA Today (2001). Taliban flees Kandahar. *USA Today World*, December 7, 2001. Accessed August 11, 2018 at http://usatoday30.usatoday.com/news/attack/2001/12/07/handover.htm#more.

US Census Bureau (n.d.). About international programs. Accessed July 8, 2016 at https://www.census.gov/programs-surveys/international-programs/about.html/.

US Department of Defense (2008). Pentagon public opinion poll of Iraqis. Accessed August 11, 2018 at http://musingsoniraq.blogspot.fi/2008/10/pentagon-public-opinion-poll-of-iraqis.html.

US Department of Justice (2001). *The USA PATRIOT Act: Preserving Life and Liberty*. Accessed July 11, 2017 at https://www.justice.gov/archive/ll/highlights.htm.

US Department of State (2004). *Patterns of Global Terrorism 2003*. Washington, DC: US Government Printing Office.

US Government Interagency Counterinsurgency Initiative (2009). *US Government Counterinsurgency Guide*. Washington, DC: Bureau of Political-Military Affairs.

US Government Printing Office (various years). *Public Papers of the Presidents*. Accessed August 13, 2018 at https://www.archives.gov/federal-register/publications/presidential-papers.html.

Van Creveld, M. (1991). *The Transformation of War*. New York: Free Press.

Van Evera, S. (1994). Hypotheses on nationalism and war. *International Security*, **8**(4), 5–39.

Van Linschoten, A.S. and Kuehn, F. (2012). *An Enemy We Created: The Myth of the Taliban/Al Qaeda Merger in Afghanistan, 1970–2010*. London: C. Hurst & Co.

Van Wauwe, V. (2018). Presentation at the University of Bath, at the launching of the documentary *Voices from the Mine: Artisanal Diamonds and Resource Governance in Sierra Leone* by Roy Maconachie.

Vincent, R.J. (1974). *Nonintervention and International Order*. Princeton, NJ: Princeton University Press.

Vincent, R.J. (1986). *Human Rights and International Relations*. Cambridge, UK: Cambridge University Press.

Wæver, O. (1996). European security identities. *Journal of Common Market Studies*, **34**(1), 103–32.

Wallerstein, I.M. (2004). *World-Systems Analysis: An Introduction*. Durham, NC: Duke University Press.

Waltz, K.N. (1968). *Man, the States and War: A Theoretical Analysis*. New York: Columbia University Press.

Waltz, K.N. (1979). *Theory of International Politics*. Reading, MA: Addison Wesley.

Washington Post (1984). The Weinberger Doctrine, November 30, 1984. Accessed August 13, 2018 at https://www.washingtonpost.com/archive/politics/1984/11/30/the-weinberger-doctrine/c7f20ffe-b591-4189-ad05-a704aac1935d/?utm_term=.ffd8c05c97ef.

Watt, N. (2015). Tony Blair makes qualified apology for Iraq war ahead of Chilcot report. *The Guardian*, October 25, 2015. Accessed February 26,

2018 at http://www.theguardian.com/uk-news/2015/oct/25/tony-blair-sorry-iraq-war-mistakes-admits-conflict-role-in-rise-of-isis.
Wendt, A. (1987). The agent–structure problem in international relations theory. *International Organization*, **41**(3), 335–70.
Wheeler, N.J. (2003). Reflections on the legality and legitimacy of NATO's intervention in Kosovo. In K. Booth (ed.), *The Kosovo Tragedy. The Human Rights Dimension.* (2nd edition) (pp. 145–63). London: Frank Cass.
Wight, C. (2006). *Agents, Structures and International Relations: Politics as Ontology*. Cambridge, UK: Cambridge University Press.
Wilkerson, J. and Casas, A. (2017). Large-scale computerized text analysis in political science: Opportunities and challenges. *Annual Review of Political Science*, **20**, 529–44.
Williams, B.G. (2010). The CIA's covert predator drone war in Pakistan, 2004–2010: The history of an assassination campaign. *Studies in Conflict & Terrorism*, **33**(10), 871–92.
Wood, E.A. (2016). Hypermasculinity as a scenario of power. *International Feminist Journal of Politics*, **18**(3), 329–50.
Woods, C. (2017). International airpower and the myth of risk-free airstrikes. Lecture at the University of Bath, UK.
Wyn Jones, R. (1999). *Security, Strategy and Critical Theory*. Boulder, CO: Lynne Rienner.
Young, M. (2000). The mad bombers. *Diplomatic History*, **24**(2), 365–70.
Zakaria, F. (2017). Zakaria: Trump just became president [Video]. *CNN*, April 7, 2017. Accessed March 29, 2018 at https://edition.cnn.com/videos/politics/2017/04/07/fareed-zakaria-trump-became-president-syria-newday.cnn.
Zalewski, M. (2003). *Feminism After Postmodernism? Theorising Through Practice*. London: Routledge.
Zartman, I.W. (2011). Greed and grievance: Methodological and epistemological underpinnings of the debate. *Studies in Ethnicity and Nationalism*, **11**(2), 298–307.

Index